Witchcraft

witchcraft

9482

Charles Williams

Meridian Books

THE WORLD PUBLISHING COMPANY

NEW YORK AND CLEVELAND

A MERIDIAN BOOK

Published by The World Publishing Company
First Meridian printing February 1959
Ninth printing 1971
First published in March 1941 by Faber & Faber Limited.
Library of Congress Catalog Card Number: 59-7178
Printed in the United States of America.

WORLD PUBLISHING
TIMES MIRROR

To the immortal memory of
ALONZO SALAZAR DE FRIAS
NICHOLAS DE LA REYNIE
ANDREW ELIOT

PREFACE

These pages must stand for what they are—a brief account of the history in Christian times of that perverted way of the soul which we call magic, or (on a lower level) witchcraft, and with the reaction against it. That they tend to deal more with the lower level than with any nobler dream is inevitable. The nobler idea of virtue mingled with power either worked itself out eventually as experimental science (but the extent to which experimental science was at any time denounced has probably been exaggerated), or it was kept carefully secluded in its own Rites (and to know these one would have had to share them), or it did in fact degenerate into base and disgusting evils (as I have here and there tried to suggest). No-one will derive any knowledge of initiation from this book; if he wishes to meet 'the tall, black man' or to find the proper method of using the Reversed Pentagram, he must rely on his own heart, which will, no doubt, be one way or other sufficient. I have not wished to titillate or to thrill; so far as I can manage it, this is history, and (again as far as I can manage it) accurate history. I have tried to make no statement that was not justified by reputable editions of original documents, and neither to exaggerate nor minimize events or contemporary opinion on events.

There are two authors who have laid the most casual student of the subject under heavy debt—the late Dr. Montague Summers and the late Dr. Henry Charles Lea; the first chiefly by his various translations, especially of the *Malleus Maleficarum*, the second by the great collection which was edited (after his death) by Professor A. C Howland and published as *Materials towards a History of Witchcraft*. The relevant chapters in his *History of the Inquisition* and *History of the Inquisition in Spain* also illuminate the subject. Both Dr. Summers and Dr. Lea held fixed views; those views, it is true, were in absolute opposition. I am not myself convinced either by Dr. Summers's credulity or by Dr. Lea's contempt. But both were sincere and learned men, and neither of them would willingly have altered a single fact in order to support his own view.

The double acknowledgement is the chief purpose of this preface. I have given other references in their proper place. The whole subject, however remote it may seem, is not without value at the present time. It is one exhibition among many—and more flagrant than some—of a prolonged desire of the human heart; few studies of the past can present that heart more terribly—whether on one side or on the other—in its original and helpless corruption.

CONTENTS

Chapter One

THE BACKGROUND

In the years of the Divine Tiberius Christendom had already come into being. There existed, scattered over Southern Europe and the Near East, companies of united disciples. They were known by certain beliefs and certain rites; they were also known by a certain mode of life which aimed at a particular and, it was thought, eccentric strictness. The centre of those beliefs, rites, and manner of life was asserted to be their peculiar and intense individual relationship to a historic (though almost contemporary) being. It was this, and one other thing, which distinguished them from the followers of the many mystery-religions and the many philosophies of the time. There were other groups which depended on rites, and there were many others which aimed at a strict moral life. The conflict of man's worse desires with his better was not confined to Christians. It was a commonplace of the Roman world as it had been a commonplace of others. Conflict and division were obvious to all moral thinkers.

What distinguished Christendom was (i) its relation

to the Crucified Jew, and (ii) its assertion of a supernatural Will. The use of the word supernatural has been rebuked, and indeed it is a little unfortunate. It did not imply then, nor should it ever have implied since, any derogation from the natural order. But it did imply that that order was part of and reposed on a substance which was invisible and which operated by laws greater than, if not in opposition to, those which were apparent in the visible world. Substance was love, and love was substance. And that substance of love was disposed by conscious and controlling Will, which had yet so limited itself, by its own choice, as to leave the wills of men and women free to assent or not to assent to its own. The nature of that final and supernatural Will was not at all clearly imagined or defined by the passionate thinkers and orators of the early Church, except in two or three points. It was absolute; it had created all things; and in that historic being Jesus it had set itself in a special relationship of love to mankind. It had, by a sacrifice of what was more and more beginning to seem itself, operated to restore to men a state of goodness and glory of which they had miserably deprived themselves. It intensely and individually desired the salvation of all men. The one thing necessary, besides its own sacrifice, was the will of the creature to accept and unite itself with that sacrifice. And the death of Jesus, called Christ, had been that sacrifice.

Such ideas were in no sense repugnant to the age. The introduction of the supernatural was common enough. What was not so common was the single absolute Will, the historic personality, and the intensely exclusive demands which the new bodies of believers promulgated.

It was not the mysteries of Christendom but its defini-tions that were alien to contemporary thought and feel-ing. The supernatural was allowed, was even welcomed, so long as it was not intellectually and dogmatically de-fined. The half-allegorical gods of Rome, the symbolical and feverish divinities of the East, were very ready to welcome another god. It was the new god who refused to welcome them. On the whole the Roman world might accept myth, but it refused metaphysic as part of a religious creed, and dogma, in its repelling and formu-lated sense, was utterly alien to it. There was therefore at best a symbolism, at worst a cloudiness, about its divine beings; whether those beings were the lords of Eastern rituals or the even less credible gods of Roman public tradition. They could almost be believed to be idealiza-tions of man's desires and emotions. The highly sceptical section of the great world found no difficulty in that interpretation. It was content to allow the mass of men to believe as they chose—always assuming that the safety of the Empire was preserved.

There was therefore, in our sense of the words, hardly any 'good' or 'evil' about the world of divinities. Myths of evil supernatural beings might exist. The Furies might, in Virgil's poem, chastise the souls of sinners. The mys-teries might supply means by which the devotee entered into 'blessedness'—of one kind or another. There were rites of a dangerous nature, invocations of awful and appalling deities. There were ghosts and curses, night-travellers and night-pestilences. But all these came rather under the head of Power than of Will. And if that were true even of the more respectable gods, it was much more true of the less respectable. Charms and amulets, necromancy and divination, were popular, and their makers and professors were many. Popular also, though perhaps chiefly among a different and smaller class, were the literary reflections of such things; to the incredulous an amusement for their leisure, to the credulous a thrill of delicious fear.

In the very great poem in which, some fifty years earlier, Virgil had celebrated the restoration of the Julian line and the re-foundation of Rome, there is much of the supernatural. There indeed the Will of Jupiter might almost seem to approach the Christian idea of omnipotence; especially in the noble passage where the vocation of the Roman Empire in the world is related to the necessity of the Jovian commands. But perhaps the final resolution is never made. Or if it is, then it is made precisely in terms of justice here and not of supernatural substance nor of love. Piety and propriety Virgil understood; he pushed both very far; the very feel of his verse seems to hover on some greater mystery. But, could he have heard of Christianity, there seems little doubt that he would have recoiled from it, and would have relegated it to the train of obscene evils which attend on the traitor Antony and his Egyptian paramour.

But he knew much—at least he knew much poetically and for his literary purpose—about the darker power of enchantments. The beautiful, dangerous and fatal Queen of Carthage who nearly captivated Aeneas and prevented Rome knew about it. In her distress she had recourse to a woman of occult power. 'I have found', the queen said to her sister Anna, 'a priestess who was the guardian of the Hesperides, who can use spells to free minds from love or to bring them into slavery to love. She can stop flowing streams and turn the stars back in their courses. She can call up those spirits who wander by night; she can cause the earth to shake and trees to fall from the mountains. Be witness, gods, and you, sister, how unwillingly I turn to these sorceries.'

And now (the sacred altars placed around)
The priestess enters, with her hair unbound,
And thrice evokes the powers below the ground.
Night, Erebus and Chaos she proclaims,
And threefold Hecate, with her hundred names,
And three Dianas; next, she sprinkles round
With feigned Avernian drops, the hallowed ground;
Culls hoary simples, found by Phoebe's light,
With brazen sickles reaped at noon of night;
Then mixes baleful juices in the bowl,
And cuts the forehead of a new-born foal,
Robbing the mother's love. The destined queen
Observes, assisting at the rites obscene:
A leavened cake in her devoted hands
She holds; and next the highest altar stands;
One tender foot was shod, her other bare;
Girt was her gathered gown, and loose her hair.
Thus dressed, she summoned with her dying breath
The heavens and planets conscious of her death,
And every power, if any rules above,
Who minds or who revenges injured love.[1]

This example is from literature, and literature does

[1] John Dryden's translation.

not always directly and accurately reflect the social or moral content of a culture. In fact, however, the activities represented in that image, whether or not they existed, were certainly feared in the public life of the time. The newly established Empire took measures against invisible as well as visible dangers. The invasion of Rome by religions and superstitions from the East was still regarded, as it always had been, as undesirable and improper, and the *Aeneid* itself had with great power denounced the rallying of the East at Actium. The imperial government, as much as was possible, barred its door against the intrusion, though it could not prevent the oriental myths and rituals drifting in not so much by the back door as by a thousand windows. The Emperors, with some reluctance, allowed themselves to be deified, at first in eastern cities, presently in Rome; and the deification, which had been so reluctant, presently became the very test of every Roman's fidelity to the State. But this ceremonial godhead, however it might conflict with the Christian Faith, did not much involve the idea of supernatural power or supernatural knowledge. It was indeed the practice of supernatural knowledge against which the government set itself, from motives of public policy. The insatiable curiosity of the Divine Julius might examine, with a detached mind, all matters of the intellect with which he came in contact. His successors were compelled to guard their interests more carefully. The enemy, for them, was divination, the foretelling of the future, by whatever means. It was highly undesirable that recourse should be had to diviners, whether by groups or individuals. Such diviners might too easily become centres of disaffection. Inquiries concerning the probable length of life of the Emperor, for example, whether made of the heavenly bodies or of the souls of the dead, might obviously become dangerous to the stability of the State; much more might inquiries concerning the immediate future of the Empire. The great Maecenas, cautious of the newly instituted peace, advised his master Augustus to forbid all kinds of divination and sorcery. Augustus consented to the decree. He rebuilt the ancient Roman temples; he restored the ancestral rites; and at the same time he caused all books of divination to be burned—to the number, it is said, of some two thousand. All consultation of sorcerers and diviners was prohibited on pain of death. Neither the Emperor nor any of his subjects were to be harried by any power or knowledge derived from another world. His successors from time to time renewed the decrees and put them into action.

Nevertheless, it was the political result and not the religious with which the government was concerned, whether public or private; the *maleficium*, the evil acts done against life or property. In principle the government had no objection to anyone studying the stars any more than to his studying the Greek poets, just as in principle it had no objection to the Christian worshipping Jesus instead of Jupiter. As things worked out, it had to take measures to suppress both Christians and diviners, and for the same reason—the political danger they were thought to involve. An example is given in Tacitus's account of the conspiracy of Libo Drusus. This youth was deliberately inveigled by a friend Firnicus

Catus into dangerous paths. Catus talked to him of the greatness of his family; he urged him to magnificent living; and he encouraged him to turn to sorcery and divination—astrologers' promises, magicians' rites, and interpreters of dreams. Libo at last went so far as to approach a certain Junius, 'for the purpose of evoking by incantations spirits of the dead'—perhaps Libo's own great-grandfather Pompey, his aunt Teribonia, who had been married to Augustus, or other great ones of his house. The necromancer betrayed him to another informer, who went to the consuls. Libo was summoned before the Senate and invited to explain. The prosecution, amid other evidence of his dealing with diviners, with inquiries whether he would be so wealthy that he would cover the Appian Way to Brindisium with gold, produced a paper on which had been written the names of Caesars and of Senators, and against them signs of dreadful and mysterious significance. Order was given that his slaves should be formally sold, in order that they might be put to the torture, which could not legally be done otherwise in any case affecting a man's life. The case was adjourned; and that evening the unhappy young fool killed himself. As a result fresh decrees were passed against all practitioners of magic. Some were seized; one was flung from the Tarpeian Rock; one was put to death by the consuls, to the ceremonial sound of trumpets, outside the Esquiline Gate. Yet the official consultation of omens continued, and even the official consultation of magians. Astrologers were frequently found in the imperial train and even in the close imperial circle. There they were harmless and even useful, since the

occult dealing of the Emperor was, by definition, no treason, being part of his dutiful care of the State. And when
even darker things were rumoured to have happened,
the same excuse was invoked. In the reign of the Emperor
Hadrian the young favourite Antinous died mysteriously
in Egypt. It was whispered that his death had not been
accidental; the master of Antinous was learned in the
arts of magic, and his best-loved servant had been
awfully sacrificed to ensure the good estate of the Emperor himself.

In the second century both the literary and social
aspects of sorcery were represented in the career of
Lucius Apuleius, a Roman and an African; he was born in
Numidia, about A.D. 125. He had travelled in the Near
East, and had been initiated into the mysteries of Isis and
of Osiris. He had written one of the most famous novels
of the world, the *Metamorphoses* or *Golden Ass*, which
(as a modern novel might do) dealt both with religious
initiations and with black magic.

It is a romance in the best style; it not only demands
the 'willing suspension of disbelief', but also defeats it.
The first description of a witch is after the earlier Vir-
gilian manner—'She can call down the sky, hang earth
in heaven, freeze fountains, melt mountains, raise the
spirits of the dead, send gods to hell, put out the stars,
and give light to Tartarus itself.' But this is not to be
taken seriously; the examples of her art which follow are
meant for laughter. 'She turned a neighbouring innkeeper, whose competition damaged her trade, into a
frog: and now the poor old fellow swims about in a
vat of his own wine and, squatting deep in the lees,

summons his former customers with hoarse importunate croak.' The next example is wilder yet. 'She turned another—a lawyer—into a ram because he had spoken against her, and now he pleads in the shape of a ram.' It is a world where such things can happen, a world of every-day shot with fantastic twirls of metamorphosis. That, however, does not prevent the world from being at times terrible; the very style hints at the reality of those awful powers, and the laughter, even when apparently whole-hearted, is found to be half a defence against the energies which, were they once believed in, would be effectual. The ninth book holds what is perhaps the best example. There a certain adulterous wife, driven from her husband's house, plots with a witch against his life. It is the means which are frightful. A dead woman, herself murdered, is evoked and sent to the house. 'About midday a woman suddenly appeared in the mill. She was clad in the garb of mourning worn by persons accused of some crime; her face was strangely disfigured by grief, while her raiment hardly covered her and consisted of deplorable shreds and patches. Her feet were naked and unshod, her countenance hideously thin and pale as boxwood, and her grizzled hair was torn and foully besprinkled with ashes, and hung over her forehead so as to cover the greater part of her face. She laid her hand upon the miller as though she would speak to him in private and led him to his chamber.' When, at last, the slaves break into the room where the two are supposed to be, they find their master hanging dead from a beam and the woman gone.

Such a passage might certainly be paralleled by many

modern 'ghost' stories. In these, however, the victim is usually himself a sinner; a supernatural propriety exercises itself through the apparition, and 'the manner of the death', in the words of Apuleius, 'that sends him as a ghost to dwell in the world below' is justified by the nature of the original sin. Here, however, there is no such justice; there is only malevolence made powerful by rare control of secret means. In the mill, to the slaves grinding the corn and the honest miller, 'an excellent fellow of a very modest disposition', the evoked phantasm of the unfortunate dead appears, and, like the later vampires whose bite drew their victims without their will into their own company, works on the living, in ways which Apuleius will not describe, till the dead body hangs strangled from the beam. Against such malevolence, in that world, it seems there is to be imagined no protection, except perhaps in the end for those who, like Apuleius himself, have been able to concern themselves with the other mysteries, the sacred ritual of the supreme goddess—Isis, who among all her divine manifestations is also Proserpine, 'to whom men render shuddering reverence with howls by night, whose three-fold visage awes the wild rages of the goblin-dead, and holds fast the gates of hell, who wanders in many a diverse grove and is propitiated with varied rites.' It is this goddess who frees Apuleius at the end from his own metamorphosis, reminding him that when he at his proper term descends to the world below, he shall see her 'shining in the darkness of Acheron and reigning in the inmost halls of Styx'.

The solemn conclusion, coming so to a tale which had

played with every kind of emotion, bestows on them all an additional seriousness. The three-fold visage overlooking the goblin-dead accentuates the earlier terror of the dead woman. There is, certainly, no reconsideration; there is no suggestion that the miller is blessed among the dead, and we have no right to ask for it. Apuleius was writing a romance, not a philosophy. But the dead are made more real by that great office of Isis, and therefore, as it were upon the edge of her divine operations, the loathly operations of witchcraft are made more credible. And this, in that particular age, was one of the books the world enjoyed.

It would be easy to dismiss the book as a mere literary *tour de force*, a metaphysical holiday, if there had not fortunately been preserved to us another work by the same Apuleius, his *Apologia*. His literature, it seems from this, was then too much like life, and what was fearful fun in the study might be a serious danger in the law-courts. Apuleius, at a later period of his life, came to Tripoli, and there married one Pudentilla, a wealthy widow. An action was brought against him by her relatives, accusing him of immorality and sorcery, of having used magical arts to ensnare Pudentilla, and of having married her for her money. The case was tried at Sabrata, which is now called Zowara, in the ordinary courts, before the proconsul Claudius Maximus, somewhere between A.D. 155 and 161. The defence remains.

As far as the sorcery charge went, he began by arguing that it could not necessarily be said that the magic was harmful. A magician was nothing but a priest, for the word (he said) was the Persian word for priest, and

meant therefore one skilled in ceremonial law and the
sacrificial practice of religion—'an art acceptable to the
immortal gods, full of all knowledge of worship and
prayer, full of piety and wisdom in things divine, full
of honour and glory since the day when Zoroaster and
Oromazes established it, high-priestess of the powers of
heaven'. The common herd, he said, thought that a
magician was one who by 'communion of speech' with
the immortals, had power to do such marvels as he
would. The 'communion of speech' is noteworthy. It
is the sense which is at the bottom of all incantation, of
all 'words of power', the power which powers acknow-
ledge, the right utterance of sounds whose energy drives
supernatural things to obedience. Apuleius himself
pointed out, in defence, what was afterwards to be so
widely and dreadfully felt, the fear that must lie on all
who dare to attack a magician of such a kind. The man,
he said, who really believed in the charge he brought
should be the last to bring it; 'no escort or care or guard
can save him from unforeseen and inevitable disaster'.

But in fact his enemies did not accuse Apuleius of
such tremendous energies. Their complaints and their
evidence dealt with lesser images and practices. They
declared that he had procured certain curious fish for
his spells. Apuleius retaliated by declaring that fish
were not mentioned in the magical authorities as having
any value. The second charge, that he had bewitched a
boy with a magical incantation, was more dangerous;
the boy, it was said, had gone mad. Apart from the
facts of his own action Apuleius was less certain about
the principle. He held that there were certain divine

powers, midway between gods and men, from whom all divination and magic came; also he held that a child or young lad—healthy, beautiful, intelligent—might be cast into a trance, or what we should no doubt call the hypnotic sleep, 'and be reduced to its primal nature, which is in truth immortal and divine'; and thus, as it were in a kind of slumber, it might predict the future. But it was not such a solemn rite that had here happened; and if it had belonged to the other kind of magic, that long since forbidden in the Twelve Tables, 'mysterious, loathsome, horrible, needing night-watches and darkness, solitude and murmured incantations'— would he, as his accusers declared, have allowed fifteen slaves to be present? On another charge of the same kind the evidence was only that there were reported in a certain room to have been walls blackened by smoke and feathers of birds sacrificed in evil rites. For such purposes also he was said to have fashioned from rare wood by secret means a seal in the form of an eviscerated body, and adored it and called it *basileus*, king.

On all these things, and others, Apuleius had little difficulty in showing his innocence. The accusations were false and factitious. But they were brought in a court of law in one of the chief cities of the Empire, before the proconsul Claudius Maximus, under the Emperor Antoninus Pius. They were therefore possible and even plausible charges. He was accused of having used magical influence to cause his wife to marry him and to give him her property. In similar cases of a not dissimilar kind concerning wills, the modern English phrase is 'undue influence'. The difference between 'undue' and 'magical' is the difference between two kinds of imagination.

This then was the air which, in that intellectual world, the young Church breathed; these were the sounds she heard, the sights—in spite of the fact that her eyes were fixed on her own Divine Hero—she half-saw, ceremonial initiations, magic thought of as a high art, 'high-priestess of the powers of heaven', but also magic as a secret and loathsome ritual, dangerously communing with other deities by means of horrid sacrifices and barbarous chants. Apuleius, in his own eyes, was a humble student of an art known to Zoroaster and Plato, of the 'communion of speech' which set men in touch with divine things. His enemies saw him in different attitudes—bribing fishermen to bring him coarse fish as charms for gross purposes, or secretly honouring in his own room the image of a skeleton-like corpse worked on a seal and calling it his king. This was the world of Rome.

But there was another tradition of which the Church was aware, and one closer to her. The Gentiles to whom the Apostolic missionaries went in the second place had their divinations and art-magic. But the Jews, who might often be ignorant or scornful of this, had no less their own. Deep in the Law itself lay the Divine command—'Thou shalt not suffer a witch to live'—'Maleficos non patieris vivere' (Exodus xxii. 18), and others followed—denunciations of those who sought after the Magi, those who observed trances and auguries, those who consulted 'pythonesses' or diviners, those who sought truth from the dead. The curse is directed mostly against two classes—diviners as such, and *malefici*—workers of evil, but evil here not in the ordinary human sense but by supernatural means. The prophets of the Lord were sent out by Him alone; for the rest—'regard not them that have familiar spirits, neither seek after wizards, to be defiled by them: I am the Lord your God.'

There had not then been developed, in that old Jewish tradition, the full-fledged figure of the Devil himself. It would not be true to say that evil came late into the Jewish inheritance, but the metaphysical formulation was late, the myth was late. Diviners and wizards had existed, relics of the world from which the Jews had morally extricated themselves—the world that was around them in Egypt and Assyria and Rome. But the spiritual world in which that learning worked was not so clearly known. The canonical books of the Old Testament are practically silent on the subject; nowhere does the Devil appear, and even in the story of the Witch of Endor, though there is necromancy, there is, as such, no diabolism. The allusion in Job is unique, and that allusion does not necessarily imply spiritual malignancy. The earliest myth of the origin of evil and of apostate spiritual beings was that given in the story in Genesis vi. It declared how 'the universal sinfulness with which mankind appeared to be infected flowed like a dark turbid river from a single fount, namely, the unholy unions of angelic and human beings, and the commixture of mortal and immortal essences effected thereby'.[1]

[1] N. P. Williams, *The Ideas of the Fall*.

'The sons of God saw the daughters of men that they were fair'; there, and not in the Adam and Eve story, was the attribution of the Fall to a sexual origin, and that derives its real force—its horrible force—from the conception of angelic beings plunging into an alien and separate mode of existence. The whole point of an angel was that he was not a man, and in that sense no man ever could or can be an angel, as the whole point of Christ was that he was Man. The union of angel and woman was an outrage on their natures. Others might have legends of gods and goddesses loving mortals, but the Olympians, when they were not abstractions, were human. It might (in our view or in the view of the great sceptics) be absurd or immoral to conceive of gods acting so, but it was not, primarily, impossible. But it was impossible that angels should, and yet it happened, or was supposed to have happened. The celestial beings who continually watched the Throne had eyes and sense deflected. The Watchers turned aside, ten-score of them, and descended. From that mystery sprang the giants who 'devoured mankind'; and from that mystery also sprang artistic knowledge and occult knowledge. The secrets of the making of weapons and armour, of magic and divination, passed into man's keeping. One writer 'ingeniously adds the art of writing with ink and paper as one of the chief causes of human corruption for which the apostate Watchers were responsible'.[1]

The Church had, very early, felt within itself the reverberations of magical arts. In the very tales of the

[1] N. P. Williams, *The Ideas of the Fall.*

Nativity itself it was said that 'there came wise men from the East to Jerusalem'. There was nothing said then about kings; the strange travellers who finally adored in the house at Bethlehem were of another kind. They were learned in astrology; they foretold destiny by the stars; and the star that slid through the sky to guide them was itself a destiny, a portent of judgement or of joy. 'The god, an angel, a familiar spirit, a star, seem to be interchangeable terms.'[1] In an Egyptian magical papyrus it had been written that 'a shining star shall descend and place itself in the midst of the chamber and when the star has descended before thine eyes thou shalt see the angel whom thou hast invoked, and immediately shalt know the counsels of the gods'. The practitioners of the high art in the Gospel narrative saw a similar thing happen; they saw a route traced in heaven; they took on earth a similar way; and though they delay a little, mistaking their guide, in Jerusalem itself, they emerge from the city and go on until the star hovers in the air over the place of destiny. They go in and contemplate the adorable God; they offer sacred and symbolic gifts. But whether consciously or not, the young Church saw the Magians there as, in effect, abandoning their art. The wise men belonged to the class described by Apuleius; their wisdom was 'high priestess to the powers of heaven'. Nevertheless, for good or for evil, that office of astrology and divination was taken now to be for ever ended. There could be no more foretelling, and that for two reasons at least. The

[1] Dr. Lowther Clarke, *Divine Humanity: the Rout of the Magi*; to which I am indebted for this knowledge.

30

first was that the future should not be foretold, since it depended on the Will of God and the free will of men. God might know what would happen, but even if He did He knew it as much because it was already present to Him as because He merely foresaw it. But no-one else should; the future had to be treated as unknown if man was to be treated as free. But secondly the future, apart from man's moral choice, could not *matter*. 'All luck was good'; whatever happened was fortunate. Knowledge was not so much immoral as irrelevant to the reality of Love loving and being loved at every moment. That was what did matter.

The Magians were the first conquest of the Child-God. 'They departed', wrote Justin Martyr afterwards, 'from that power which had taken them as spoil.'[1] It was, one might say, the first intellectual victory of the Faith. The first victory, however, did not settle the campaign. Our Lord did not greatly deign to concern himself directly with magical opponents after that victory. The apostles, however, passing out into the Graeco-Oriental world of the Empire, found themselves confronted on all sides by such opponents.

Of the tales of their conflicts the one which achieved most popularity was that of Simon Magus. He appears in various documents of the second and third Christian centuries, and by the fourth the tale had taken its shaped form. It was then properly romantic, involving shipwrecks, family separations, recognitions, and (a new thing in romance) arguments on doctrine. The Apuleian tradition in literature is being converted to edification

[1] Dr. Lowther Clarke, *Divine Humanity: the Rout of the Magi*.

more thoroughly than even the serious conclusion to the *Golden Ass* had allowed. This is partly due to the fact that the Simon story has one great magical figure, whereas the *Ass* has various disconnected magical incidents. But this again is partly due to the fact that there is now a recognized universal supernatural Will against which the 'villain' can set himself. Isis could never be, for all the earlier cultured readers, quite so universal a figure as Christ was for the later Christian readers, and she was quite certainly not so historical. Simon is therefore much more of a depraved magian than of an elevated sorcerer. The magians, as such, were already being thrust into opposition to the Redeemer, and as that happened there was necessarily attributed to them a deliberate egotism. They were caused to desire to rival God.

Simon, the romance began, 'wished to be thought an exalted power, which is above God the Creator, and to be thought to be the Christ, and to be called the Standing One'. 'God the Creator' here is the old Gnostic deity which was so unwisely responsible for the creation of the worlds. Above it and remote from it the high and passionless Godhead of the true nature existed, to which Christ was to draw the elect. It was this nature, and nothing lower, to which Simon professed he belonged, though he was compelled to profess that his body was also 'composed of divinity'. He, as he was, could endure for ever. He began, however, in a small way, by joining the band of disciples of a teacher called Dositheus. There were thirty adepts of the inner circle, as it were representing the time of the passage of the moon, and one woman with them who was herself called Luna, or according to some accounts Helena. Besides this inner circle of lunar symbols were other followers waiting and hoping for advancement into it. Simon succeeded, after the death of an adept, in being made a member, and he followed this up by drawing a party to himself and proposing to set up relations with Luna. He presently succeeded in evicting Dositheus and being recognized through the sect as the 'Standing One', the blessed and incorruptible in every man (he called it) which stood, stands, and shall stand. Of Luna he taught that she had 'been brought down from the highest heavens, and that she was wisdom, the mother of all things, of whom the Greeks and barbarians, contending, were able in some measure to see an image; but of herself, as she is, the dweller with the first and only God, they were wholly ignorant'.

The accounts we have are, of course, opposed to Simon, and they are very late. But it is clear what they suggest: that Simon, taking over the headship from Dositheus, who afterwards died, formed a symbolical school of adepts, he himself being the pillar transfused, body and soul, with compact divinity, the woman being the moon and visible wisdom of that source, and the circle of the order of time in terms of the month. He himself knew all arts—he could become invisible, ascend into air or descend through rock, control matter, direct fertility, and make and unmake kings. He was a master of necromancy also, and for this purpose he had once 'turned air into water, and water into blood, and solidifying it into flesh, had formed a new human creature—a boy'. He made an image of this boy, to stand in his own bedchamber, and then killed him, because the mortal soul, once free from the body, acquires prescience, and that is why it can be invoked for necromancy and all divination. 'He made use', says the romance, 'of the soul of the boy, after he had been slain by violence, for those services which he required'. Thus he imposed necessity upon heavenly places, and not even the angels could prevent that soul from coming down at his command.

The conflict with Peter followed. Simon at one point turned the face of another man, by magic, into the likeness of his own in order to evade his pursuers, but eventually both he and Peter came to Rome and were brought before Nero. Simon reached the city by moving in a cloud of dust, 'like a smoke shining with rays stretching far from it'; it vanished, and there suddenly was Simon standing among the people. Peter, however, came from Jerusalem by sea. Peter and Simon contend by signs and wonders; a great dog and a sucking child bear witness against Simon. Eventually Simon promises to fly; he begins to do so. Peter prays; Simon's power deserts him, and he falls to the ground.

The conclusion is uninteresting. Simon Magus degenerates from a symbolic master of adepts into a vulgar worker of marvels, and Peter is not much better. His strong point, of course, is doctrine, of which Simon by now is empty. It is, intrinsically, this which is significant.

The doctrine of the single Supernatural Will, and of the Incarnation, had launched itself on a world in which supernatural powers were believed to exist. It was believed that men could, if they wished, operate by means of those powers. The executants were in the main of four kinds: (i) there were the merely vile kind, the night-hags, the potion and poison makers, malefical wizards of the lower sort; (ii) there were the grander kind, such as the priestess in Virgil, learned in conjurations, who by knowing, as it were, the mathematical pattern of the universe, the proper balance of sound and movement, could control the heights and depths of things, change kingdoms, and even terrify the gods; (iii) there were the diviners and astrologers, those who forecast the future and read the purposes of the stars; (iv) and besides all these there were, it seems, some few to whom the magical art was indeed 'high-priestess of heaven', who, pushed on by a pure learning, followed in honour and chastity towards a sublime union with the final absolute power; there was a means of doing this, but it was very secret.

Finally, from one source and another, but largely from the myth of the angelic Watchers who turned their watch on the daughters of men, there was a tradition of a great and awful blasphemy—of the sexual union of alien and opposed natures. Yet it was this tradition which resembled most closely the central dogma of the Church, where something (neither alien nor opposed, but utter spirit) entered into the womb of a woman.

Chapter Two

THE ARRIVAL OF THE DEVIL

It has been recorded by Saint Luke that Christ, on the return of the seventy disciples, cried to them: 'I beheld Satan as lightning fall from Heaven.' If the word heaven there might be taken to mean the kingdom of Heaven which Immanuel so constantly proclaimed, then there was already present to Him that state of things from which evil had vanished, and indeed it is asserted that He followed up that cry with a promise that nothing should hurt those blessed ones who were with Him. Some such consciousness seems to have been present in the early Church; they knew by direct experience what their inheritors mostly knew only by faith. A kind of complete freedom leapt into being. Saint Ignatius, at the end of the first century, speaking of the conversion of the Magians, or Magicians, at Bethlehem, said: 'From that time forth every sorcery and every spell was dissolved.' The foretellers could bind no more, nor the grand controllers of conjurations shake the earth and the hearts of men at will, nor the creeping haunters of cemeteries. In the new state such things could not be, and there was no such great need to make war on them. Satan had dropped, like lightning, from that Heaven.

It is true there were other phrases. Immanuel had also spoken of Satan desiring to sift Peter like wheat, but He had not then encouraged the Apostle to believe that he himself could do much. 'I have prayed for thee, that thy faith fail not, and thou, when thou art converted, strengthen thy brethren.' Peter was rather to confirm than to curse, to build rather than to fight. Saint Paul had, it is true, spoken of wrestling with principalities and powers, and after Saint Paul the notion of a grand spiritual conflict became (not, in the circumstances, unnaturally) even more vivid to the Church than the renewed and perfectly achieved glory. At the end of the second century it seemed clear that every sorcery and every spell had not been dissolved. Irenaeus, thinking of Antichrist, wrote: 'Let no-one imagine that he performs these wonders by divine power; it is by the power of magic.' Some simplicity of triumph had passed away; some complexity of trouble endured. Heaven was beginning to look more like the skies and less like the soul; if Satan had fallen like lightning, it had been to earth, and his effects had been precisely like lightning, he had burnt and blasted and more, for he ran up and down the world, 'seeking whom he might devour'.

The Church, in fact, had begun to need an opponent whom it could divinely hate. It might spiritually oppose, but it certainly was not allowed to hate, its persecutors. The crosses went up; the torches flared; the wild beasts were loosed. In a world full of strange sects, wild legends, and horrible ceremonies, in a world full of indistinguished invisible *power*, the Church began, rather in detail than in principle, to define the nature of that power as being a conflict of powers. Apocalypses, including the canonical, began to exist. *Maleficium*—evil work against the Empire or evil work against a neighbour—was already abroad in the world. Divination was abroad; and there was also, of course, a certain amount of 'white magic', healing spells, charms of protection, jewels and amulets worn against disease and the evil eye. But it was not held seemly for the Church to use such methods; besides, her power for healing was within herself, her charismatic ministry had been given by Christ. The power of the Holy Ghost moved among the faithful, and where it did not choose to protect, a rejoicing submission was the only—and a most blessed—alternative. 'White magic' could be neglected. But the other things were not so easily neglected.

The new energy was hostile both to divination and sorcery. They would have been, for reasons already given, discouraged separately. But in fact they tended to be regarded as one, and to be discouraged together. The romance of Simon Magus shows the process at work. *Maleficium* was expanded to cover more than a neighbour, more even than the Empire itself. Love could love and could be loved; that was a great discovery—say, a revelation. But the revelation was at least accompanied by another discovery—more energetic in its exploration than perhaps the Revealer had altogether approved. If Love could be loved, Love could be hated. If a single supernatural Will existed, then there could undoubtedly be an extension of *maleficium* against that single Will.

It must, technically, exist in all unbelievers. 'He that is not with me is against me.' It might not always be deliberate or even conscious. But it might. The *maleficium*, in fact, might be actuated by malice. Whose malice? Primarily, the Church more and more tended to feel, the malice of that flash which had fallen from Heaven and of those in whom still living that fatal lightning burned.

'The prince of this world cometh who hath nothing in me.' He was allowed, he was even encouraged, to come. The great developing rituals did not attend to him overmuch; they converged on their single Centre. But the developing fancies of the Church began to pay a good deal of attention to him. Nor indeed was the Church alone in doing so. Philosophers were doing the same thing. Duality had arrived out of Persia. Plutarch toyed with the idea of an evil world-soul. The Gnostics construed creation itself as evil. The Manicheans declared matter at least to be evil. Heresies saw the frontier of good and evil drawn between spirit and matter. But the Church saw it drawn both in spirit and in matter. The Empire and the Church might be at war. But as the Empire forbade *maleficium*, so the Church denounced malice—'spiritual wickedness in high places'.

The more earnest Christians saw the images of that spiritual wickedness in all the temples, streets, and private houses of the Empire—wherever an altar or a statue recalled the names of the old gods. So metaphysical had the Church been from the beginning that it had always been regarded as criminal to eat 'meats offered to idols'. The immorality of such eating accentuated the immorality of the gods to whom the food had been offered. Their existence was encouraged in order that they might be the more passionately rejected; they gave to the dreams of the supernatural evil local habitations and names. The notion that they were all inadequate ideas of God was not popular in the young Church. Aphrodite and Ares, Hera and Heracles, were not then easily recognized as types of the Incarnate Redeemer; and if they were not gods, if they were but images of inner desires and emotions, they were even less easily recognized as types of the Incarnate Redeemer. Even the huntress Artemis, with such strange variations as her thousand-breasted sister Diana of the Ephesians, was not then easily observed to be but another type of holy chastity from the blessed Mother of the Divine Hero. Philosophize as, after two centuries, Christians might, they could not then achieve a synthesis which, even after twenty, remains a little forced. The gods of Virgil began to look not unlike the unclean spirits of the Book of Enoch. The developing theology of the Church created a more patterned heaven and a more patterned hell. The great arguments slowly determined the Nature of Christ. The Holy Spirit was known to exist. The tradition of angels was taken over from the Jews.

This development is perhaps particularly noticeable in two places: the one being the tales of the Thebaid, the other being (of course) the works of Saint Augustine, especially the *De Civitate Dei* or (as we call it) the *City of God*. The first will serve as examples of the kind of detail in which the diabolic nature showed itself in its relations with men. When the great humanist Athanasius wrote the *Life of the Hermit Anthony*, he described how 'in his first strife' the Devil appeared to Anthony in the form of an Indian boy. So dark, so young, so slender, enters into Christendom one of the first, if not the very first, of those 'black men' who were afterwards to be so prevalent in the works of witchcraft. But here he is not only and entirely the individual Devil; he is also the exhibition of Anthony's own inner evil nature. The division is not, and is not meant to be, completely drawn; and Anthony's answer is to either: 'Thou hast done well to appear in the form of an Indian, for thou art black in thy nature, and thou art as pitiably weak as a boy brought low by punishment.'

The apparitions throughout these tales are sometimes actual and sometimes phantasmal, and are meant sometimes to terrify and sometimes to seduce. Not only the flesh but the intellect is tempted by such 'forms and similitudes'. Those whose minds cannot otherwise be turned aside, those who are beyond the trial of sensual indulgence, are ruined more subtly. The angels of the abyss say to them, 'Look, we will show you the things that are to happen,' and they fill the place with mighty phantasms. The test of such apparitions is always the challenge, the sceptical inquiry, as it has been in Christendom since the adorable Virgin challenged with a question the prophecy of the archangel. The hermits were instructed to say, when these phantasms appeared: 'Who art thou? whence comest thou? Art thou some god, some angel, or some devil?' And if the apparition is of God, then our courage and confidence will increase; but if it is not, then it will itself be confounded and fade away. Such was the experience of Anthony himself when the Enemy, who finds it easy to create apparitions, sent against him a whole host of phantom creatures—lion, wolf, panther, serpent. Anthony only laughed at and teased them: 'If you can hurt me, come and do it! If you could do it, one of you alone would be enough, but you know very well you only look like these ferocious things; you are not anything at all.'

Another hermit, Macarius, dispelled sorcery. A magician 'had made a woman appear in the form of a mare'. Her husband led her to Macarius. He looked at her and asked: 'What ails her?' He was told that she was a woman who had been changed into a mare, but he said: 'She has not been changed from her nature of a woman except in the sight of those who have made a mistake.' Then in the style of the sorcerers of the *Arabian Nights*, he took water and blessed it and threw over her; then he prayed and her form was restored.

This dance, as it were, of evil hallucinations went on for long in the Church. Sorcerers, and even good angels, produced or sought to produce results first in the imagination; that done, the body received the effect of those results, in its emotions if not in fact. Thus a certain Elijah was vexed by lustfulness, and in a dream saw three angels who took him by the hands and feet and 'one of them took a razor and mutilated him, not indeed in very truth but only apparently and in a phantom-like manner, and he imagined in the vision that he had been cured of his malady.' Nor was he again physically disturbed; his prayers and sorrow had their influence in the spiritual world and his sensuality was subordinated to it.

But perhaps the most striking of all these phantasmal beings is one which appeared to the holy Pachomius and his disciple Theodore. It is worth giving at some length.

It is said that Pachomius and Theodore were walking through their desert monastery by night when they saw before them a great phantom 'full of the deepest deceit'. It was like a woman of great beauty, but its beauty was so indescribable that no man was able to talk of the beauty or the form or the appearance of the phantom. They prayed against it, but it drew nearer, and became more solid, and when it was close to them, it asked why they were praying so vainly, 'for I have received power from God, who sustains the universe, to tempt whom I please, and I have time to do this, for this I have asked from God.' Pachomius asked who she was. She answered, 'I am the daughter of the Calumniator, whose great power cannot be described, and unto me the whole company of the devils is subject. It was I who brought down the holy stars to the earth, and it was I who snatched Judas from the Apostolic power. I have received authority to make war against thee, O Pachomius, for I am not able to endure the reproach of the devils, and no man hath made me as weak as thou. Thou hast made me to be trampled under foot by youths, and by old men, and by young men, and thou hast gathered together against me a congregation such as thou hast, and hast set for them as a wall which shall never fall the fear of God, so that my ministers are not able to approach with boldness and freedom unto any one of you.'[1]

She went on to warn the two monks that they would presently die and that then their co-inherence with the other monks would break down, and she would have power over those for whom they now laboured. Pachomius answered that those who followed would labour even better, and better confirm and strengthen the faithful. The phantom answered that she knew otherwise, 'for the beginning of every matter is in love and knowledge, and it receiveth confirmation from the things which are provided, and especially through the divine care and the calling of heaven, and by the Will of God it becometh confirmed by wonderful things and signs, and it is confirmed also by various powers which are exercised therein; but when that beginning waxeth old and becometh grey, it falleth away from growth, and when growth hath ceased, it perisheth of old age, or languisheth through sickness, or decayeth through neglect.'

'And afterwards Pachomius asked her, saying "Why hast thou come, according as thou sayest, to tempt these and not all the brethren? If it be as thou sayest, the destruction of souls resteth with thee to work." And the phantom answered and said unto him, "I have already told thee that when the strength of the Sustainer of creation, the Redeemer Christ, appeared upon the earth, we were brought so low, that, like a sparrow, we were mocked and laughed at by men such as those who are clothed with the Spirit, and who seek to learn the

[1] E. Wallis Budge, *The Paradise of the Fathers.*

Lord; but although we have become feeble through Him, we do not cease to work as much as we possibly can against you, and we never cease from opposing you by every means in our power." '

After this Pachomius drove the phantom away and forbade it to return to the monastery. He could not have known that that strange, lovely, and diabolical apparition had indeed prophesied the history of the conquest of the church (in all but the last things) by the 'mighty ones and cruel devils whom it is exceedingly difficult to defeat'.

Widespread as the belief in visions of the fallen world became, it yet needed an adequate formalization by an adequate authority. That it received; it received indeed almost more than that. At the moment of most awful crisis in all that once Imperial world, at the moment of the fall of Rome, and the disappearance of the City, Augustine defined the other, the sublime, City. He reformulated the doctrine of grace; he declared men's co-inherence in sin. His grand metaphysic absorbed and arranged all tales of divine and diabolic beings. He did not perhaps himself believe in them more greatly than many others, but he believed in them as much and he had a place for them. He built up the celestial City of God; he exhibited around it the raging demons; he overthrew them and all the 'arts magic' of which men boasted. And therefore wherever the authority of Augustine went, there went also an acceptance of the 'arts magic' he claimed to have overthrown. It would have perhaps been possible, at least theoretically, up to his time that the world of magical effects should have been dissolved by incredulity and faith and love rather than retained for combat. 'We Christians', it was said, 'have not acquired the mystery of life through the wisdom of strange words, but by the power of faith which has been given to us by God'. Might not that faith have avoided all this annexation of a world of dark powers? Might not Ignatius have been, by such sweet grace, justified—'every spell and every sorcery was dissolved'?

One cannot say that it was absolutely impossible: 'I saw Satan as lightning fall from Heaven.' But one can with some probability say that it was relatively impossible. Augustine was not concerned with delicious literary ingenuities, nor with the intellectualisms of conjuration. In his world magic was not confined to base slanders on poor old women by villagers, women afterwards scandalously tortured by priests. It was not only a world of occult philosophical inquiry. Astrology might be 'the queen of the sciences', but her sisters were less noble. It was a world of love-philtres and death-philtres, a world in which secret compulsion by magical means was, or was pretended to be, exercised on ignorant victims. It was a world of high scepticism, but it was also a world not at all unlike the worse kind of African village. Neither Augustine nor any of the other great doctors felt this as anything less than the direct challenge of hell, and they answered it in the name of the Freedom of the Will. 'Christianity', says Dr. Inge, whom no one will suspect of an undue partiality for the Fathers, 'may claim at least some of the credit for reducing a permanent nightmare of the spirit to a discredited and slowly dying superstition.'

46

It is in the Seventh Book of the *City of God* that Augustine comes down to this discussion. He has been talking about Plato, and the philosophy which holds propinquity with the Catholic Faith, because of its end, which is God. But, he says, many Platonists, and even Plato himself, adored many gods—and he names 'Plotine, Jamblichus, Porphyry, and Apuleius, an African'. It is Apuleius with whom he proceeds to take issue, both on the matter of the gods and of the arts magic. The works of Apuleius which he discusses do not remain to us, except the *Apology*.

Apuleius, like other neo-Platonists, distinguished between the gods themselves and 'airy spirits' whom he calls *daemones*. These are they who inhabit middle air, and are centres of communication between men and gods; 'to them also', says Augustine, quoting his author, 'belong divinations, dreams, auguries, prophecies, and all magicians' miraculous works.' They are unlike the gods, who cannot be moved by passions; these are subject to such perturbations as men are, and Augustine sweeps on in a scornful comparison of these perturbed spirits with Christians aiming at a true beatitude. 'They are moved by wrath (as Apuleius for all his adoring and sparing them affirms); but true religion bids us not yield to wrath, but rather resist it. They are won with gifts; we are forbidden to take bribes of any. They love stage-filth which chastity loathes; they love all the villainies of witchcraft which innocence abhors.' Such tales are told of them that their name, *daemones*, is already brought into disrepute even among the heathen. 'The name of a daemon was by good doctrine brought into hate.' The

47

word daemon has universally come to mean demon, he says; and the demon is indeed a *daemon*, one who knows, but he knows without charity, and thence is puffed up big and proud. There follow the distinctions between angels and devils. The world of Neo-Platonists—gods (or God) and airy beings and men—is transformed into the Christian World of God, and angels and devils, and men, and the One Mediator Christ Jesus.

As for all magical arts, with the sacrifices, they are, of course, wholly condemned—things done 'by charms and conjuration, tricks of damned curiosity, by Goetia or (to call it more honourably) Theurgy, which whoso seeks to distinguish (which none can) they say that the damnable practices of all such as we call witches belong to the Goetic; marry, the effects of theurgy they hold laudable. But indeed they are both damnable and bound to the observations of false filthy devils, instead of angels.' This is the old business of black and white magic, and Augustine attacks Porphyry for allowing that certain theurgic rituals may help to purify the soul, making an effective point in an argument that rites can cancel rites. He quotes from Porphyry himself an anecdote of a Chaldean, a good man, who was prevented from all such advance of purgation by a greater magician, who, envying him, forbade the invoked powers to grant the other's prayers. 'O goodly theurgy! O rare purgation of the mind, where impure envy does more than pure devotion.'

Apuleius's own defence of himself against the accusation of magic came under Augustine's logical censure. He had admitted the propriety of ancient theurgic practices; he had condemned the lesser magical miracles, which, if done at all, must be done by virtue of those very aery powers Apuleius was otherwise content to invoke. It is not quite clear that Augustine did in fact cover the whole field; for the great rituals, the mysteries of Isis and the rest, the operations of that 'high-priestess of heaven' were not so much to control the Divine Ones as to exhibit to the Divine Ones the pure heart, the pious act, the calm yet passionate entreaty. The conclusion of the *Golden Ass* is hardly magical at all; or if it is, the magic is symbolical only and not compulsive. Initiative remained with the gods. In so far as this was so, Augustine might have retorted, Apuleius had thrown over the nature of magical art—as indeed he had.

As the centuries passed and the world became more confused, as the business of administration passed more and more into the hands of the clergy and became more difficult, so the expectation of a change even more terrible than that of the Fall of Rome entered men's hearts. The colour of that expectation is in the *Dialogues* of Saint Gregory the Great. These were composed round about the year 600; they became popular; they were presently translated into Greek and into Anglo-Saxon, and they were to remain one of the best-known books of the Middle Ages. They were the work of a devout and administrative mind, and they were written for edification. It seems probable that Saint Gregory himself accepted all the miraculous stories they contain. They describe—like the tales of the Thebaid—a world of miracle, which does not mean a world of haphazard. It means a world in which other classes of beings beside men operate materially, and a world in which the immediate intervention of Almighty God counterpoints the habitual movements of the universe—a stricter rather than a less strict world than that we know. But Saint Gregory saw that world as existing under the approach of doom, a final doom. There is a story in which a bishop had a vision of a dead saint crying out, 'The end of all flesh is come! The end of all flesh is come!' It was his own feeling; in his first papal sermon he proclaimed it, and the sense of it was in the organs of his body while he fashioned his book. He was not subject to our modern sense of the grotesque; a soul might be damned because of a lettuce as easily as because of a gold-mine. But it must be admitted that his awful sense of responsibility pressed so far as to introduce irresponsibility. When any smallest piece of casual carelessness in the lightest matters may result in damnation, we faint under the strain. Sanctity may be encouraged but sanity is lost. There is already present in the *Dialogues* the first exhibition of a fatal logic. There was a nun who wished to eat a lettuce from the convent garden, and she forgot to make the sign of the cross over it first. She was immediately possessed of the Devil. In that world the miracles of heaven may (since most of the stories are about saints) be more frequent than the miracles of hell. But the intervention of the miracles of heaven has usually to be invoked deliberately, the miracles of hell may be invoked by accident. A certain priest, coming home, called casually to his servant: 'Come, sir devil, and pull off my hose.' At which suddenly his garters began to be loosened, and his hose to be pulled down by invisible hands. Terrified, he cried out: 'Away, miserable rascal, away! I was speaking to my servant, not to you.' The movement of the stockings ceased. 'By which we may learn', wrote Saint Gregory, 'that if the Devil be so officious in things concerning our body, how ready and diligent he is to observe and note the cogitations of our soul.'

The moral may be sound. But the danger is too frightful; it cannot, by others than the most austere of holy men, be believed—not quite like that. To any other age than his own, and those that immediately followed, Saint Gregory unintentionally restored what he intentionally omitted—disbelief. His world is the world of Apuleius, except for two things: scepticism is absent and an intense moral choice is present. Even Augustine had not gone so far. Witches exist in both worlds alike; there is no need to explain or confirm them. 'At such times', begins one story, 'as divers witches were here in this city of Rome apprehended, one Basilius, a principal man in that wicked art took on him the habit of a monk.' In that habit he commended himself to the bishop, and was by him put into a monastery, much against the will of its holy abbot Equitius, who, staring at the newcomer, spoke his mind: 'This man whom you commend to me seems to me to be a devil and not a monk.' However, under pressure of the bishop, he yielded. When later he had gone on a journey, a nun in a neighbouring convent, 'who in respect of her corruptible carcase seemed beautiful', fell into a fever, and kept on crying out for Basilius to come and cure her. Basilius was willing—the suggestion is that his secret spells had caused the fever—but the other monks would not have it. Eventually all ended well; the nun was cured by the intercessions of Equitius; Basilius was expelled from the monastery, and afterwards burnt by the Romans.

It is not only such darker magicians who are denounced. Healing enchantments are equally sinful. There was a young lady in Tuscany who was invited to a great festival, the dedication of an oratory of the blessed martyr Saint Sebastian. On the previous night, being much in love with her husband, she took her pleasure with him. In the morning she was assailed by pangs of conscience; it had been a breach, it is clear, of the accepted ritual purification; it had been like eating before Communion. But to stay away would mean that everyone would guess: 'shame drove her forth'. When the relics were brought in, she was possessed by the Devil. The priest threw 'a white linen cloth' over her, but because he 'presumed above his strength' he too was possessed. This is a little obscure, but what follows is clear. The young lady's parents and friends carried her off to 'certain witches'. These were obviously white magicians, for not only did they set about healing rites, but to do so they carried the patient to running water, to a river, where, bathing her, they laboured long by their enchantments to cast out the devil. They seem to have at first succeeded, but because they had worked by unlawful means, a legion of other devils entered in. She was tossed about in as many different ways, she spoke with so many different voices, as there were devils in her. Her parents saw, repented, confessed, brought their daughter to the bishop, and the true healing miracle followed.

The point, of course, is not the half-successful cure. The witches were not early doctors, though they may (if they existed) have been the local 'wise women'. The point is precisely in their sorcery; they were invoking supernatural powers outside the ordained machinery of grace. It was this which was evil; it allowed the opening for hell to enter. That nature of hell is already displaying certain characteristics which were to remain for a thousand years.

As it can be drawn in by accident, so it can be defeated by a sign. Also it is hierarchical. Both these points are clear from the story of a Jew, who, being belated one night, slept in an old temple of Apollo. But, a little anxious, in that horrid and obscene place, though he did not believe in Christ, he made over himself the sign of the cross. During the night he woke to see a troop of evil spirits enter, walking before one 'of greater authority', who presently sat down in the body of the temple and began to inquire what his subordinates had been about, how they had spent their time, and what villainy they had done. When the recital was ended, they became aware of the Jew, and the master-devil sent some to view him. 'When they had come, they found that he was marked with the mystical sign of the cross, and they marvelled and said, "Alas, alas, here is an empty vessel, but yet it is signed," upon which the whole company suddenly vanished away.'

The goat is a sign of the Devil. The pagan Lombards 'did after their manner sacrifice a goat's head to the

Devil, running about with it in a circle, and by singing a most blasphemous song, did dedicate it to his service'. The great goat was later to sit at the Sabbaths, adored and obscenely kissed by the gathering, but here it is so far separate from the god, being the sacrifice to him.

Also there are the faint beginnings of another sacrifice. There is a physical appearance of innocence about many young children—no-one who has had much to do with them will suppose it is more than physical, but in that world of intense phenomena, in which the childhood of the Saviour was a high centre of imagination, the inevitable fantasy of a grand contradiction, of perversity, had already crept in. It was perhaps natural, but it was certainly unnaturally developed, even (one would think) to the point of heresy. It is, I think, generally held by the Church, that under the age of seven or thereabouts children cannot seriously sin. 'It is certain, by God's word,' says the Rubric in the Book of Common Prayer, 'that children which are baptized, dying before they commit actual sin, are undoubtedly saved.' At five years old, one would suppose, a child could hardly blaspheme voluntarily and deliberately, or at least that the nightmares of hell need not be invoked against it. There is, it may be admitted, something horrible, and something fascinating, in the idea. Saint Gregory himself may not have felt anything outside the fervour of the moral missionary. One child of five, he recounts, was so carelessly brought up by his father that whenever he was thwarted, he began to blaspheme. The household may, conceivably, have been too severely religious;

where God is invoked to justify parents, children are apt to denounce God as well as their parents. This child fell ill. His father had him in his arms. The child fell into what we should call delirium. 'He beheld certain wicked spirits coming towards him; at which sight he began to cry out in this manner, "Keep them away, father, keep them away", and crying out he turned away his face, and hid himself against his father, who asked why he was so afraid. "O father, there are blackamoors come to carry me away!" After which, he straight blasphemed God and gave up the ghost.'

The blackamoors were to have many successors. So also, though sometimes in a happier manner, was the old tale of the dead man inhabiting earth. As the innocence of the child was involved in a great contradiction, so also was the body of the dead. A virtuous priest used to wash himself in certain hot baths. He found an attendant there to do the necessary service, and after a while began to feel that he ought to do something in the nature of tipping. He therefore took with him one day two 'singing breads' or unconsecrated hosts (*duas oblationum coronas*), which he offered, 'desiring him to take courteously what for charity he did offer him'—an admirable phrase for an admirable temper. But the apparent man answered: 'Why do you give me these, father? This is holy bread, and I cannot eat of it, for I, whom you see here, was sometime lord of these baths and am now appointed for my sins to this place; but if you desire to pleasure me, offer the bread unto Almighty God, and be an intercessor for my sins, and by this I shall know that your prayers be heard, if at your next coming you find me not here.' It was so done, and the result was so.

But of all the details of the stories that prepared and were prepared for the Middle Ages, perhaps the one of most consequence was summed up in the little word *pact*. It is not in Gregory, but it is contemporaneous with Gregory. The originating text is to be found in Isaiah xxviii. 15: 'percurrimus foedus cum morte et cum inferno fecimus pactum'—'We have made a covenant with death, and with hell are we at agreement,' says the Authorized Version, but it was the *pactum* of what became the Vulgate that created in men's minds the possibility of such a certain seal. Augustine had supported that view, and before Augustine the rumours of it had gone abroad. Devils or gods, or gods who were devils, had still something to give and would give it only on their own terms. The first agreements were not written. Among the tales of the desert was one of a certain brother who fell in love with the daughter of an Egyptian priest. He went to the father; the father consulted his god. The god demanded the renunciation, on the part of the Christian, of 'God, baptism, and his cross'. It is a sign of the change that Christianity had brought that such a demand (say, on the priest's side) should have been possible; no god in ancient days would have been so intolerant, unless indeed some consular of Rome had in his high respectability refused to allow his own daughter to become entangled with the unsavoury priesthoods and adorations of the East. In a frenzy of love the Christian promised—and saw something fly from his mouth as he uttered the words which vanished like a Dove into heaven. When, however, the priestly father returned to his own altar with the promise the deity only answered: 'No; his God has not left him; He still helps him; He will receive him if he repents.' So that the apostate was driven away unsatisfied, but afterwards by repentance, fasting and the prayers of others he found salvation, and the flying shape of the Dove returned—once so that he could almost touch it with his hand but it disappeared, but the second time so that it seemed to pass again into his purified mouth.

This is rather the preparation for the Pact than the Pact itself. The heathen god was wiser, or perhaps more despairing, than later devils; he had no real hope that the madness would last. But as the notion of a Pact grew, the evil powers were more easily satisfied. The real purpose of the Pact can be discussed later; it will suffice here to refer to one of the earliest developments of the idea of a formal contract. It is the story of Theophilus of Adana. The earliest manuscripts are said to date from the seventh century, and the story itself from the sixth, roughly from the time of Saint Gregory, and like the *Dialogues* it became one of the famous medieval tales. Theophilus was a moral, devout, and distinguished Christian in the City of Adana in Cilicia. He was a steward of the Church and was put especially in charge of the almsgiving. He was even proposed for bishop, but refused; *noluit episcopari*. Later on, however, some of the clergy who disliked him intrigued to get him dismissed by the new bishop from his office as steward. When this happened his Christianity was put to its great test, and (as so often happens in affairs of some importance) failed. In a state of bitter anger he had recourse to a Jew, a practitioner of all kinds of black art. The Jew, finding him now of a proper disposition, took him by night to the middle of the Circus of the City, warning him whatever happened not to fear and not to make the sign of the Cross. When he had sworn to this, he saw suddenly before him 'creatures clad in white robes, among a multitude of candlesticks, uttering loud cries, and having their prince seated in their midst.' Theophilus was brought before this lord, to whom he made his appeal. The prince of the living creatures spoke to the Jew. 'Let this man', he said, 'renounce the Son of Mary and those other things which are offensive to me, and let him set down in writing that he absolutely denies them, and as long as he denies he shall have from me whatever he will.' Theophilus said, 'I deny Christ and his Mother.' He wrote it down; he put wax on it; he sealed it with his ring.

Almost the next day the bishop sent for him, and to his astonishment he found himself re-appointed steward. But when this happened, he was by no means happy. He had acted, but it seems he had not realized his choice; or else, having his desire, it seemed a poor thing. He was distracted to think of what he had done, of the pact, and of the eternal fire. He appealed to the Mother of Christ for help; he invoked and entreated her for forty days, and at last—also in the middle of the night—she came. She rebuked him for his apostasy; he solemnly revoked it. On the third day afterwards—the interval being spent in tears and penitence—he fell asleep and dreamed. He dreamt that the August Maternity appeared to him again, and that she gave him back the parchment he had so wickedly signed. He awoke; it lay on his heart; and he knew that she had torn it for him out of the gates of hell. In pure gratitude he went on the next day to the church and there made confession of his sin before the congregation and held up the parchment for all to see. Then it was solemnly burned. An additional detail, made in the thirteenth century, declares that the bond had been written in Theophilus's own blood.

Such then was the transformation of the universe—from power to distinction of power, from fear to belief and fear. The supernatural will dominated all, and other wills rebelled against it. Many questions were to arise, but they were problems within that universe. Hardly till our own day was that universe itself to be widely disbelieved.

Chapter Three

THE DARK AGES

The development of the idea of the Devil was the subordinate centre of the whole great transmutation of general supernatural power into the two schools of divine and anti-divine power. But the Devil, whether as angel or as blackamoor, was not alone. Other demons were with him, and the shapes and images, whether of demons or of witches. The Egyptian desert had been full of them, rather diabolic than sorcerous. Certain kinds of beasts were already particularly associated with them—goats, cats, all vermin. But there were also other strange creatures who, in the folk-fables or the inventions of poets, had been used as images of destructive power, and the names of them hovered for long over Christendom. Thus there was a particular kind of being known as Lamia, who was known originally to classical tradition, but the name of her, being drawn into the Vulgate, became a general title for some of those organisms of hell. Lamia was a queen of Libya, and she had been loved by Zeus, but the jealousy of Hera had slain her children, and Lamia in despite and malice robbed other mothers of theirs. She tore them with her nails or else she sucked their blood, and presently the cruelty of her blood-lust changed her face from the beauty which Zeus had loved to mere bestiality. And though there was only one of her, yet there were many of her; the horrible mad figure of creatures neither quite woman nor quite beast wandered through the night. Witches were like the Lamia; they were *lamiae*, for it was an old belief that witches sucked blood from the living, from living children; they were like vampires in that, though they were not vampires, for their powers were greater. The *lamiae* could take again the appearance of beautiful young women, the shape, as it were, of the Lamia whom Zeus had loved.

The most famous story of these (a story made more famous by Keats) occurs in the life of Apollonius, the philosopher of Tyana. A young Corinthian met upon the highway 'a ghost which took the shape of a woman', who made love to him and whose lover he became. It was Apollonius who at the wedding banquet denounced her. 'Madam the bride is an Empusa, such as are commonly called Lamias. They have amorous appetites, but their chief appetite is for human flesh, and they ensnare their intended victims with the bait of love.' In Keats she dies, but in the original she confesses her true nature: 'her wont was to feed upon young and beautiful bodies, because their blood was fresh and pure.'

The name was introduced into the Vulgate by the translators, into a verse of Isaiah (xxxiv. 14): 'ibi cubavit lamia et invenit suam requiem'. It was used as the nearest Latin for the name of another terror in the Jewish tradition, the name Lilith. The translators were not far wrong, for Lilith was the first wife of Adam and (as some said later) the daughter of Samael the accursed; she was driven from Adam because she would not obey him, and she too is a dangerous lover and a murderess of children. She, however, became a queen of devils, which the Lamia did not, and she did not take on a bestial face, which the Lamia did. But it is thus from both sides that the idea of the woman of the darkness who loves and kills entered Christian mythology.

In Isaiah the Lamia is named among other monsters—demons and centaurs of ass-form and satyrs. The Authorized Version has for 'lamia', 'screech-owl'; the Revised has 'night-monster'. The Authorized Version seems here to have confused the lamia with another creature of the night, the screech-owl proper, or at least improper, the Roman strix. This also was said to suck the blood of children; it was related to sorcery, its cry was a malediction, and its feathers magical. Both the lamia and the strix were popular shapes in the 'nightmare of the spirit'; both were shapes of demons, therefore shapes of the followers of demons, therefore shapes of those supposed to be followers of demons. The night was given up to its riders, and these were among them.

But the night had other riders also. In an age when the high air has become unfriendly to us, it should not be difficult to understand the feeling of those earlier centuries. They too feared and set watches against the noise of hordes by night; only their fear was, in a way, worse than ours, because we know our enemies and they did not know theirs. The danger was concealed—

in the street; nay, nearer, in the home. It is not true to think that it was only poor old women who fell under suspicion; beautiful women, noble men, priests, were quite as likely to be centres of doubt and mistrust. Doctrine and literary tradition and popular rumours mingled in the general mind; and the roar of the wind at night—or of more than the wind—stirred everywhere an ancestral terror. In the old days, gods, of one kind or another, had passed through the air, and among them had been Diana the night-huntress. Another invention had grown up in Christian times; the moralists recounted, for edification, tales of great hosts met upon country roads, the damned pouring towards hell. The screech-owl, the lamia, the ghost, the lost soul, the demon, these transported themselves by night. It was not long, as these things go, before all these began to draw together; it was not even long before men and women began to hint at what they knew of such things, what they could say if they would—before little brags and secret boasts began to be heard. Men must be interesting to themselves, and therefore necessarily to others; very few men and women can nourish themselves only on their own self-interest. The Christian religion, on the whole, tends to discourage self-interest and self-importance; against that discouragement there are two methods of fighting—one is to go on being interested in oneself under cover of that religion; the other, to go on being interested in oneself under cover of another religion. The desire for self-importance which had caused many fools in earlier times to nourish themselves on their neighbours' envy and fear, the secret satisfaction of pride, passed over, with so much else, into the Church. It was not the orthodox alone who took a thrill from the thought that X was indeed a witch.

Transmutation of bodies remained a frequent thing —at least in fable. It may reasonably be doubted how many actual men and women through all the centuries of Rome were transformed into beasts, but at least the myths were full of such tales. The taking-up of these tales by the Christian Fathers, for whatever purpose, gave them a validity they might not otherwise have had. Thus the *City of God*, in the short history of the world given in the thirteenth and fourteenth books, collects a number which, if it does not say they are credible, it yet does not declare to be incredible. For when, after speaking of Diomedes and his followers turned into birds, and of Circe, and of the Arcadians turned into wolves by swimming a certain lake, and of the power of Pan and Jupiter to turn men into wolves, it turns to the new metaphysic, it goes on to discuss whether the Devil has any power of this kind. Augustine refers again to the *Golden Ass* of Apuleius, and he says he has himself heard a report that women of a certain place in Italy know of a drug which they will sometimes give, concealed in cheese, and whoever eats it becomes an ass and carries burdens, but still retaining his human reason, and being re-transformed at the end. He does not give this on general rumour alone; he says he talked with a man whose father had undergone the magic, 'one Praestantius'. The victim 'took the drug in cheese at his own house, whereupon he lay in such a sleep that no man could awake him; and after a few days he awoke of himself and told all he had suffered in his dreams in the meanwhile, how he had been turned into a horse and carried the soldiers' victuals about in a budget. Which was true as he told, yet seemed it but a dream unto him.' Another tale was of an actual personal experience. A friend of Augustine's related that he had asked a certain philosopher, an old acquaintance of his, to explain certain 'Platonisms' to him while they were together in the philosopher's house. The man refused at the time, but afterwards just before Augustine's friend went to sleep one night, in came the philosopher and did as he had been entreated. The next day, asked why he had done then what he would not do before, he answered: 'I did it not; indeed I dreamed I did it.' Augustine is a little uncertain of the explanation. His sense of the omnipotence of God and the dignity of man does not allow him to believe that the devils can either create or can really change men 'from any soul or body into bestial or brutal members or essences'. If such things happen, they are due to diabolic action in the following manner. Men have certain fantasies in their minds, and what the Devil can do is to induce deep sleep in a man, while they themselves 'transport the phantasy to other senses'. The dream having occurred, the devils can themselves, in the shape of the dream, appear elsewhere, and even themselves do the actual corporeal work of the dream. Why they should do so, Augustine does not very clearly explain; except that it is 'to delude men's eyes'. It would seem, even so, that the women who gave the drug in the cheese must have been of the nature of witches, since (whatever they themselves believed) they must have taken advantage of supernatural spells.

Here, however, we have a point of view which was to become, in part at least, for some centuries the official explanation of the Church. But it was not against the haunted sky of the Mediterranean alone that the Christian doctors maintained their protest, offered their explanation, or issued their defiance. There had been, while the City stood, a kind of repugnance to all this —the repugnance of Lucan, of Philostratus. These lucid minds might accept astrology and the knowledge of great cycles of events, learned through much care, vigil, and noble practices of the soul; as when Philostratus makes his Apollonius define magical science as 'divination, and how to pray and worship the gods'. But they did not conceive that you could, or should, buy from a sorcerer for money the name of the winner in the two o'clock or an aphrodisiac philtre for the cruel beloved. The distinction might not be altogether logical, but it was at least gentlemanly. A gentleman might study the influence of the stars to discover the future or not, but he did not allow himself to hire the supernatural in order to gain an advantage over his fellows, nor did he traffic in curses, in poisons, in necromancy, or in human sacrifice. Neither Apollonius nor Apuleius would have thought it decent to take part in a magical and cannibal feast; how much less Porphyry or the Emperor Julian himself! But now, from outside the contracting Empire, precisely these evils began to reinforce the more disgusting evils within.

Here again the first thing that strikes the reader is

precisely the *commonness* of the idea, and here again twenty centuries of Christianity have removed that ordinariness from our understanding. Even if we do not think sorcery, human sacrifice, and cannibalism wrong, we still do not think them common. On the rare occasions when something of the sort—or as near it as comes out—appears in the Law Courts, the judges are obviously astonished and even bewildered. It is true that they are so often bewildered, or allow themselves to be, at ordinary human behaviour, that one cannot press that too far. But in general the thing is true; the dark rituals are not an accepted thing, and are punishable (if at all) by fine and imprisonment—certainly not by death.

In the movement of the peoples that then surrounded the Empire they were exactly that. It is true that frightened minds attributed the very birth of some of the invaders to art magic. The Goths held the still more terrifying Huns to be the children of sorceresses and unclean spirits, spirits who wandered in the marshes of Asia, small and emaciated, and having only 'the shadow of human speech'. The coming of Attila seemed the coming of a lord of sorcery, especially because of the number of magicians who accompanied him. Before his battle with Actius, 'Attila assembled the sorcerers. There in a great tent lit by torches gathered together a council of magicians; the Ostrogothic aruspice, his hands plunged into the entrails of the victim whose palpitations he watched; the Alaric priest shaking in a white flag his divination sticks, according to the interminglings of which he read out their prophecies; the Hunnish sorcerer whirling round beating a drum and evoking the spirits of the dead until, with foaming lips, he rolled over exhausted and grew rigid in catalepsis; while at the far end of the tent sat Attila on his stool, watching these convulsions and listening to every cry of these interpreters of hell.'[1]

Against such groupings the groupings of the high officers of the Church themselves seemed half-magical. The Pope Leo I, when he met Attila and saved Rome, came as a form of enchantment—robes and chants and incense. There went with him on each side great supernatural figures, guardians of the City, princes of power, holy Peter and holy Paul, visible (it was said) to human eyes. Attila half yielded to and half compromised with the power of a greater sorcerer than himself, and allowed terms of peace to be imposed upon him. Sometimes the Pope himself had to compromise, as when Pope Innocent was compelled by the passionate anxiety of the people of Rome to allow Etruscan augurs publicly to work divination in the Forum.

But also there was the mass of secret, and yet open, dealing with the black arts which was so private as to kill a man by enchantment and so widespread as to be generally recognized in the penal codes. As the Church mastered the peoples, so the ecclesiastical government, like the secular, made rules against all such practices. It was not, however, recognized as different in kind from any other sin—even from the sin of false accusation of witchcraft. The Salic Law of Charlemagne decreed that anyone who was convicted of witch-cannibalism

[1] Quoted from Jornandes by Major-Gen. J. F. C. Fuller, *Decisive Battles*, vol. i.

should be heavily fined, but also that anyone who was found guilty of bringing such an accusation falsely should be fined an amount equal to about one-third of the other. Incantations of all kinds were denounced everywhere; so was the making of images to bring harm on the original. 'An actual case of such a murder is mentioned in an Anglo-Saxon charter of c. 963–75. A certain widow and her son had forfeited an estate at Ailsworth, Northamptonshire, "because they drove iron nails into Alsi, Wolfstan's father". The image was apparently discovered in the woman's chamber. She was drowned at London Bridge and her son fled and was outlawed.'[1]

Three years' penance was ordered for such offences if the magic failed, seven years if it succeeded and the victim died (of which years three were to be a fast on bread and water). Periods of penance of differing length were laid down—one year's penance for those who offered at wells and trees; five years for one who drove a man out of his right mind by the help of demons; seven years for those who raised storms; ten years for those who had great commerce with evil spirits. King Canute ordered banishment or death for all 'wizards, witches, soothsayers, perjurers, secret murderers (probably by enchantment), and harlots', unless they altered their lives and did what they could to make amends. He also included in one proclamation the word *walcyries* for witches; it was not the gods of Greece only who rode dangerously through the air by night, but more and more the 'gods of folk', they who 'all beth

[1] Kittredge, *Witchcraft in Old and New England*.

fenders, and they beth yclept strange gods, other alyen gods.'[1]

But did they? This is not a modern but a contemporary question. All over the Empire the Church had found itself confronted with such beliefs, and as its own dominions increased, as it conquered (if it did not wholly convert) the tribes and peoples, it still found itself confronted by the same ideas and the same tales. In the northern parts of Europe witches raised and subdued storms; they tied winds in knots and hung them on the masts of ships; in the more southern parts the more amorous attention of young men and maidens sought for philtres—the distinction is not absolute but it existed as a tendency of division. But malice was everywhere. The Church, it is now clear, was then fighting much more violently against Goetia than against almost anything else. She did not invent Goetia; that was there already. But so was the tendency to scepticism, 'the quality of disbelief', and this was converted as belief in the old gods had been converted. The Devil having been developed, it could hardly be denied that he and his friends and worshippers could do (under the Permission) very remarkable things. But they were also very severely limited. The malice of men and women was unbounded. But it was impossible to believe that the practice of that malice was also unbounded. Saint Augustine had checked his belief over the matter of the maidens of Italy. By the end of the Dark Ages an accident—or what seems to us an accident—determined for centuries the formal law of the Church.

[1] Kittredge, *Witchcraft in Old and New England.*

The bishops did their best by examinations to check not only Goetia but belief in Goetia. Just as under Charlemagne it was an offence to be a witch and an offence to say, untruly, that anyone was a witch; that is, just as accusations as well as sorceries were discouraged, so the bishops, with intellectual inconsistency perhaps but with the best possible intentions, often attempted to discourage both sorcery and belief in sorcery. 'Si credidisti aut particeps fuisti' is a recurrent phrase; 'if thou hast believed or taken part in'. It might possibly be argued that 'credidisti' implied an active intelligent consent to the sin, but then sometimes the word is used alone. There is, for instance, a very stringent interrogatory against belief in werewolves, which begins: 'Hast thou believed as some are accustomed to believe that those who by the vulgar are called *parcae* are able to do what they are believed to do ... namely so to affect a man at birth that afterwards when he chooses he can transform himself into a wolf ['quod vulgaris stultitia werwolff vocat'] or into any other form? Or, that you could yourselves change?' And if you have believed that this is done or 'that the divine image can be changed into any other form or species by any other power than by Almighty God', you shall do penance for ten days on bread and water. Another interrogatory inquired whether any women had got ready a table with meat and drink and three knives, in case those three sisters should come 'who were by ancient folly called the *parcae*'; penance was to last a year on lawful feast-days. And so for those who thought that they could harm poultry and pigs either by incantation or by the evil eye. There, however, is obviously a point at which belief and act come very near together. In fact, the authorities seem rather to have taken the view that to believe that anyone could do it, to believe that one could oneself do it, and to do it were three degrees of preoccupation with the same evil. They were concerned to change the whole form of the invisible world; they were concerned to direct the attention of the visible world to Christ. There were two ways of doing so, and the mind of the ecclesiastical rulers swung between them. One was to prevent people thinking about Goetia; the other was to frighten them with the Devil that lay behind Goetia.

There was in the diocese of Prum a bishop in the tenth century by the name of Regino. He drew up a number of interrogatories and he also made a collection of what may be called Rules on the subject. He included one which he attributed to a certain Council, or Synod, of Ancyra. It seems that the attribution is incorrect. It was not, however, the rule's past, but its future, which became important. For it was taken up by other collectors, and presently when Gratian, the first great editor of Canon Law, drew up his own work, this canon —the *Canon* or *Capitulum Episcopi*, as it was called— found a place there. Gratian's collection became, about 1234, the accepted law of the Church, and so therefore did the *Canon Episcopi*. It ran as follows:[1]

'Bishops and their officials must labor with all their

[1] The translation is by H. C. Lea, from *Materials towards a History of Witchcraft*.

strength to uproot thoroughly from their parishes the pernicious art of sorcery and malefice invented by the Devil, and if they find a man or woman follower of this wickedness to eject them foully disgraced from their parishes. For the Apostle says, "A man that is a heretic after the first and second admonition avoid." Those are held captive by the Devil who, leaving their creator, seek the aid of the Devil. And so Holy Church must be cleansed of this pest. It is also not to be omitted that some wicked women, perverted by the Devil, seduced by illusions and phantasms of demons, believe and profess themselves, in the hours of night, to ride upon certain beasts with Diana, the goddess of pagans,[1] and an innumerable multitude of women, and in the silence of the dead of night to traverse great spaces of earth, and to obey her commands as of their mistress, and to be summoned to her service on certain nights. But I wish it were they alone who perished in their faithlessness and did not draw many with them into the destruction of infidelity. For an innumerable multitude, deceived by this false opinion, believe this to be true, and so believing, wander from the right faith and are involved in the error of the pagans when they think that there is anything of divinity or power except the one God. Wherefore the priests throughout their churches should preach with all insistence to the people that they may know this to be in every way false and that such phantasms are imposed on the minds of infidels and not by the divine but by the malignant spirit. Thus

[1] Later texts added Herodias to Diana, which looks as if Herodias had been of an importance once which is now lost.

Satan himself, who transfigures himself into an angel of light, when he has captured the mind of a miserable woman and has subjugated her to himself by infidelity and incredulity, immediately transforms himself into the species and similitudes of different personages and deluding the mind which he holds captive and exhibiting things, joyful or mournful, and persons, known or unknown, leads it through devious ways, and while the spirit alone endures this, the faithless mind thinks these things happen not in the spirit but in the body. Who is there that is not led out of himself in dreams and nocturnal visions, and sees much when sleeping which he had never seen waking? Who is so stupid and foolish as to think that all these things which are only done in spirit happen in the body, when the Prophet Ezekiel saw visions of the Lord in spirit and not in the body, and the Apostle John saw and heard the mysteries of the Apocalypse in the spirit and not in the body, as he himself says "I was in the spirit"? And Paul does not dare to say that he was rapt in the body. It is therefore to be proclaimed publicly to all that whoever believes such things or similar to these loses the faith, and he who has not the right faith in God is not of God but of him in whom he believes, that is, of the Devil. For of our Lord it is written "All things were made by Him." Whoever therefore believes that anything can be made, or that any creature can be changed to better or to worse or be transformed into another species or similitude, except by the Creator himself who made everything and through whom all things were made, is beyond doubt an infidel.'

This was the great achievement of the 'quality of disbelief'. It applied chiefly to the riding by night; other credulities were not so firmly and canonically reproved. It was not entirely consistent with itself, nor perhaps with the Christian Faith, for it might be thought to involve a suggestion that the body was not capable of heavenly things. But even if all that is allowed, it has a nobility of effort in it. Unfortunately the great vision of the One Mover could not be adequately communicated to all the men and women of Europe. The Church, three centuries after, went back on its own law. But it must be admitted that the inquisitive and iniquitous minds of a rumoured Goetia had made nonsense of it first.

WITCHCRAFT AND HERESY

At this point, before the Middle Ages open, it is perhaps worth while considering what, setting aside any pact with the Calumniator, the causes of magical sensation were. What is it, in experience, that habituates men's minds to the idea of magic? Any such discussion of secondary causes in experience is open, of course, to frank contradiction. It is one of the difficulties of all intellectual argument that all intellectual argument reposes on, and is carried on amongst, an immense amount of valid or invalid predispositions, emotions, and sensations, which can hardly be properly taken into account until the argument is ended—the purification, the validity or invalidity of which, it is the purpose of the dispute to discover and ensure. The argument must always proceed, of course, on the basis of something in common; if no more, at least that the intellectual process is, in some way, relevant to phenomena. The fundamental challenge to this—namely, that there is no reason to suppose that our intellectual processes are relevant to phenomena, can never be refuted; it can only be denied on the general basis that, as regards the lesser things of existence, they seem to be. But whether, because we can to some extent rely on repetition, we have any reason to suppose we know anything of that which repeats is another matter.

The predisposition towards the idea of magic might be said to begin with a moment which seems to be of fairly common experience—the moment when it seems that anything might turn into anything else. We have grown used—and properly used—to regarding this sensation as invalid because, on the whole, things do not turn into other things except by processes which we realize, or else at least so frequently that we appreciate the probability. But the occasional sensation remains. A room, a street, a field, becomes unsure. The edge of a possibility of utter alteration intrudes. A door, untouched, might close; a picture might walk; a tree might speak; an animal might not be an animal; a man might not be a man. One may be with a friend, and a terror will take one even while his admirable voice is speaking; one will be with a lover and the hand will become a different and terrifying thing, moving in one's own like a malicious intruder, too real for anything but fear. All this may be due to racial memories or to any other cause; the point is that it exists. It exists and can be communicated; it can even be shared. There is, in our human centre, a heart-gripping fear of irrational change, of perilous and malevolent change.

Secondly, there is the human body, and the movements of the human body. Even now, when, as a general rule, the human body is not supposed to mean anything, there are moments when it seems, in spite of ourselves, packed with significance. This sensation is almost exactly the opposite of the last. There, one was aware that any phenomenon might alter into another and truer self. Here, one is aware that a phenomenon, being wholly itself, is laden with universal meaning. A hand lighting a cigarette is the explanation of everything; a foot stepping from a train is the rock of all existence. If the first group of sensations are due to racial fear, I do not know to what the second group are due—unless indeed to the Mercy of God, who has not left us without a cloud of witnesses. But intellectually they are both as valid or invalid as each other; any distinction must be a matter of choice. And they justify each other, at least to this extent, that (though the first suggests irrationality and the second rationality) they both at first overthrow a simple trust that phenomena are what phenomena seem.

But if the human body is capable of seeming so, so are the controlled movements of the human body—ritual movements, or rather movements that seem like ritual. A finger pointing is quite capable of seeming not only a significant finger, but a ritual finger; an evocative finger; not only a finger of meaning, but a finger of magic. Two light dancing steps by a girl may (if one is in that state) appear to be what all the Schoolmen were trying to express; they are (only one cannot quite catch it) an intellectual statement of beatitude. But two quiet steps by an old man may seem like the very speech of hell. Or the other way round. Youth and age have nothing to do with it, nor did the ages that defined and denounced witchcraft think so. The youngest witch, it is said, that was ever burned was a girl of eleven years old.

Ordered movement, ritual, is natural to men. But some ages are better at it, are more used to it, and more sensitive to it, than others. The Middle Ages liked great spectacle, and therefore (if for no other reasons—but there were many) they liked ritual. They talked in ritual —blazons declared it. They were nourished by ritual— the Eucharist exhibited it. They made love by ritual— the convention of courtly love preserved it. Certainly also they did all these things without ritual—but ritual (outside the inner experience) was the norm. And ritual maintains and increases that natural sense of the significance of movement. And, of course, of formulae, of words.

The value of formulae was asserted to be very high. The whole religious life 'as generally necessary to salvation' depended on formulae. The High God had submitted himself to formulae. He sent his graces, He came Himself, according to ritual movements and ritual formulae. Words controlled the God. All generations who have believed in God have believed that He will come on interior prayer; not all that He will come, if not visibly yet in visible sacraments, on exterior incantation. But so it was. Water and a Triune formula concentrated grace; so did oil and other formulae; so— supremely—did bread and wine and yet other formulae. Invocations of saints were assumed, if less explicitly guaranteed, to be effective. The corollaries of the Incarnation had spread, in word and gesture, very far.

The sense of alteration, the sense of meaning, the

evocation of power, the expectation of the God, lay all about the world. The whole movement of the Church had, in its rituals, a remarkable similarity to the other rites it denounced. But the other rites had been there first, both in the Empire and outside the Empire. In many cases the Church turned them to its own purposes. But also in many cases it entirely failed to turn them to its own purposes. In many cases it adopted statues and shrines. But in others it was adopted by, at least, the less serious spells and incantations. Wells and trees were dedicated to saints. But the offerings at many wells and trees were to something other than the saint; had it not been so they would not have been, as we find they often were, forbidden. Within this double and intertwined life existed those other capacities, of which we know more now, but of which we still know little—clairvoyance, clairaudience, foresight, telepathy. Joan of Arc told the Dauphin the secret of his heart and Agnes Sampson told James VI of Scotland the words he had said privately to his wife Anne oversea in Denmark. Joan of Arc had one explanation and Agnes Sampson had another. It is not perhaps wholly loss that our more modern explanations do not compel us either to approve or disapprove (on those grounds alone) of either Joan of Arc or Agnes Sampson. Even in those centuries there were many who were shy of either approving or disapproving. There was a movement towards discouraging attention to such things. 'Credidisti'—'hast thou believed . . .?' Don't. Be kind to your grandmother; believe that Love loves; go to your religious duties; and be glad. Perhaps it failed. But if so, it was not altogether the fault of the Church or of the ecclesiastics. There were a few who wanted power, who wanted fear, who wanted something—some actuality? some illusion?—more certain than all. In the year 1600 Rollande du Vernois, taken to be burned alive, amid great and violent rain, and entreated to repent and be reconciled to God, said only that she had had a good master, and died.

One cannot altogether have it both ways. The du Vernois had confessed after being badgered and imprisoned and cross-examined and threatened with torture, if not actually tortured. She may have been in a state to confess anything. But then one would expect her to be so broken as to be reconciled. There are, of course, a dozen explanations. She would not, at the very last, give her executioner that satisfaction. She was past everything, tied to the stake, amid such rain that the fire could hardly be lit, and she broke out only into a few delirious words. She had come to believe in her own confessions. She had been shown (is it past belief, if she were indeed innocent?) something of the inscrutable mercy of Almighty God. Or she knew her master indeed, and her master was not God.

That extremely intelligent man, King James I of England, in his book on demonology, wrote that men and women were lured into this 'sin against the Holy Ghost' commonly by three passions: 'Curiosity in great ingines: thrist of revenge, for some torts deeply apprehended: or greedy appetite of gear, caused through great poverty'. One ought perhaps to add one more—the longings of sex and what other energies arouse variable phantasms in the human mind—the strange eidola of dreams and waking fancies, of horror and desire. It was held by the Canon Episcopi that the riding by night was fantasy, diabolic fantasy but still fantasy. But it was spoken of more realistically: 'all such ben led at night with gobelyn and erreth hither and thither'. And as the centuries pass, with the more general coming of rumours of incubi and succubi, with the growth of universal obscenities, with the examinations and cross-examinations, the possibility of such fantasies being in every mind increased. Secret dramatizations of longing, yearnings, efforts not to 'nurse unacted desires' combined with the grand tradition that desires need not be unacted.

As the metaphysical civilization established itself, those matters which had been so strongly felt emotionally (whether by the pious or the impious) began to be defined. Leisure and communication gave the intellectuals a chance to argue and to define. That reluctance to define which has been one of the graces bestowed by God on the Church has had, like all graces, its sincere opponents. The Middle Ages had their fill of people like the late W. G. Ward in the nineteenth century, who was said to desire a new papal decree every morning at breakfast. These people, generally then clerics, began to pay concentrated attention to error. This was nothing new, but the universal organization in which it operated was new, and the capacity of that organization to issue authoritative statements was new. Centres of definition existed, and the most important of those centres, the overruling source of definition, was the See of Rome.

At first, however, this operation was not particularly

aimed at witchcraft. That came under the moral law. It was a rather peculiar and horrid immorality, but discussion no more centred upon it than upon the technique of murder or theft. There were those who made wax images and destroyed them in order to destroy their enemies. It was said that a Bishop of Treves, in the eleventh century, had been killed in this way by the Jews; the image was put to the fire while he was baptizing one Easter Sunday, and the bishop collapsed and died. There were those who caused storms of rain and hail in order to destroy crops; also in the eleventh century a Pope (Gregory VII) protested to the King of Denmark against the attribution of all storms to priests and old women. Dead wizards called the living to follow them, so that the living also died; there was a case on the borders of Wales, which only ceased when Sir William de Landon pursued the living corpse and struck it through the head with his sword.[1]

Such things were habitual. But the attention of the medieval mind was paid at first not to them but to heresy. Even the great fundamental text, *Thou shalt not suffer a witch to live*, was explained to refer to heretics. 'We may take the word *malefici* as applying to heretics, who, actuated by the[2] malign spirit, perversely deceive men', wrote one Father.

[1] Dr. Kittredge points out that this is a case of vampirism; 'it is noteworthy that the vampire was a wizard in this life.' But the two traditions, though obviously related, did not, so far as I can see, often cross so definitely.

[2] Or 'a'—*spiritu maligno*. It is an interesting consideration how far the lack of an article in Latin, and therefore the doubtful use of 'a' and 'the' may have helped, in those of popular intellect, to hasten the conception of the devil.

The definition of heresy involved an obstinate persistence in a particular opinion against the known authority of the Church. This was, not unnaturally, for long regarded by the authorities as much worse—being fundamental—than any other sin, and dealings with devils did not involve such a particular obstinacy. Heretics deliberately refused an intellectual obedience; witches merely disobeyed. There were, no doubt, a number of witches; there were also a number of adulterers, murderers, thieves, and what not. It was, no doubt, shocking. But since the idea and image of the Devil had grown popular, a certain amount of carelessness as well as care existed in the matter. The two great schools of those who thought it happened and those who thought it did not happen had not yet come to blows. Everyone thought that the witches thought it happened; most thought it was wicked of them; some thought it was silly of them. But there was, so far, no general formulation of the evil or of its characteristics or of its cure.

Nor was the distinction between divination and witchcraft, between control of demons and submission to demons, very much discussed. The great schoolmen had not yet arisen, nor was the Inquisition yet a working concern. In the earlier periods of the Middle Ages there was a great deal more looseness than after the grand formulating period of the thirteenth century. There was a much wider no-man's-land where magic and science rubbed shoulders. Great men, even great ecclesiastics, might have their personal 'wise man'—something of an astrologer, a worker at alchemy, learned in divination

84

—and no-one (unless a particularly Puritan bishop) was likely to inquire too closely into what exactly his relations with the spirits were. It seems likely that, apart from his general use of adding reputation to the court of his employer, the use of such a man was aimed chiefly at foretelling fortunate days, casting horoscopes and prophesying, and at least suggesting the possibility of more money, either by alchemy or by discovering hidden treasure. He was sometimes set to find other things. The Abbot of Whalley in 1280 was excommunicated for having paid much money to a supernaturalist, 'whom he employed to discover the body of his brother, drowned in the Ouse'.[1]

There was in fact almost no limit to the various practices or to those who practised them. From reputable sciences like astrology to the lowest traditional charms, from metal plates inscribed with complicated symbolisms to bags containing toads or toads' feet, from bishops and marshals to vagabonds and gypsies, the preoccupation moved universally. Like the early Christians under the Empire, such practitioners or guardians of practitioners were officially regarded as liable at any moment to legal action, and sometimes the law was indeed put into action. More often it was no-one's business to start it. Sometimes it was. A murder plot might be discovered, and magical working be found to be involved. Sometimes an accusation of magic was used to undermine a man's position; thus Hubert de Burgh was accused of magic in the thirteenth century; and in the early fourteenth a Bishop of Troyes was accused

[1] Kittredge, *Witchcraft*.

of murdering the Queen of France by piercing an image, and a Bishop of Cahors was actually put to death for conspiring to murder the Pope by the same means.

The change which took place may be said to be largely due to the gradual identification of sorcery and heresy. This identification of what had been for long two different categories was due, it seems, to several causes. The first, the overt cause, was in the secret gatherings of heretics—'heretics' šabbaths', as they were called. The Ages of Faith were infiltrated by doctrines which were not those of official belief, and those who held them came together to hold their own worship according to their own rites. The most famous of these were the Albigenses of the south of France at the beginning of the thirteenth century, but the Albigenses were only one group, though certainly the largest. Europe held many others. They were attacked in different places at different times: in France, in Germany, in Italy. The Luciferans, for example, carried on the semi-pagan dream of the unjust Creator and the just rebel—Prometheus Gnosticized. They were said to meet 'in loca subterranea', and to abandon themselves, after their rites, to those indescribable orgies of which the later descriptions of the Sabbath are probably as near a definition as the European imagination has found. It would be rash to say that nothing of the sort happened —though it is true the Romans had said something like it about the early Christians. Even according to Saint Paul, however, some of the Christian gatherings had a non-Christian side to them. The test of judging the tree by the fruit has never been very certain in Christendom, and it has been made more difficult by the popular habit of attributing undesirable fruit to an undesired tree. It may have been in some such popular attribution that the tales of the tall black man and the great cat began to be repeated about any reputed gatherings of secret worshippers. 'In loca subterranea' became metaphysical as well as spiritual, whether they were said to be occupied by Luciferans or Cathari, Bogomils or Albigenses.

An example, in the fourteenth century, of these secret gatherings, and of their attributed acts, is to be found in the history of the destruction of the Templars. The accusations brought against them in 1307 exhibit what might be called the preparation for sorcery. They involve the renunciation of Christ, the obscene kiss which afterwards became such a marked feature of the evil Rites, the worship of an idol or of an idol's head, and in some cases the worship of the cat. The confessions acknowledged these evils in varying degree. The cat was not generally admitted; the head more frequently; the kiss and the apostasy very generally—one hundred and eighty-three admitted apostasy and one hundred and eighty obscenity out of the two hundred and thirty-one Templars examined by the Papal Commission.[1] One witness declared that after he had renounced Christ, he had been commanded to believe instead in 'the great omnipotent God'. Others testified to sacrilegious acts against the Host or to the omission of part of the Canon of the Mass. The head was reported by

[1] E. J. Martin, *The Trial of the Templars.*

some to be the head of the first Grand Master, 'who made us and has not left us'; it was 'pale and discoloured'; it was so terrible that it looked like a devil's; it was covered with gold and precious stones; it was carried in procession with lights. A few said that the members wore girdles which had been bound round the head and distributed, which has a certain resemblance to the magical link so common in sorcery.

It does not seem, however, that the accusations were pressed to the actual practice of sorcery as such. The aim of the Order is not stated to be more than to enrich itself by all means; there is no definite invocation of devils, nor any *maleficium* aimed at the lives or property of others. There are occasional hints of a further secret rule among the more experienced brethren, but if it existed it was never brought out. This makes it seem, on the whole, that there was no such rule. The Order was not really concerned with the discovery of supernatural and diabolical operations. But there was a general tendency in the various houses to create an atmosphere in which, had the intention to operate existed, it could easily have been carried out. That it was not generally supposed to have done so is clear, not only from the confessions, but from the fact that the destruction of the Order was not afterwards regarded as one of the victories of the Church against witchcraft. But it may easily have excited the sense of the secluded congregation, the secret worship, and the degraded and disgusting buffoonery.

The overthrow of the Templars was conducted largely by the Inquisition. The rise of the Inquisition helped in the identification of heresy with sorcery and witchcraft. It involved a distinction between cases of which it could itself take cognizance and those which had to be remitted to the bishops' courts—or, of course, to the ordinary secular courts. The Inquisition was supposed only to deal with 'the Heretical Evil'; any cases of witchcraft or sorcery remitted to it therefore must have in them an element of intellectual error. One point on which the decision could be made was this: was there, in the sorcery, any attribution of power to the Devil as such? It was orthodox belief everywhere that the Devil could only do what God permitted. Any assumption that he had power in himself was heretical. The distinction, if a sacrifice had been offered to the Devil, depended on the witch's confession in regard to that abstract point. If the witch meant only a repudiation of God in her inmost soul, if she were, so to speak, perverse and irrational, then she was not heretical. But if she believed that she repudiated God in favour of another power, if she were, so to speak, rational and dualist, then she was heretical. Other points were the use of sacred things in the evil invocations, or indeed of a parody of sacred things. Thus the perverse baptism, whether of human beings or of witches, was regarded as heretical. To observe chastity in honour of devils was heretical; so was fasting—it implied adoration. On the other hand the invocation of devils to seduce women from chastity was not heretical. God had allowed that to be within the power of devils; therefore adoration was not implied. But the more cautious theologians refined a little there: an invocation by command was not heretical; an invocation by entreaty was.[1]

Cases involving doctrine took place during an outbreak in the south of France in the early fourteenth century, about a hundred years after the Albigensian war. In 1335 two women, Anne-Marie de Georgel and Catherine Delort, both of Toulouse, confessed (one after torture) to both heresy and witchcraft. Anne-Marie had first been seduced by a tall dark man who had come to her 'while she was washing'; Catherine had been inveigled into the group by her lover. They had both been at the gatherings, and had adored the goat; they had done, afterwards, what harm they could. They both believed that God and Satan were equal, and that there was perpetual war between them, but that it was the turn of Satan to gain the victory. Catherine added that Antichrist would soon destroy Christianity. It was such cases that tended, in spite of some checks, to enlarge the jurisdiction of the Inquisition to include all forms of witchcraft and sorcery. Nor were the definitions of the schoolmen lacking. Saint Thomas Aquinas declared that the denial of sorcery was heretical; he defined even magical control to be impermissible; 'no power is given to man over demons to use them as he will, for he is required to fight against them'. The University of Paris declared that sorcery

---

[1] At a later date the refinement went still further. It was not heretical (though it might be wrong) to use the consecrated Host in a magical attempt to divine whether, for example, a certain woman loved the inquirer, because God knows the secrets of hearts; but it was heretical to inquire by magical command of an evil spirit, because evil spirits do not know.

was actual and that pact was actual. The doctrine of ambivalence worked in the Middle Ages. They made haste to enlarge the Devil's power, even while they denied that the Devil had power. They denied that Antichrist could conquer and burnt Catherine Delort for saying so. But they implied that only by the most extreme measures could they be certain that he would not. Pact loomed everywhere, either explicit or tacit; in either case, close to heresy. The combined efforts of the Inquisition and of the theorists ended practically in the decision that it was either direct heresy or worse than the worst heresy. Nicholas V in 1451 committed all such cases in France to the Inquisition, even if they were not 'manifestly' heresy.

By that date a change was coming over the whole manner of thought. There lay in the way of the great new formulation one document—a document of uncertain origin, of dubious credit, except that it was included in the Canon Law of the Church. That document was the Canon Episcopi. It was there clearly laid down that the 'riding by night' (and all that was then in the minds of the orthodox shaping itself into the tale of the Sabbath), the transmutations of bodies, or the alteration of bodies, by diabolic power was false. The evil powers were deceiving the women who dreamed of such things. During the fifteenth century the two answers to this were discovered. The first was that, even if the dream were only a dream, yet intentional recollection and intentional consent to or delight in such a dream made the subject as guilty as if the dream had been actuality. The second answer was that the Canon

Episcopi was correct, for the women to whom it referred. But times had changed. A new sect had arisen. It might be true that women in those past days had not been transported on beasts, because beasts could not move over such distances or so fast; and did not ride with Diana or Herodias, because Diana did not exist and 'the most damned of adulterous women' would not be let out of hell to ride with them. But in these present days, the argument ran, the new sect were transported by devils, and did not believe that the spirits with whom they rode were Diana or Herodias, but knew them to be evil spirits.

Along these lines the old position was attacked and turned. The Canon Episcopi became of less and less importance. It is true that the full details of the Sabbath had not yet been discovered or invented. But the great condition necessary for a formal belief in the Sabbath had been laid down; namely, that the accused of to-day were not like the accused of yesterday; that to-day's crisis was deeper and darker and in every way more dangerous than any crisis of yesterday; that the world was worse than it ever had been, and much more desperate means must be undertaken in order to deal with it. If Satan had fallen from the kingdom of heaven he had already almost returned there. And indeed he had.

Chapter Five

THE CENTURIES OF THE NOBLE TRIALS

As has been said, accusations of divination and sorcery were by no means brought only against the poor or the unprotected. Even in the later times of the great persecutions the rich were liable to attack; merchants and burgomasters and their families were arrested and presently burnt. In the earlier period neither rank nor riches were any protection. The grand metaphysical theory operated in all classes, and the use of rank in safeguarding and riches in hiring wizards and witches was well recognized. Nor in fact was the Christian Faith always involved in more than the technique. Secular governments, exactly like the government of Augustus, looked with high suspicion on all divination, but now they were supported by the ecclesiastical power. The colleges of the Mysteries cursed what the courts of the kings forbade. At that time, however, accusation was not always followed by condemnation. Acquittal in the secular courts was always possible, and even in the ecclesiastical it seems that death was not altogether certain.

The great formulation of the Middle Ages, which

happened after the Council of Lateran in the thirteenth century, took some time to work itself out in practice. The idea of Pact was still rather accidental than essential; that is, whereas in many actual cases it was naturally expected to exist, it was not yet an all but defined certainty. France had by 1350 seen many witchcraft trials, yet in Italy by 1340 the inquisitorial courts 'had no precedent to follow'; in 1350 a secular court in Moravia allowed two women, accused of witchcraft and homicide, to clear themselves by their single and separate oaths. The effect of the scholastic intellect had not yet been felt, and there was no universal decision on what happened in the witch-centres or what ought to happen in the courts. Naturally those definitions first affected the ecclesiastical courts; it was not until about 1400 that they began to be felt as patterns in the secular. On the other hand, the pressure from Rome on its subordinates began to be increased; in the early part of the fourteenth century John XXII issued several declarations against offenders, besides in the year 1318 ordering a special inquiry into the behaviour of certain members of the Papal Court, 'accused on good authority of necromancy, geomancy, and other magic arts . . . invoking spirits in circles, confining spirits in mirrors . . . and using *Dianae*'. Benedict XII in 1337 issued a similar commission against certain clerks and laics who had slandered the Bishop of Beziers by accusing him of having attempted the life of John XXII by magical images. It seems as if, one way or another, a particular mass of magical rumours and operations gathered round that Pope.

At times a trial of some particular distinction stood out. In 1232 Hubert de Burgh was accused of gaining King John's favour by means of charms and incantations. In 1315 a certain Enguerrand de Marigny, once chamberlain to Philip IV of France, was accused under his successor Louis X of treason, embezzlement, and witchcraft (this was the waxen image method of killing), and was hanged, though afterwards rehabilitated. The natural attribution of royal affection or displeasure to such means was obviously bound to be widespread. It was as difficult then as it is now to understand why anyone should love (in whatever sense) anyone else, and when the beloved was a man of outstanding parts or indeed of no outstanding parts, either fact contributed a promising element of suspicion to the distracted and frustrated minds of other courtiers. The presence of learning in the beloved or in any of his friends, servants, or clients accentuated such suspicion. Clergy indeed, had it not been for their generally privileged positions as far as prosecutions went, might have suffered more than they did. Control of blessed formulae might not be far from control of accursed, and the knowledge of holy ceremonies might disguise even better acquaintance-ship with black rites. In 1374 Gregory XI was lamenting to the Inquisitor of France the prevalence of the evil thing among the clerics of that kingdom.

In 1324 a famous case took place in Ireland—that of the Lady Alice Kyteler. She lived near Kilkenny and was accused of various forms of witchcraft by the Bishop of Ossory. The accusations included almost every sort of evil-doing of that kind. It was declared against her and her companions that, in order to obtain their desires, they had (i) denied the Faith of Christ and his Church, agreed to believe nothing that the Church believed, and neither adored the Body of Christ nor entered churches nor heard Mass nor taken blessed bread or holy water; (ii) offered to demons sacrifices of living creatures, tearing them asunder and distributing them at crossroads; (iii) sought advice and answers from demons by casting lots; (iv) held gatherings by night ('in suis conventiculis de nocte'), when in the light of wax candles they had solemnly excommunicated and cursed the husbands of the Lady Alice and her companion, from the foot's sole to the head's top, naming expressly all their members, and extinguishing the candles on the final Amen; (v) from the intestines of cocks offered as aforesaid, and certain horrid worms, various herbs, nails from dead bodies, hairs, and brains of boy-children dying without baptism—all boiled together in the skull of a robber who had been beheaded—made by incantation powders and ointments to cause love and hate, to kill and to harm the bodies of faithful Christians and also to make the candles of the ceremonies; (vi) by such means destroyed the Lady Alice's first three husbands and debilitated her present; (vii) had as a familiar spirit a demon called Robinum filium Artis, or Robin Artisson—'ex pauperioribus inferni', one of the proletariat of hell—whom the Lady Alice knew carnally as an incubus, and who appeared to her as a cat or as a black and shaggy dog or as an Ethiop (but then with two companions like himself but greater); from whom also she received all her riches and everything she possessed. It was said also that between compline and twilight she had been seen in the streets of Kilkenny, raking the filth and garbage towards the door of her son's house and murmuring:

> To the house of William my son
> Hie all the wealth of Kilkenny town.

In her house, when it was searched, was found 'a wafer of sacramental bread, having the Devil's name stamped thereon instead of Jesus Christ, and a pipe of ointment, wherewith she greased a staff, upon which she ambled and galloped through thick and thin, when and in what manner she listed'. The information, however, concerning the sweeping and the hid magical properties, is of later date than the accusations, and may be decoration.

The Lady Alice fled and escaped. Of her two companions one, a woman named Petronilla de Midia, was seized and, after confessing to the truth of the accusations, was burnt. The other, Petronilla's daughter Basil, also escaped. Petronilla, in dying, maintained the equal guilt of the Lady Alice's son William, who was arrested and for some time imprisoned, but afterwards released.

In the same year, 1324, there was a celebrated case in England. Edward II was on the throne, the two Despensers were his favourites, and the friends of the Despensers were in power. There was living in Coventry, in the previous November, a certain Master John de Notingham, and in his house a lodger, Robert le Mareschal of Leicester. John was known as a necromancer, or magician. There came to the house, 'on the Wednesday before the feast of St. Nicholas', a band of some twenty-seven men, who 'demanded of the aforesaid Master John and Robert le Mareschal if they could keep counsel and they should have great profit'. John and Robert swore they would. One of the leaders of the band, Richard le Latoner, assisted by the others, opened the secret. He said that they were all tired of the exactions put upon them by the Prior of Coventry, who had for patrons and backers the King and the two Despensers. They wanted to know if John would undertake to free them by killing 'the King, the Count of Winchester (the elder Despenser), Monsieur Hugh le Despenser, the Prior of Coventry, and others whom they named, by means of his necromancy and his arts'. John 'dict qe oye, et se assentit'; so did Robert, who was presumably a similar craftsman. John was to have £20 and his maintenance in any English house of religion that he chose; Robert was to have £15. In a few days the burghers paid a part of the money, and also supplied materials, seven pounds of wax and two ells of canvas. The two magicians made seven images—of the King, of the two Despensers, of the prior, of the prior's cellarer, and of his seneschal. The seventh was of a certain Richard de Sowe, and this, it seems, was made only that it might be used as a test, to see if the work were well done. This making took place in an old house half a league away from Coventry, from the Monday next after the feast of Saint Nicholas, when they began 'faire leur mestries', and with whatever other rites were necessary occupied them until the Saturday next after the feast of the Ascension. During all that time they 'demorèrent continuellement sur leur œuvre'. Towards the end of the period, one midnight, John gave Robert a piece of lead with a sharp point, and bade him strike it into the forehead of the image of Richard de Sowe, which he did. The next day Robert was sent round to Richard's house to see if the experiment had succeeded. It had succeeded very well; the image had been properly identified with its human original. De Sowe was in a dreadful state. He could remember nothing; he could recognize no-one; he was screaming and crying out 'harrow!' He remained in that state for about three weeks, when Master John, in his old house, before the image, pulled out the sharp-pointed lead from the forehead, and struck it in again, but this time into the heart. De Sowe died in a few days. 'Proof was made of the said Richard in the form aforesaid, by the assent of the aforesaid Richard (le Latoner) and others, and those knowing the fact.'

All this is from a legal deposition by Robert le Mareschal before the Coroner of our lord the King. He was then 'appellor' against both John de Notingham and all the aforesaid men of Coventry, who had all been taken into custody. The case went to the King's Bench, and was tried by a jury in 1325. John of Notingham had died in prison. All the Coventry men were declared by the jurors to be 'in nullo culpabilis de feloniis nec maleficiis sibi impositis'. And the aforesaid Robert le Mareschal 'remittitur prisonae marescalli in custodia'.

There the fantastic thing ends. It is all incredibly legal

and correct—Hilary Term, writs of certiorari, the prisoners 'putting themselves on their country', and the rest. But what *happened*? The younger Despenser is found afterwards complaining to the Pope (the same John XXII) that he has been threatened by magic. The Pope assures him that if he keeps his religious duties he is quite safe, though the Despenser letter may have encouraged the papal denunciation of sorcery. But still what *happened*? Did Robert le Mareschal invent it all? Or was the feeling against the Despensers so high that the jury would not convict? Richard de Sowe, one would suppose, must have died in strange circumstances; was there some magical rite and were the Coventry men involved to give it an air of respectability? What is clear is that, even if Robert were lying throughout, still he thought those lies might be swallowed. He thought that that operation was credible, and so did everyone else. But he thought also that respectable men—and many of them—might be quite quietly involved in such 'malice'. And so did everyone else. Of course, in this case no formal Pact was involved; what was involved was hiring a murderer by supernatural means. Between that case and that of the Lady Alice Kyteler all the medieval tales of magic sway— between the Ethiop dwarf 'ex pauperioribus inferni', the torn cocks, the devil-stamped sacramental wafer, and the bourgeois group hiring a wax image and the necessary accompaniments, to put a stop to the exactions of priors and nobles.

These two kinds of sorcery proceeded all through the century, but it is not until the next century that what was regarded as the great war between Christendom and the Devil seems to open. By about the year 1400 the opinions of Saint Thomas and other great school-men had begun to produce their effects. The logical arguments, based on dogmas and on texts, could hardly be denied, once the powerful orthodoxy of their pro-posers was admitted. The emotional strain of the closing Middle Ages, the Black Death, the Great Schism, the exhaustion of the long concentration on the super-natural, had perhaps something to do with it; perhaps those three or four remarkably notorious trials which took place in the early part of the new century. In 1419 King Henry V of England caused it to be publicly de-clared that his stepmother Joan of Navarre had made attempts on his life by means of the evil arts. In 1430 Joan of Arc was accused of demon-worship by trees and fountains. In 1441 the Duchess of Gloucester, the wife of the Regent of England, was found guilty of magical practices. In 1440 Gilles de Rais, one of the greatest lords of France, was put to death for devil-worship combined with the murder of children. All this time there went on, all over Europe, a quickening of the suspicion, a hurrying on of trials, an increasing use of torture. Con-fessions were more rapidly extracted, and confessions became more and more similar. More and more books aimed at the grand evil appear, quoting, discussing, defining, insisting. But also there appears on the orthodox side a very dangerous and awful thing—a sentence peculiarly increased according to the offence. It might be held necessary to put to death; it might be necessary—by an effort of the mind one can believe it

—to use torture in order to extract particulars of the danger, of the array of the diabolic war. As for burning, incineration was the habit; it did not occur to anyone to go against it. But a particular and horrible sense of retaliation begins; the question over, the death near, something *extra* must be done. A vengeance creeps up and runs whispering among the exact scientific judges, and hell looks out of their faces, they who thought nothing less! In 1462, in a trial of four men and four women at Chamounix, the accused had first denied and then confessed under torture. Sentence was pronounced by the secular court; they were all to be burned. *But—* one of them, a woman and a widow, called Peronnette, who had committed 'unspeakable crimes' (giving herself to incubi, eating children), was for that cause to be made to sit naked for three minutes on red-hot iron before being burnt; and another, a man, named Jean Grehaudi, who had trampled on our Lord in the Sacrament, was to be taken naked to the spot, there to have his foot cut off, and to be made to kiss the sign of the Cross on the ground, also before being burned.[1] And so, presumably, it was done.

It is perhaps worth while to note some particulars of the noble trials (including Saint Joan's) mentioned above, since they present the idea of the enemy against which (as a cause), and in favour of which (as a result) these horrors grew up. The episode of Henry V does not help much, except that, like so many other cases, it involved a priest. The chaplain of Queen Joan confessed that he had conspired, under instructions from his

[1] Lea, *Materials.*

mistress, to kill the king by sorcery and necromancy; it may have been by making an image, as in the case of John de Notingham and Edward II, or it may have been by saying a Mass against him. It was held that either a Mass said over wax images with the intention of death, or else the Mass for the faithful departed, would suffice. If this last were said a certain number of times, the victim was thought to die before that number of days had passed. There is a terrible inversion in that vision of the ordained priest chanting, with his thoughts on a living man, 'Requiem aeternam dona ei, Domine', and meaning it. Queen Joan was said to have 'compassed and imagined the death of our lord the King in the most horrible manner that could be imagined' She was relegated to Leeds Castle, and her lands and goods confiscated; Friar Randolph was sent to prison. He was afterwards killed by a mad priest. The king, however, caused the queen's lands to be restored.

The case of the Duchess of Gloucester, twenty-two years later, had more particulars. It was one of those ambiguous affairs which could be presented, after one manner, as an innocent if rash effort to achieve permissible things; after another, as a matter of inquiry into forbidden knowledge, but without any evil intention; and, after a third, as an activity in the worst kind of sorcery and *maleficium*. It suggests that the Church was right when it forbade all unauthorized dealing, whether theurgic or goetic. Theurgy has a curious way of taking on darker colours, and the use of magic for personal knowledge has, like so many other uses, a way of degenerating into a use for personal profit. What follows is, of course, an arranged presentation of the facts, and must be read with that caution.

Eleanor Cobham, wife of Humphrey, Duke of Gloucester, brother of King Henry V, uncle to the young Henry VI, and Regent during his minority, was a woman of some passion and some ambition. She was reported, during the trial, to have gained the love of the duke originally by magical means. For this purpose she had recourse to a woman named Margery Jourdemayn. This woman was known as the Witch of Eye, which was the name of a manor near Westminster, and could therefore be got at easily when the court was in residence at Westminster. Henry V appears to have caused his council and officers to take pains to search out all sorcerers and witches, possibly after his actual or reputed experience of his stepmother, and among others a number of priests were from time to time arrested on this charge. In 1430 a certain Friar John Ashewell, 'ordinae Sanctae Crucis London', was so seized, and with him a clerk named John Virley, and the said Margery Jourdemayn. It seems to have been a London group, but what exactly the relations between the friar, the 'cleric' (of unknown degree), and Margery were, it is impossible to say, except by guessing from what eventually followed. The three of them were sent to Windsor and there kept in custody for some time. They were presently released, on security given, Margery on that of her husband. The warrant directing their dismissal was sent by the Council in May 1432.

The Duke of Gloucester was married to Eleanor by 1431, possibly earlier. There is no evidence that this group was connected with her use of drinks and philtres (if such there were). But if the future duchess were indeed obtaining such things from the Jourdemayn, it is very likely that the clerks were the intermediaries. Something of the same kind was certainly now to happen. A period of nine years went by, during which the Jourdemayn was presumably at Eye, and may have been practising her craft in more concealment. The duchess appears to have found that love-philtres may attract but cannot retain love. On her own showing she desired to have a child by her lord, and she had recourse to the same old trick of magical images. This time, however, she certainly moved through two priests, Roger Bolingbroke and Thomas Southwell, Canon. Margery became part of the conspiracy.

Bolingbroke's evidence, however, had gone farther than that of the duchess. He did not admit to high treason; indeed he urgently denied it. But he said he had at the duchess's request worked necromancy in order to discover what her future should be. This is the old divination for which young Roman nobles had suffered death under Tiberius, and it was regarded by the Government in the same light. Bolingbroke confessed that he had presumed too far in his knowledge—a knowledge which would evidently involve questions of the life or death of the king. There were, there could be, only two matters about which the Duchess of Gloucester's future estate was in question; the one was, would she be queen? the other, would she have a child? It is very likely that she desired to know both, that she aimed at being the royal mother of a dynasty. The king's death and her husband's love were equally necessary for that.

The two priests were quite certainly using magical practices for this 'presumption of knowledge'. Canon Southwell had said a secret Mass over the instruments that Bolingbroke was to use. It need not be supposed that there was any question of Pact or submission to the demons. On the contrary it seems likely that both of them professed and thought themselves to be of the great line of controllers of demons, masters of the infernal spirits by arts of measurement and incantation, priest-princes whose rites compelled hell to discover its own secrets and those of earth. Bolingbroke's instruments were seized with him when he was arrested, and were displayed about him when he was exposed on a scaffold against Paul's Cross. He was clad in his strange dress, the robes in which he exercised necromancy, the magical sword in his right hand, and the magical rod in his left. There also was the painted chair in which he was accustomed to sit, and there were other swords at each corner of the chair, with copper images hanging from their points, 'and there was hanged round about him all his instruments which were taken with him, and so shewed among the people'. It is quite clear that Thomas Southwell and Roger Bolingbroke had been attempting commerce with those powers for whom the copper images stood, commerce by command perhaps rather than submission, but undoubtedly commerce. It must, when all is said, be acknowledged, on behalf of the ecclesiastical and secular authorities, that the antique tradition was still in operation. They had the perfect answer to any objection (except to that single last objection to logic culminating in horrible and superfluous pain): 'Que messieurs les assassins commencent.'

For beyond Southwell and Bolingbroke appeared again the figure of the Jourdemayn, released on security, left in peace for years, but still with that earlier shadow of sorcery over her; and it is not perhaps to slander her if one feels that with her a sudden sense of *actualizing* that inquired future enters in. The Jourdemayn was none of these robed and sworded lords; philtres and such things were her commerce, and if she knew how to make images, they were likely to be not copper images of devils who could be controlled but waxen images of men and women who could be destroyed. The great arch through which the power of conjuration floats out over the unwilling inheritors of hell dwindles to quite a different thing, the door of a house behind which Margery practised very different—and yet not so different—rites. For the step from intellectual magic and knowledge to the practice of envenoming and inebriating is very short and very easy. Bolingbroke and Southwell, when the first Mass was said over the sacred instruments, may have—as Bolingbroke insisted—meant but the one; they became dangerously connected with the other. The great masters, sooner or later, always seem to be in that danger; some need of immediate help, some promise of profit, lures them; they condescend, but for once, to invoke the help of the lower magic; and they are lost.[1]

[1] Bulwer Lytton put it into *Zanoni*—if that odd, pretentious, but intelligent book were ever read now.

Among the waxen images exhibited with Bolingbroke was one which the prosecution said was of the
young king; the accused said it was of the hoped-for
child. Death or life, it was either way interference with
the human will. The king must not be killed to give
Dame Eleanor Cobham the throne; the duke must not
be compelled to return to his wife's bed—not though
he sinned by staying thence. Sentence was given against
all the accused. Southwell had died in prison. But
Bolingbroke was 'drawn from the Tower of London
to Tyburn, and there hanged, headed, and quartered,
and the head set upon London Bridge, and his one
quarter at Hereford, another at Oxford, another at York,
and another at Cambridge'. (Were the two universities
included this time a little to warn practitioners of
that dangerous learning?) Margery Jourdemayn was
burnt at Smithfield. The duchess did penance by walking
three times through the streets of London, barefoot,
white-clad, her hair hanging, carrying a candle of two
pounds' weight in her hand, and was afterwards sent to
perpetual prison, at Chester first and afterwards to Peel
Castle in the Isle of Man; there to ponder how she had
urged her priestly servants to discern the future, and
how in the end they had all—priests and duchess—
had recourse to the spells and drinks of the Witch of
Eye.

The two great French trials of about the same period
deal with other sides of the subject. They are, as it
happens, connected by the relation of their subjects,
though the development of those subjects' lives, once
the relation was established, was very different. In the

late afternoon of the 23rd of February 1429, among the crowd that thronged the Great Hall of the Castle of Chinon, where the Court of the Dauphin of France was established, were two persons of note, a man and a woman. The man was twenty-five years old, one of the great lords of France, cultured, and a soldier, Gilles de Rais. The other was a girl of seventeen, a peasant, uncultured, ardent, Joan of Arc. She was received by the Dauphin, and Gilles de Rais, in the train of the Dauphin, saw her. It seems that, like the Dauphin himself, he was taken captive by her personality. When she was accepted by the Court and the Army, he too had accepted her. He was devoted to her; he rode by her side; he took eager part in her battles. He was one of those to escort a convoy of food into Orleans. He abandoned himself to her; he was allowed to be one of those who brought the Holy Oil to Rheims for the coronation of the Dauphin, and rode with it into the church, escorting the Abbot of Saint Rémy, who actually carried it; there, within the church, he dismounted. She, with the high and princely comradeship that distinguished her, loved him as she loved Dunois and D'Alencon, and her other soldier friends, and called him 'true and bold'. He brought her money; he defended her person in battle. Together they swept with her banner against the English. For those efforts he was created a Marshal of France, and the Maid and he were permitted to show in their coats of arms a border of fleurs-de-lys.

He was not, however, with her on the day when she was taken; he had been sent on some other military errand. Their lives were separated, and, it seems, more awfully, their souls. She was conveyed to her prison. In that prison and during the process of her trial she had two things to depend on—her belief in the Faith and her belief in her Voices and Visions; perhaps, until the end, some faint hope also that the Dauphin would move, since that last belief that the temporal horror may change dies very hard, and when it is at last gone there is nothing left but despair or the Kingdom of God. It was the effort of the court before which she was tried to set the Faith against the Voices, to persuade her that they could not both be accepted at once. She maintained that they could, and that, by her, they must be. The final decision of the authorities, years afterwards, was that they could be, and, centuries afterwards, that she was blessed in her decision. But at the time? The Universal Church was then, and has always been, chary of private revelations; its feeling was expressed by that bishop who said to Wesley: 'Sir, this pretending to a special revelation of the Holy Ghost is a horrid thing, a very horrid thing.'

The conduct by the Maid of the war against the English was the occasion of suspicion, and provided a special energy in the courts. But the suspicion itself was aroused by other things, by the direct supernatural instruction which the Maid claimed. It is possible that the Dauphin—then, through Joan, the king—ought to have moved; other kings, in such circumstances, would certainly have moved. But it is not to be overlooked that the court which tried her was an ecclesiastical court acting in due discharge of its functions. Even the French ecclesiastics had never been quite easy about Joan, and her trial was to them a very real trial. They were intelligent enough to know that the mere fact that Joan had done what they wanted done did not prove anything about the nature of the help extended to her. Hell may give one what one wants as easily as heaven; and, oddly enough, the French, especially the French ecclesiastics, did not wish to be indebted to hell for their gains. The hush and the quiet that lay over the whole French Court and Army during the trial is due partly to the fact that it was indeed a trial.

The process was long and laborious. The very opening included two points which suggested the worst against the prisoner. She had, it is to be remembered, already behaved in a way conducive to the heaviest suspicion of improper dealing with the invisible. She had claimed such help; she had been taken in male dress, riding in an army as its leader—all against order and decency. She was asked about the revelations which she claimed; she quite definitely refused to submit them to the Inquisitorial Court. 'I will not reveal them to you, even if it cost me my head, because I have had them in visions and by secret counsel, and am forbidden to reveal them.' But this was the very description of the normal witch; she too—in Carcassonne, in Toulouse, in Switzerland, in England—had received 'secret counsel'. They bade her say the Lord's Prayer; she refused—at least she refused to say it in the open court. They insisted; she still refused. She said: 'Hear me in confession and I will willingly say it.'

The process continues: 'To this same question, which We many times put to her, she always answered: "No,

I will not say my Pater to you, unless you will hear me in confession."

"Willingly", We [that is, the bishop] said to her, "we will give you two well-known men, of the French language, and before them you shall say your Pater."

"I will not say it to them, unless it be in confession." '[1]

Each of the first few days of the process opened with a wrangle between the court and the prisoner; they demanded that she should swear to tell the truth absolutely, and she refused. She was, no doubt, within her rights; indeed her canonization has shown that the Holy See approves her action. But her continuous refusal naturally did her harm in the mind of the court, who could imagine no reason for her obstinacy apart from the serious likelihood of her being mixed up with the only powers who would wish to hide their operations from the Church of God.

It was in these conditions that the court proceeded to the question of the Voices and the Visions. She spoke of the light and the Voice. It may have been very different from the other meetings with Ethiops or tall men which were already beginning to be recounted in so many places. The Voice, she said, had woken her; they asked her if she was touched; she said she was not. They asked her if it had a face and eyes; she answered: 'You shall not know yet: the children say

[1] T. Douglas Murray, *Jeanne d'Arc: from the Original Documents*. It was Miss Margaret Murray who first, I think, drew attention to this curious attitude on the part of Saint Joan. I am not here supporting all Miss Murray's deductions, but it must be admitted that the episode was sufficient to increase the suspicions of any court. It seems uncertain if she eventually consented to say it.

"Sometimes one is hanged for speaking the truth".'
But afterwards she spoke of the Visions—the Apparitions of Saints. It is most likely that in the minds of
some of the Assessors of the court the possibility of an
incubus was already present. The question was not put,
though they came near it; they asked: 'How do you
know if the object that appears to you is male or
female?' They asked of her embracing the Visions, and
if she felt any heat in them. They asked her of her
sword, of her banner, of her knowledge of the future
and if her Voices had revealed her fate; conjuration and
divination hung in the air. They asked her of her rings,
of the secret sign she gave the king, of her reported
healing of a child; they went back to her exclamation
that the Bishop of Beauvais would be in great danger
through her trial; they asked: 'In what peril or danger
do We place Ourselves, your Judges and the others?'
Once the thought of those other trials is in the mind,
once it is recollected what was going on in many cases,
and more and more speedily and intensely, much of
the process becomes clear.

Saint Joan, of course, remained steadfast. She said that
the first Voice bade her be good and go to church; she
said, 'Never have I asked of it any recompense but the
salvation of my soul.' She identified her Voice with the
high duties of a Christian. But it was known that
priests could be warlocks and devout women witches.
Even the word 'God' was ambiguous. They asked her
whether, if a devil appeared in the form of an angel, she
would know if the apparition were good or evil; she
said she should know quite well if it were Saint Michael

or a counterfeit. They were only half-satisfied; beyond all her orthodoxy, all her devotion, all her answers, lay a reserve, a secrecy, a communion with something not of that order. But of what order then?

They had had news of her childhood. They interrogated her on it. There was a tree near the village of Domrémy; it was called 'the Fairies' Tree'; near it was a well with healing waters. 'I have often heard old folk say that the fairies haunted this tree.' Her godmother had told her so, 'a good woman, neither divineress nor sorceress'. She would not say whether she thought that fairies were evil spirits. It was admitted that she had hung garlands on the tree, and that she had sung there, 'more sung than danced'. She claimed that she had made garlands for Our Lady of Domrémy; people had said that she received her mission at the Fairies' Tree—her brother had said so, but it was not true. They asked her concerning 'those who come in the air with the Fairies'; she answered: 'I have never done nor heard anything about them, but I have heard of them, and that they came on Thursdays. I do not believe it; I think it is sorcery.' She was accused of carrying a mandrake about with her; she denied it, though she admitted that she had heard there was one, with a hazel growing over it, close by the Fairies' Tree.

It is clear that (her canonization apart) there was a great deal that any court would find highly suspicious in all this. We are quite accustomed to thinking that her spirits were either no spirits or good spirits. The court thought they might be evil spirits. Domrémy was a place of doubtful reputation; 'those who come in the air' is enough to show that. And in the last, the very last, resort, she would not submit. She referred herself to the Pope; but she would not promise unconditionally to submit to the Pope. The Promoter of the Cause asserted that her adoration of her Visions (whom she ought to have considered evil spirits) was equivalent to a pact with demons. In the end the court, driven to acquit or condemn, decided to condemn. She was pronounced a divineress, guilty of idolatry, invocation of demons, and other enormities. It was half a legal habit, but the other half was not. All Christendom was beginning to grow agitated and tremble under the fear of 'those who come in the air'.

Meanwhile, except that he made in November 1430 some sort of an effort against Rouen, where she was, nothing is heard of de Rais until after the Maid was burned in May 1431. By the end of the next year he was back at his own castle; he was then twenty-eight, and the second part of his life lay before him. He was one of the richest lords in France. He had grown up as the heir to a great name and a great position, but apart—especially apart from women. In that solitary youth, treated with almost royal ceremony, but largely alone, he had developed a taste for fine manuscripts and was himself an adept at illuminating them. He said afterwards in his confession, speaking of his crimes: 'I do not know why but I, myself, out of my own head without the advice of anyone, conceived the idea of acting thus, solely for the pleasure and delectation of lust; in fact I found incomparable pleasure in it, doubtless at the instigation of the Devil. This diabolical idea came to me eight years ago; that was the very year in which my relative the Lord of Suze died. Now being by chance in the library of his castle, I found a Latin book on the lives and customs of the Roman Caesars by a learned historian called Suetoñius; the said book was ornamented with pictures, very well painted, in which were seen the manners of these pagan emperors, and I read in this fine history how Tiberius, Caracalla and other Caesars sported with children and took singular pleasure in martyring them. Upon which I desired to imitate the said Caesars and the same evening I began to do so following the pictures in the book.' If he remembered rightly, he was aware of it as an imperial indulgence, especially suited to himself. In rank, in wealth, in power, he was already almost such a Caesar; he would be so in his tastes.

But also, as was proper, he would be so in arms. Before the Maid had left Domrémy on her mission to the Dauphin, de Rais had fought on behalf of his overlord the Duke of Brittany. He had already become a leader. He was married, to the increase of his wealth, but to his own boredom and the unhappiness of his wife. He was known to have entered upon a life of supreme magnificence, of homosexual relations, and at moments of cruelty. It was at this moment that he met the Maid.

He had never cared for women; he was consumed with a yearning for the strange non-sexual beauty of children; the clarity of earth's body in them oppressed and provoked him. There appeared suddenly before him one who was undoubtedly a woman and a maid, and yet in man's dress, young, fresh, exquisitely strange;

one who was a devout child of the Church, and yet was in direct touch with spiritual apparitions; a maid touched by—nay, familiar with—that other air and yet a maid capable of charging with the spears through this air; a kind of supernatural Caesar of airy and earthly powers. He was touched by a militant energy of body and spirit; his imagination woke to the unique glory.

He lost her; he knew she had been burnt, as heretic, schismatic, idolator, diviner, adorer of demons. What he had himself believed her to be God only knows— what, and on whose side. Perhaps it did not greatly matter. Only the sight of those two together fighting outside Paris seems for a moment to bring together all the worlds. When she was gone, he lay, it seems, silent in his castle for a while; then he moved. Besides his great households he had accumulated round him a few very private friends. It was these whom he called to help him when he determined to enter on his grand career as an image of the Caesars. The moment came when he heard a boy singing in the Church of Saint Hilary, Poitiers.

Beautiful voice and beautiful face—he was bribed incredibly to come to the castle. He came, and his voice saved him; his new lord could not bear, immediately, to lose it. Others instead were found, and persuaded to the special set of rooms in the castle; they themselves— two-score or so in all—ended in a dry well. De Rais said in his confession, of the 'amusement of the Caesars':

'I took the mystery to several persons, among others to Henriet and to Pontou, whom I trained for this sport. The said individuals aided in the mystery and took charge of finding children for my needs. The children killed at Chantoce were thrown into a vat at the foot of a tower, from which I had them taken out on a certain night and put in a box to be transferred to Mâchecoul; and at Nantes, in the Suze mansion, they were burned in my room except for a few handsome heads I kept as relics. Now I cannot say exactly how many were thus burned and killed, but they were certainly to the number of six score per year.'

Presently the lord of the place moved on to another castle, this time that called Mâchecoul. There at first he varied his pleasures, but following still the same dancing star of non-sexual, or rather of twi-sexual, beauty. He established a Foundation in honour of the Holy Innocents. He gave great lands to support it, and put them in trust to dukes, kings, and even the Emperor himself, and the Pope if those others failed. For, he said, none could requite the Creator for all his benefits, and it was highly desirable to accumulate intercessors. He put himself under the protection of those holy and adorable creatures whom the Church has canonized, as it were, by universal acclamation and only because they suffered unknowingly in direct substitution for Christ.

He continued also an artistic—perhaps a more than artistic—devotion to the Maid. The Foundation of Holy Innocents had been in the early part of 1434; towards the end of the year he presented at Orléans a play called *The Mystery of Orléans*. It went on for ten months—free. Those who could not afford to leave their work to attend were paid to do so. It was in verse; it was produced with the utmost possible richness and unstinted largesse. The king came to the opening. There, on the stage, moved the figures of himself and the Maid and their companions, and among them the Lord Gilles de Rais played the part of the Lord Gilles de Rais.

It was at this point that de Rais began to explore other capacities of man's mind as the time presented it. He desired money, much having been spent on his theatrical productions, and on his devotions of the Foundation of the Innocents (which eventually failed precisely for lack of money). But also he desired some further experience; the torture and killing of young boys was not enough. He sent one of his group to Italy—to Florence, where he was brought into touch with a strange circle of diabolists. The messenger who had gone was a priest; the adept who returned with him, Francesco Prelati, was a priest. There seems here to be one of those real unions between the Christian priest-hood and the black arts which are part of the curious imagination of Christendom. Such was the case of Urban Grandier in 1634; such of the Abbé Guibourg in Paris in 1673.

Under this direction the full magical ritual of in-vocation of the Devil was entered on, with, later, the final addition of the human sacrifice. The confession later made by de Rais presents the attempt he made, while still retaining his hold on salvation, to procure graces and gifts from the figures of damnation. It was, perhaps, not altogether a fantastic egotism that drove him both ways; it was the sense that he did not wish to lose irretrievably either way of dealing with the beauty of youth. They must be, those victims, spiritually available either as Innocents for invocation or Victims for immolation; let Prelati commit himself to the diabolic Rites, but de Rais would ambiguously seek a greater thing. No doubt there may have been mixed with this a real fear of committing himself to damnation. But it is a generally valid rule, in considering the actions of these figures of the past, to look for the positive imagination rather than the negative; desire has always its own dream, and the attempt to retain two opposites is not so uncommon that we need deny it to de Rais.

The Rites proceeded; the sacrifices were offered. At times there seems to have emerged something very like a hostile manifestation. Gilles heard voices and fled from the room; when he dared return he found Prelati lying bruised and unconscious outside the magical circle. Such violence is not uncommon in the accounts of witchcraft. At the Sabbaths it was reported that the presiding demon often beat those who had not done enough evil; and even in some of the lesser meetings of the covens the directors would strike those who failed to keep in with the ceremonies; it happened in the famous North Berwick meeting of 1590. Prelati took long to recover.

All kinds of means were used to procure the boys; some were persuaded, some bribed, some hunted. It was not easy, whatever suspicions were aroused, to set any machinery in action against anyone in de Rais's position. But at last the Bishop of Nantes began to move; he made an episcopal visitation; he collected evidence; he appointed commissioners. It was done privately, but rumours got about; Gilles's servants heard them and began to take measures for their own safety. At this moment Gilles rashly committed himself, in the course of another quarrel, to the forcing of a church and the seizure of a priest. He was persuaded to release him, but it was too late. In July 1440 the bishop drew up an accusation of sacrilege and sent it to the Duke of Brittany and to the King of France. In September de Rais was arrested at Mâchecoul, with such of his circle as had remained; the castle was searched and the remains of at least one body immediately discovered. Prelati was in hiding.

The Ecclesiastical Court, presided over by the Bishop of Nantes, held a session on the minor charges hitherto put forward. Meanwhile the Civil Court, presided over by Pierre de l'Hôpital, had been making its own inquiries, and as soon as these had reached a sufficient stage, the ecclesiastical charges were amended and enlarged. Gilles, brought before the Civil Court, professed that he was anxious to give away his property to the Church and to the poor, and to vow himself to the service of God. Pierre de l'Hôpital answered that the justice of man as well as the justice of God must be served. The two courts worked, as they generally did, in complete harmony. The accomplices of the prisoner were seized in their hiding-places, including Prelati. Prelati's confession was read. De Rais denied it all. He was threatened with torture. He confessed. He was ordered to read the confession in open court. He assented. In the scene that followed, the whole horror and goodness of the Middle Ages were displayed.

Gilles began to read. He was dressed in black; his

voice was heavy; the confession was full and detailed. The voice continued; murder after murder, pain after pain, loathsomeness after loathsomeness. Once someone screamed. The voice continued; murder after murder, pain after pain, animalism after animalism. The Bishop of Nantes stood up; the voice paused. The bishop went up to the Crucifix that hung over the seats of the judges, and veiled it. There were some things men could not bear that that carved image should see. The voice broke into repentant cries, to God, to the Church, to the parents of the dead. The bishop came down to the prisoner and embraced him, praying aloud that he might be purged and redeemed. There, clasped, the two stood. That, as well as torture, was the Middle Ages.

He was condemned and executed, with two of his companions, on the 26th October 1440. He was to be hanged and burned, but his body not to be entirely consumed but to be given to his family. Before the execution he preached penitence, faith, and hope to the other condemned men; he implored again the prayers of the parents of the dead. He invoked Saint Michael. He died. A great fast was held and intercession by the populace offered for his soul.

In spite of the official secular rehabilitation that followed, it seems likely that the whole tale was true. It was to prevent such things that the laws against sorcery were aimed. Those laws, and all the beliefs that lay behind them, were now to be codified. But it is desirable, in reading of that codification, to have in mind the murders, the devotions, and the public scandal of Gilles de Rais, Marshal and Peer of France.

Chapter Six

THE MALLEUS MALEFICARUM

When Gilles de Rais was executed in 1440 there was already alive at Bâle in Switzerland a boy of from two to four years old. His name was James Sprenger; in 1452 he became a Dominician novice at Bâle. About 1480 he became Provincial of the German Provinces and was made General Inquisitor for Germany. In 1484 another Dominican was associated with him in the work, Father Henry Kramer. These two devout priests were the authors of the grand volume called the *Malleus Maleficarum*. It was published somewhere about 1490 or a little later; the Bull by which Innocent VIII declared the jurisdiction of the authors in the Germanic countries was printed with it; it spread widely and became for centuries the great formulation of the Catholic attack on sorcery.

The *Malleus Maleficarum* is a very remarkable work. It is long, carefully detailed, and (allowing for its hypotheses and its particular appreciation of evidence) extremely scientific. It is in many ways repugnant to our minds, but then our minds would have been repugnant to the minds of its authors. It refers continually to certain first principles which, its authors supposed, would be accepted by any clear and educated mind. Had they supposed that their work would have been read by minds which wholly or partially refused those principles, they would perhaps have begun by a demonstration (to their ability) of the truth of those principles, or perhaps —and more probably—they would have referred their readers to other works in which they conceived that demonstration adequately to exist; to the *Summa* of Saint Thomas or some other similar exhibition of a great philosophic system. They did not do so because they assumed that one or other of those systems would be accepted, and that in any case the contemplation of the Faith, some knowledge of its history, and some recognition of its doctors, was common ground. They knew that they had philosophical opponents even in the matter with which they were dealing; that was why they wrote the book.

As an intellectual achievement the work is almost of the first order. Nothing less like the common notion of the self-indulgence of half-mad sexual perverts can be imagined. They deal with sex, of course, as any examination of a great part of human life must, but there is no sign that they were particularly interested in sex. They were interested in the Catholic Faith and its perpetuation, and they were, also and therefore, interested in the great effort which it seemed to them was then in existence to destroy and eradicate the Catholic Faith. They proceeded with great care to examine the nature of that effort, its successes and its defeats, and the best methods of orthodox operation against it. They corrected error, instructed ignorance, and directed action.

It may certainly be held, in spite of all this, that the book is one of the most appalling that has ever been written. Such a view depends on one or more of three things. First, the principles of the *Malleus* may be entirely denied. They can be denied by dogma, but hardly by anything else. Secondly, it may be maintained that, though their general principles are correct, yet this presentation of them is, in fact, disproportionate; that their system, like so many others, has got out of hand. And thirdly, it may be held that their evidence is insufficient and unreliable.

They were aware, or they thought they were aware, of a growing arrogance and intensity in the attack on the Faith. In our modern language they demanded 'security' and they distrusted 'appeasement'. They were afraid, not in any mean or personal way, but with a generous and lofty fear—if fear can at all be lofty or generous, with the kind of fear Saint Paul had on behalf of his converts or John Wesley on behalf of his disciples. This, of course, was because they believed human souls to be capable of damnation, and because they believed the moral and sacramental system of the Catholic Church to be appointed for the redemption of souls to beatitude. And they believed that there were directed against that system a number of wills in energetic operation, and among those wills one especially malevolent, powerful, and intelligent, which they called the Devil.

The attack which the Devil so directed was consonant

with his own nature. They defined this nature, and they exhibited the Devil's sin. This particular exhibition is of great interest in the consideration of witchcraft. It was not that the Devil wished generally to be equal with God. He desired it in a particular way. 'He wished and asked that the blessedness and goodness of all the inferior creatures should be derived from him. And he sought this in his own natural capacity, that just as he was the first to be endowed in nature with those qualities, so the other creatures should receive them from the nobility of his nature. And he sought this of God, in perfect willingness to remain subject to God so long as he had that power granted to him.' This, and only this, was his error and his sin; he desired to be, to those related to him by a certain dependence, the only source of good. It is, among men, a not very unusual desire.

It would seem that it is this desire of his which is carried out when he allures men and women to follow him as wizards and witches. For there is a difference between the ordinary, and even the extraordinary, temptations of men, and this particular enticement. 'His principal motive', says the *Malleus*, 'is to offer the greatest offence to the Divine Majesty by usurping to himself a creature dedicated to God, and thus more certainly to ensure his disciple's future damnation, which is his chief object.' But the result of this usurpation is to attribute to the Devil a power upon which, as if from a Creator, the power of his subordinates depends. The phrase which was said to open the infernal parody of the Dominical Prayer, 'Our Father which wert in heaven', intends the first two words as it intends the rest, and the paternity of the Devil is the object of all the pacts. Witchcraft, according to the *Malleus*, depends upon pact, either tacit or expressed. But even if only tacit, it is a defined thing; it purposes directly to profane God and to harm his creatures. It intends malice, not merely in particular but in general, and not only in general towards men but also absolutely towards God.

It would seem therefore that the effort of this grand conspiracy is to discover or create an organic relationship other than the organic relationship which exists in the divine principles of the universe. The Devil desires, against those principles, to be an utter organic source; the witch desires to relate herself to the Devil as father and source. It is stated in the *Malleus* that for witchcraft to exist three things must concur—the Devil, the witch, and the permission of God. Three spiritual wills exist—the first two in operation, the third suspending its active judgement. In that suspension—a suspension not perhaps other in kind, but, as it were, more intimate and intense, than His normal suspension under any sin, since here the sin is aimed more peculiarly at Himself—in that suspension the effort to establish organic relationship takes place. Four points are normally characteristic of the effort: (i) the renunciation of the Faith; (ii) the devotion and homage to the Devil; (iii) the offering up to him of unbaptized children; (iv) the indulgence of carnal lust with incubi or succubi. Not all these are always to be found in the examinations, but the *Malleus* declares that these are the four activities 'generally necessary to damnation'.

There is a point of some interest raised here which the *Malleus* does not directly discuss; that is, the relation of the Devil to matter. There are, of course, all kinds of discussion as to how far spirit, or spiritual beings (not being God) can move, change, or influence matter. But this is not quite enough. It is impossible not to feel, as one reads, that this desire for an infernal (because profane and malicious) organic universe desires also to extend itself into matter, to absorb matter also into itself. The old fable of the birth of Merlin, by impregnation of the Devil, crude as it was, is another example. Certain writers have spoken of the desire of God to unite Himself with matter; and it has been held by great Christian doctors that the Incarnation would have taken place even had man never fallen. Spirit lusts towards matter as matter towards spirit. The fallen angels are pure spirit. It is not enough for them. Good angels may properly desire, and be permitted, to influence men's bodies, and this they can do by certain works such as the heightening of imagination, or even the bringing about of visions. But the essential body they cannot enter, either as a part of it or as a quality of it. 'The angelic and the human essence are entirely distinct from each other.' Nor will the angelic powers desire to outrage those holy limits; they subdue, as it were, the movement of their natures. But it is not so with the evil angels. As in the old myth of the Watchers of Israel, so in the newer myths of Christendom. A surge towards matter passes through the hierarchy of the abyss; they rush towards it; they seek the bodies of men and women; they desire to incarnate. They desire it with the more passion the more they are frustrated. And the *Malleus* does certainly assert that one of the surest protections against the injuries of witchcraft is the Name of Jesus followed by the great and triumphant assertion of the Divine John :'Et Verbum Caro factum est', 'And the Word was made Flesh'. It recounts how a man, walking with two companions, saw them suddenly struck by lightning, and heard in the air above him voices crying: 'Let us strike him too!' But he understood another voice to say: 'The Word was made Flesh'! This, of all the Eucharist at which he had been present that morning, was the phrase most potent to save. So the 'key' trial of witches consisted in setting a key within a Bible at the first verse of the same passage —'In the beginning was the Word'. The Bible was then tied and hung from the suspect's finger; if she were indeed a witch, she could not support the burden and it fell.[1] The test was indeed inadequate, but the passage chosen is significant.

It is true that the strife which proceeds, by the Permission, between the true organism and the false organism is not confined to the battle round the place of generation. But it may be said that there, in the imagination of the time as represented by the authors of the *Malleus*, it raged most fiercely. It was round the most secret organs of body and soul that the effort to pervert body and soul went on. The two great sins were fornication and idolatry, and they were in some sense the same sin. Each consisted in the deliberate substitution of another image for that of Almighty God—

[1] Van der Leeuw, *Religion in Essence and Manifestation*.

fornication in the body when a mortal image was allowed and encouraged to set itself in the place of the law, idolatry in the soul when a spiritual image was allowed and encouraged to set itself in the place of That which is behind the Law. It is not, the *Malleus* says, for pleasure that the restless powers turn themselves into incubi or succubi; what have spirits to do with the pleasures of flesh and blood? nor do they seem to become flesh and blood for such a cause, but for malice only, and for the excitement of mortal luxury to satisfy diabolical malice. Man (as a later writer said) is the only being with whom the Devil can communicate, and malice is his only method.

Therefore, acting within their allowed limits, they can create a kind of semi-body, first taking the shape in and of the air, and they gather into it such gross vapours as they can, and the shapes thus become visible and tangible, 'partaking of some of the qualities of earth'. But the diabolisms which control them are not really united with them, for they do not speak, see, or hear through them. When they wish to seem to speak they cause a disturbance of the air, producing sounds not unlike voices, and communicating their meaning, it would seem, directly to the mind. And so also they do not see and hear corporeally, though they are able to know in both ways much more subtly than do ordinary human bodies. They are unlike the perfection of our Lord's human body in this as in all other things.

But however much they may work in that way, and however much, in a horrid parody of the holy substitutions of love, they may convey seed from one living being to another—here the succubus to receive, there the incubus to deliver—yet one thing they cannot do: they cannot themselves beget. They have no formative energy, either in the heavens above or in the earth and the hells beneath. The child born of the transferred seed is the child of the man whose seed has been transferred. The child of a wizard and witch it may be; it is not and cannot be the child of the Devil. Once only has immaterial power worked directly upon material power; when that great formative energy which we call the Spirit moved in the womb of the Virgin, and she conceived. In the diabolic schools, it seems, she was called the Anomalous woman.

But witches were themselves material and their wills were the wills of mortals. The Devil therefore could act more easily by using these instruments. If they could not be united with him by any true and organic material or spiritual connection, they could be differently united by the mere energy of malice. As malice was said to be his chief characteristic, so of his pseudo-children. In a flash of realism the *Malleus* asserted that 'the most prolific source of witchcraft is the quarrelling between unmarried women and their lovers'—the great nourishment of malice. Many witches had confessed (the two Inquisitors say) that they bore a great malice to the Faith and the Sacraments. Malice, to those writers, was the great and abiding spiritual sin. The Devil himself retained some nobility in spite of his ambition, until malice overcame him—

> he thought himself impaired,
> Deep malice thence conceiving, and disdain.

This high and proper view the Inquisitors took, and it is not to be supposed that they were themselves guilty of malice; such a view is wholly unnecessary and unjustified. Yet here they did approach a difficulty. It was undoubtedly true that some of those accused of witchcraft were, in fact, leading religious lives. They went to church, they kept their duties, they communicated. In a tract of about 1450, written in Savoy, it had already been stated that many sorcerers did precisely that—confessed often and often communicated. This was apparently drawn from the facts at the disposal of the writer; some of those executed had been people of that kind. And in the general neglect of communion towards the end of the Middle Ages such people were likely to be especially noticeable. They were put to death as sorcerers all the same.

For what otherwise followed? If such religious conformity was to be received as any evidence of innocence, the other evidence must be false. But if the other evidence were false, the whole grand scheme broke down. It is perhaps not likely that the dilemma presented itself so clearly to the minds of those two intellectualists, but nevertheless there the dilemma was. Like any other schematizers, they saw the difficulty before it appeared, and prepared for it. Saint Thomas, they remembered, had said, following Saint Augustine (O fatal, fatal name!), that deeds of infidels which arose from infidelity, though in themselves good, were in them deadly sin: thus fasting is good, but if a Saracen fasts in order to observe the rules of Islam it is mortal sin. But if a Saracen is honest, apart from Islam, by the

mere law of nature, it is so far good. A Saracen, however, has not knowingly made a pact with the Devil. A
witch has. In a witch therefore acts otherwise humanly
good are evil, because her whole life is, pseudo-organi-
cally, evil.

Thus all magic used for healing purposes by witches
is evil. If it is done by pact and consent of the Devil it
is evil, and it cannot be done otherwise if the witch is
indeed a witch. One may sometimes counter vanity by
vanity; one may sometimes use incantations, so long as
they imply no pact. What this means, however, is that
all fruit on the evil tree is evil, and all on the good tree
is good. One decides on the nature of the tree first, and
then of its fruit: a method of judgement which had been
(one supposed) reserved to God alone.

The idea of the sorcerer at communion has a certain
fascination. It is apparently the nearest the Inquisitors
got to the notion of the Black Mass. They had heard
of the seizure of Hosts for sacrilegious purposes, but
there is nothing in the *Malleus* of the blasphemous
consecration, of the black-coped celebrant, and the
triangular wafer. The Inquisitors aimed at the destruction of hypocrisy, of the pseudo-organism veiling itself
in devotion to the true; the malice of the fallen world
was never more complete than when its executants
went concealed in that hypocrisy.[1] *But* the argument
destroyed at one touch half the evidence for any defence.
A good, a religious life was no longer any proof of

---

[1] Nathaniel Hawthorne's story, 'Young Goodman Brown', has a
touch of the real horror when the two religious men pass the youth in
the wood.

innocence once a name had been screamed out by some unfortunate on the rack. Perhaps it was not. But, by the Permission, men might have taken the chance.

It was not only in the hidden connection with incubi and succubi that the propinquity to generation took place. The *Malleus* makes it clear that an interference with sexual intercourse, especially with sexual intercourse in marriage, was regarded as one of the chief activities of witches. It had been argued by some that, since marriage was sacramental and God's work, it was unseemly to suppose that the Devil could be allowed to interfere with it. This, however, they did not allow; on the contrary, they said that that Permission which was a necessary condition of witchcraft allowed it more frequently in the case of the generative powers 'because of their greater corruption'. And as much as that pseudo-organism strove to become organic after its own magical methods, so also it strove to destroy the real organism which confronted it. 'Because witches are not put down with proper vengeance, they seem now to be on the point of depopulating Christendom.' The chief means thereto were two—the sacrifice of children and the dedication of children.

Midwives, it seems, were especially liable to be witches; either because those who love the black arts have a peculiar tendency to draw towards operations by childbed, or because the Devil is peculiarly anxious to ensnare midwives.[1] The witch-midwife desires either

---

[1] No doubt also because the danger of being accused (if children were born dead, for example) was very high. But this the Inquisitors did not note.

to kill the new-born child or to offer it to the Devil. Of the first kind examples are given: in the diocese of Bâle at the town of Dann a woman confessed that she had killed more than forty by sticking a needle into their brains; in Strasbourg one that she had killed more than she could count. It was not only other women's children who were so destroyed; certain witches in Lausanne killed and ate their own. The main thing was that the children should not be baptized; this delays the filling up of the number of the elect and the coming of the Kingdom. But then comes the real usefulness of the dead babies. Their bodies are solemnly buried, by innocent or hypocritical parents. Then the bodies are stolen away, and either secretly in the witch's own habitation or at some gathering of the coven, or even at a Sabbath, are cooked in a cauldron, 'until the flesh comes away from the bones'. The 'more solid matter' is made into an ointment, both for transportation and for other enjoyments. But the liquid is poured into a flask or skin, 'whoever drinks from which, with the addition of a few other ceremonies, immediately acquires much knowledge, and becomes a leader in our sect'.

This, it seems, was the manner in which the secret knowledge was communicated; what the 'few other ceremonies' were is not communicated. A story given by the Inquisitors confirms this method. A young couple had been imprisoned in Berne on an accusation of sorcery. The husband, kept in separate custody, deter-mined to confess and obtain absolution; civil pardon he could not hope. He had been taken, he declared, misled by his wife, to a congregation of wizards, and there he

had denied Christ, baptism, and the Church. He had
then paid homage to the Devil, under the name of the
Little Master, but the Devil apparently was not then
present in person. For sometimes novices were terrified
at his appearance, and so also at his more solemn names.
This young man was one; everything was made easy.
No goat, no black man, no obscene adoration; only the
homage to an absent being under the almost playful
title of 'Little Master'. But the denial of the Faith had
to be exacted, and then after the oath there was given
to him a skin full of that grand brew. He drinks;
immediately he feels within himself a knowledge of all
our arts and an understanding of our rites and ceremonies. 'And in this manner was I seduced.' He had
made his confession; he was absolved; he died contrite
and pardoned. 'But his wife would not confess, either
under torture or in death itself, but when the fire had
been prepared by the jailer, cursed him in the most
terrible words, and so died.'

Other children were dedicated and not sacrificed.
Either the mother, if she is herself a witch, or the midwife, if she is and if she can seize an opportunity, makes
the votive offering. 'It is done by the kitchen fire,' says
the *Malleus* in a sudden flash of familiar detail. Under
pretence of warming the child the midwife carries it off;
in one case, it was done by the child's sister, at the
mother's request, they both being witches. There, in the
other room, it is raised and presented to the other God
—and to all his company—with terrible words of incantation. Sometimes strange things happened at these
times. A certain man, the husband and father of the

two women just mentioned, troubled by the mystery which seemed to fill the house, hid himself and saw his daughter carrying out the ceremony; and as he watched he suddenly saw the new-born infant climbing slowly up the chain from which the great cooking-pot hung, already practising the capacities of its infernal vocation. Aware of the disaster that had overtaken it, he determined to use the only remedy; he insisted on taking it to the nearest church, which was in the next village. He compelled his daughter to carry the child; he took neighbours with him for witnesses. On the way they came to a river crossed there by a bridge. The father turned on his daughter, saying that now either the child should cross the bridge by itself or she should be drowned in the waters; and seeing that his companions were surprised and she frightened, he swore more violently that this must be done. 'You made the child climb the chain by your infernal cunning; now make it cross the river.' The young witch trembled and yielded. She laid the child on the bridge; she pronounced incantations; suddenly the men saw the child on the other side of the river. They hurried over; the rite of baptism was performed; they returned. Afterwards the father accused both his wife and his daughter before the courts. 'They were both burned.'

These marvels, however, are accidental and rare; and due, it would seem, to some rashness or folly on the part of the witch. Satan's kingdom is, in this sense, divided against itself, for he at once desires to catch the immediate soul and yet to use it to catch others. So that his kingdom does not stand; which indeed should have been the reply of the Jews to our Lord when he asked them how that kingdom should stand: namely, that since it does not, no inferences can be drawn from any hypothesis that it does. But the Inquisitors, like the Jews, had hardly seen Satan like lightning fall from heaven; they conceived that the war was hard and long; and they may have been right. They saw around them the grand effort to create that sterile fantasy of organic life; but sterile as it might be, they saw it also as widespread, destructive, powerful, and lying in hostile circles round the beds of generation and of birth. The incubus solidified in the night; the witch-mother sighed for pleasure at the leaping in her womb of the devoted child, or the witch-midwife waited with the kitchen fire piled high that the child might be warmed and dedicated. The cauldron was ready for those who were not saved from a physical death by being devoted to the spiritual; and from the cauldron is drawn the liquid which being, 'with some few ceremonies', drunk by the neophyte, runs through him communicating to his instinct and to his mind an intimate knowledge of the forbidden arts. Or again others of those small bodies were brought to the gatherings of the sorcerers, either the Sabbath itself or something less mighty, and there were broken and shared like the Divine Body itself in the Eucharists of humble and redeemed mankind.

The effort of that false organism was to gain adherents to itself and to interfere, not only with the Church, but with the life of normal mankind. The ecclesiastical authorities tend to stress the blasphemy,

the apostasy, the renunciation of Faith and Baptism.
These things were asserted to be necessary, but they
were necessary rather as a preliminary. The tales and
anecdotes—at least those given in the *Malleus*, and
indeed most—seem not to have much to do with any
direct hatred of the Church as such. Sacrilege is there,
but it is not as common as one would expect. Whatever
the Inquisitors put into the mouths of their victims, they
did not, for whatever reason, put that in. Perhaps the
most striking example of sacrilege is given in Chapter
XVI of the Second Book, which discusses 'The Witchcraft of Archers'. Wizards who are archers are accustomed to shoot on Good Friday, during the Mass of the
Presanctified, so many arrows at a crucifix, and as many
as they shoot so many men will they kill the next day.
There may be some doubt whether the sacrilege is an
accident of the desire of killing, or the killing a result of
the purpose of sacrilege. The killing is a diabolical compact, and the conditions of it are first, that the murderer
must actually set eyes on his victim, and second, must
'bend his whole will on killing him'. These fulfilled, 'it
matters not where the man may be shut up, for he
cannot be protected, but the arrows which have been
shot will be carried and struck into him by the Devil.'
They are also promised extraordinary skill in their
general shooting; and indeed this chapter contains a
variant of the William Tell story—related of an archer
named Puneker, in the service of Eberhard Longbeard,
a prince of the Rhineland. The tale even foretells, in
its own terms, Tell's answer when asked about his
second arrow: 'If I had been deceived by the Devil and

killed my son, since I should have had to die I would quickly have shot you with the other arrow to avenge my death.' It may be an accident that Puneker would have killed the 'eminent person' who had set him the task in order to avenge his own death, not (as the legend relates of Tell) his son's.

The shooting of arrows at the crucifix is one of the rare examples of intentional sacrilege, and it is precisely one of the examples which lies at the root of a great deal of the whole problem of witchcraft. Nothing is easier than to see how the general rough and blasphemous military horse-play might lead archers to try their braggings against a mark of such a very particular form as a crucifix. The business of building or of seeing crucifixes everywhere, sometimes urged on us by the devout, has, after all, two sides. No doubt many soldiers (in the old phrase of the cloak-and-dagger novelist) 'doffed their caps and murmured a Paternoster'. But quite certainly many did not. According to the highest mind of the Church they regarded the crucifix as only an image, though they went against the highest manners of the Church when they shot their arrows at it. The Inquisitors themselves complain that many of these sacrilegious archers were maintained, in disregard of their known crimes, by kings and great nobles, 'and are permitted to boast of their deeds'. No doubt they were, but it was certainly their marksmanship that was boasted, and for which they were maintained, though a little extra notion of effective sorcery might not come amiss to their princely secular employers. It might not be inconvenient to have at hand a man who was known or reported, whether by secular or spiritual art, always to transfix his victim.

But then the question can hardly be left there. For the murderer has to 'bend his whole will on killing' his victim, and here also we touch the importance of the Renunciation and the Pact. These things were at least rumours, at most facts. But, rumours or facts, they were regarded as sacraments of will. The initiate, here as in all mysteries, pledged nothing but himself; all inventions of apostasy were to seal that pledge more strongly, to canalize the intention, to construct the awful edifice of Will. It is the Will everywhere which the sorcerers practise; the nonsensical accidents need not blind us to that; and indeed, once that Will has been imagined, the accidents are less nonsensical, no more so perhaps than the exposition of Almighty God by a thin circle of flour and water, or the waking of immortal knowledge in a human soul by 'two eyes set so strangely in the face That all things else are nothing suddenly'.

The third part of the *Malleus* is devoted to the destruction of the growing tower of Will. It had already discussed remedies for the victims of Will—remedies against incubi and succubi, against extraordinary violence of love or hate, against the loss of virility, against obsession, against hailstorms and 'dark and horrid harms'; it recommended prayers and holy offices, and it had provided a form of exorcism. But all this was but hospital work; it was the movement of the whole army which was now to be ordered. It discusses first of all the technical question of the composition of the courts which were to compose that army. It enters then upon the main direction.

There—everywhere—were the covens and the sabbaths, the conjurations and the sacrifices, the high unlawful enchanters protected by great lords, the middle-gentry and burghers practising Rites in their private and respectable homes, the wise women of villages, the archers and the pretty girls, all covering their dispositions and lending themselves to the Curse. The court existed to destroy this pseudo-organism; but how to find it? how to begin? It was directed that when any judge (ecclesiastical or secular) came to a district, he should begin by publishing a general summons, affixing the bills to public buildings, calling on all people to reveal to the judge any suspicion or belief that any person or persons were witches. Twelve days were commonly given for attendance; any who did not obey were, *ipso facto*, excommunicate. No-one who gave information was to be subject to any penalty if the accusation should prove false (unless it was deliberately malicious), because he was regarded as only laying information that such and such a suspicion did exist. Here perhaps was the first lack of wisdom; here anxiety to defeat the Devil began to grow greater than anxiety to serve God. The secular governments of centuries earlier had been wiser; they had penalized the talk as much as the act. The new effort did not do so; it encouraged the talk against the act.

The judge was set; then an informer appeared. In the presence of the judge, of a notary, and of at least two other persons, he swore to speak truth and made his deposition. He was to be closely examined both on his statements and on his own motives; he was sworn to keep all secret, and was dismissed. But in fact, though these rules were laid down, yet an informer was not necessary—public fame would serve. There the authorities were terribly democratic; they went to the *demos*. If lots of people said something, it was thought worth inquiry. 'No smoke without fire'—and indeed, indeed a fire!

But either way, how many witnesses were required? It must be left to the judge; in so grievous a matter more than two witnesses are desirable, though other rules are relaxed. Excommunicates, accomplices, criminals, and all such as would not in ordinary cases be admitted are allowed to bear evidence in matters concerning the Faith—even convicted perjurers, if they have repented. But those who are in a blood-feud with the accused, or have otherwise shown mortal hatred, are not admitted: less serious degrees of enmity may be admitted with precautions. For, the Inquisitors say, 'women are easily provoked to hatred', and therefore additional proofs are needed.[1] On the other hand, since witches were always hated, any witness would naturally feel enmity; and there all precautions disappear.

The modes of examination of witnesses which follow would be fair enough if the inquiry were into some

[1] It is clear that this question of 'mortal enmity' worried the Inquisitors. Apparently it was a plea theoretically of high validity in the courts, and it was a plea very easy for the witch to make, once she knew the names of the witnesses. If, by some chance, there were no general defamation, everything depended on the witnesses. The judge was therefore allowed to use cunning (Saint Paul had said: 'I caught you by cunning'), and various suggestions are made by means of which the accused and her advocate will be unable to decide who has said what, and may therefore fail to pick out the really damaging witness. Nor need the names of the witnesses be revealed, *if this meant any danger to them.*

abstract fact. The informer, and all others collected to give evidence, were to be asked whether the accused was reported to have spoken or acted against the Faith; how, when, where, whether in earnest or in jest; whether his family were suspected of witchcraft and whether he associated with any such; whether any others could give evidence; what he said had happened. The instructions insist that care must be taken to find out what the behaviour of the accused really was; only if he or she were acting with full purpose is notice to be taken. But if the fact is made to seem probable, then order is to be given for the arrest. The house is to be searched for instruments or tokens of witchcraft. Any friends or servants living in the house are to be seized—it is to be presumed that they know all about the doings of the accused. It is a good thing if, when she is arrested, she should be lifted off the ground and put into a basket or on a plank to be carried away; and this because witches lose their power when they are prevented from touching the earth, especially the capacity to keep silent under examination. And it is now that her examination is to begin.

It is now therefore that the great opportunities of suspicion begin to arise. The accused is asked of his family—were any burned, in that place or any other? If the informer has affirmed this and the accused denies it, that is suspicious. If he has lived in a place commonly reported to be inhabited by witches, it is suspicious. He is to be asked if he has heard talk of witches; if he denies it, he is to be asked if he believes that there are such things as witches, or that the craft can be worked. If he denies that, it is very suspicious. He is to be asked if he thinks that those who had been burned were burned innocent. 'And he or she must answer.'

All the facts seem to have been taken from the informers. The accused was not to be asked *whether* but why she had threatened[1] or touched, or had had more milk from her cows than her neighbours. It may be supposed that an intelligent judge would be able to decide how much of the farrago of report was likely to be true, but from six to ten of her neighbours generally agreeing (but not necessarily in detail) on the evil reputation of the accused were to be taken as sufficient to prove her manifestly guilty. A threat of illness, a threat of harm, if a harm followed, was sufficient. Saint Bernard, in discussing heresy, had said that 'an evident fact' was sufficient. The Inquisitors altered this to 'evidence of the fact', for the Devil works secretly, so that evident fact of diabolic relation could not be got; the judge must be content with what he could get. This was true, but with that alteration the chances of the accused were further decreased.

She may by now have confessed; it is not probable. If not, she is to be kept under arrest, unless indeed it is a very slight matter of which she is accused, and she is not reported to have done harm to children or animals. She may then produce sureties and be remitted to her own

---

[1] A threat might easily happen. The Inquisitors quote a famous case at Spiers. There a man wanted to buy something from a woman; they disputed about the price, quarrelled, parted; she called after him: 'You will wish soon that you had agreed.' It is true that there harm followed quickly. He looked back at her over his shoulder, and suddenly his mouth stretched out on either side until it reached his ears, and with that horrid grin fixed on him he remained for a long time. Where, however, the harm was slower to fall, its connection with the threat would be, of course, less obvious.

house, being sworn not to go out. Sureties cannot have been easy to come by at that time, though it may sometimes have happened in more populous or sceptical pl es. But the known nature of the coven or group-system of the witch-organization made it likely that such sureties would themselves become immediately suspect. It might have been well for the Church had there been an Order devoted to that purpose, as there were Orders for so many more usual (though perhaps as difficult) purposes, whose companions might have made themselves such sureties. It would have been worthy the Church, and, so, there might have been a greater cleansing of what was to become so great and terrible an evil.

There is much discussion whether an advocate is to be allowed to the accused; this is allowed within strict limits. He may, however, only undertake the case if he is convinced that it is just; he must not be prolix; he must not take advantage of any 'legal quirks and quibbles'; he must not bring counter-accusations. He must not, of course, defend heresy, or he too comes under strong suspicion. It is perhaps not the least achievement of our civilization that we have created the defence of the accused under any crime; that we have made an attempt to save the innocent at the risk of losing the guilty.

The accused is in prison; she is manifestly guilty. But 'common justice demands that a witch should not be condemned to death unless she is convicted by her own confession'. 'Common justice' therefore demands that she shall be tortured to compel her to confess so that she can be put to death. There can be but few sentences in all the strange and horrible past of man so difficult for

146

us to understand—really to understand. But here it is at the very root of the torture. Judge and assistants were working for common justice. A whole different mode of thought impinges on our own. A comparison would be if a man were found guilty to-day, say, of murder; he will not confess. He is removed from the dock; he is taken to the cellars; he cannot be hanged till he confesses; he is beaten, stretched, burned, torn, till he does confess. But if he does not, he must be at last let go. Justice requires it; no evidence of others is enough to hang him; only his own mouth can doom him. No-one could be put to death for witchcraft by the evidence of others. Was the idea less than noble? this was the result. In 1676 a certain learned lawyer of Innsbruck added, as it were, a finishing touch: 'The torture chamber should be constantly sprinkled with holy water and a smoke made with blessed herbs.' Could Gilles de Rais do worse?

It is to be noted, however, that confession under torture was not sufficient by itself; the guilty party must confess without torture. After torture therefore she was to be removed to another place, there to re-make or at least confirm her confession; and if she denied this, she was again to be put to the torture. But if all failed, every other kind of effort was to be made to bring her to confess; she was to be threatened, entreated, even cheated into it. Her silence—and to judge by the records, the accused often remained silent—was to be broken at all costs. Penitence they could not force, but confession they could, or all but could. To break the silence was to defeat that dark malicious power who lay vibrating in the world, and sometimes came in one shape or another to his creatures in their cells, and sometimes persuaded them to cling more closely to him, and sometimes beat them to make them fear him more than the torment and sometimes even strangled them or helped them to strangle themselves, so that death might shut their mouths more certainly than obstinacy.

In order to attack this citadel of silence, within which lay the real secrets of the life of sorcery, the following methods before torture were to be followed. First, the witch was to be adjured to weep. She was to be conjured to weep, in a set of words so terrible and awful in their full significance that by themselves they would almost persuade us of the full honest devotion and sincere passion of the judges, were there reason to doubt it: 'By the bitter tears shed on the Cross by our Saviour the Lord Jesus Christ for the salvation of the world . . . by the burning tears poured in the evening hour over his wounds by the most glorious Virgin Mary his mother . . . by all the tears shed here in this world by the saints and elect of God. . . .' In the presence of the officers of the Court all waiting, all watching, the judge, his hand on the head of the accused, pronounced those sacred and moving words, and waited in all hope for the witch to weep. She, naturally, could not. But sometimes she tried to smear her face with spittle, to redden her eyes, so that she might seem to have wept. Against this the officers of the Court were to keep careful watch. The tears must be real tears. Dry-eyed, she, also, waited— again and again.

She was to be shaved of all hair. She had of course already been searched for any small object, any material

148

thing, that might be the express magical link between herself and her lord, but a little powder, a little ash (gathered from the calcined body of a new-born child) could be hidden easily. The Inquisitors recommend the entire shaving, except in Germany, where it is not thought proper; they there adopt another method. They have the hair of the witch's head cut off, and they put a morsel of consecrated wax in a cup of water and give it to her three times to drink while fasting. This, it seems, had in their experience been very successful in breaking down silence. Relics and the Seven Words of Christ written on parchment and worn by the judge are also of very precious use in this matter.

But if she withstood all—exhortations, shaving, drink, relics, torture—one chance remained. She was to be taken away, given food and drink, and honest persons sent to talk with her. There are various ways of managing this; the *Malleus* defines them. She may even be promised mercy: 'let the judge promise that he will be merciful—with the mental reservation that he means he will be merciful to himself or the State; for whatever is done for the safety of the State is merciful'. Or if she has been promised her life, there are three ways round the promise: (i) it may be kept on condition that she helps to convict other witches, and providing that she is imprisoned for life on bread and water—but she had better not be told this; let her think she will be exiled; (ii) she may be kept imprisoned for a while and then burnt; (iii) the judge who promises her life may resign the office of passing sentence and leave her condemnation to another judge.

One thing, however, the witches might demand which must not be allowed, and that is the ordeal, as by red-hot iron. The Inquisitors reject the idea of the ordeal altogether, whether for witchcraft or not. But in witchcraft it is peculiarly improper, for the Devil has a knowledge of natural things, such as herbs, and the juice of herbs can be used to protect the hands from burning. So that witches very often demand this ordeal, because the Devil preserves them. A notorious witch in the diocese of Constance once was allowed this advantage; and she carried the iron double the stipulated distance, and had to be released, so that she was still living to the shame of the Faith.

All this having been done, the time is come for the sentence. There are four kinds of sentence, three on great suspicion (that is, where the accused has not confessed), last on conviction (where she has). Suspicion may be light, grave,[1] or violent. Those who come under the first are to abjure the 'heresy'; if afterwards any relapse, the first accusation is not to be held against them. The second class of suspects are to abjure all heresy, in particular this. If they relapse, they are to be counted as having been at first guilty. If they refuse to abjure, they are to be held excommunicate for a year, and if they still refuse condemned. Other penances may be imposed in all cases. The

[1] In the class of grave suspects come those who 'cherish some inordinate love or excessive hatred, even if they do not use to work harm'. Such persons are thought to have heretical sympathies. The point is well taken. Saint Francis had put it better with his 'Set love in order, thou that lovest me.' But the comment takes us back to the world in which, when all is said, the Inquisitors conceived themselves to be working—the world of motives, desires, spiritual excesses and negations, the powers of the other worlds rather than of this.

third class, if they confess and abjure, are to be treated as guilty but penitent; if they refuse, the strict forms of justice (on the Inquisitors' showing) are to be abandoned —they are to be condemned as guilty and impenitent.

There follow the forms of sentence, of which there are fifteen. They proceed, not without great care and consideration, from the imposition of a mere abjuration to the final sentence of handing over to the secular court, 'praying the said Court to moderate or temper its sentence of death against you'. They even provide for the unlikely event of the witnesses being struck with repentance and confessing that they have acted maliciously. In that case the accused is to be discharged, but the witnesses are to be imprisoned for life on bread and water, and to do other penance; though the bishops, as in all cases except the handing over to the secular court, may mitigate or increase the sentence subsequently. And indeed every opportunity was provided for the accused to be reconciled to the Church and be absolved, even if also burned.

At the very end come two chapters which, after so much scope of learning, legal and theological, seem almost pathetic, especially the very last paragraph of all. First, the Inquisitors protest against and denounce the secular lords who receive, protect, and support sorcerers, especially those famous archer-wizards. They threaten them with excommunication, condemnation, and eternal damnation. 'All such receivers are more damnable than all witches.' It is undoubted, however, that they exist, needlessly complicating, burdening, and nullifying the work of the courts—obstructing trials, freeing from prison, and patronizing the condemned. And after these, right at the end, is the Court of Rome itself. For sometimes, it seems, the accused put in an appeal, and the Inquisitors certainly contemplate the possibility that, occasionally, the appeal may have to be allowed, and the whole matter deferred to the Holy Apostolic See. Then the accused must be sent to our Most Holy Lord the Pope, with the process. The last sad paragraph of the whole immense work—it runs to two hundred and fifty thousand words—may be quoted complete.

'Let judges also take note that, if they are personally summoned by the appellant, and appear, they must beware at all costs against engaging in litigation, but must leave the whole process and cause to those judges, and so manage that they may be able to return as soon as possible; so that they may not be sorely troubled with fatigues, misery, labour, and expense in Rome. For by this means much damage is caused to the Church, and heretics are greatly encouraged; and thereafter judges will not receive so much respect and reverence, nor will they be so much feared as before. Also other heretics, seeing the judges fatigued and detained in the Court of Rome, will exalt their horns, and despise and malign them, and more boldly proclaim their heresies; and when they are accused, they will appeal in the same way. Other judges, also, will have their authority weakened when they proceed on behalf of the Faith and are zealous in extirpating heretics, since they will fear lest they may be troubled with miseries and fatigues arising from similar appeals. All this is most prejudicial to the Faith of the Holy Church of God; wherefore may the Spouse of that Church in mercy preserve her from all such injuries.'

Chapter Seven

THE GOETIC LIFE

What then, in theory, was the Goetic life? the imagination which, on one side and on the other, preoccupied so many minds? The most incredulous did not, for centuries, yet, altogether deny it; the most credulous, by the violence of their repulsion, assisted it to live. The evidence is suspect throughout, yet when because of that suspicion it is all rejected, some episode like that of Gilles de Rais or of Mme de Montespan exhibits suddenly the undoubted fact that there was a tradition and an operation of the most perverse kind; that in all classes of society demands were made upon hell. Whether devils were seen may be doubtful; that devils were invoked cannot be.

The Goetic life then, of one kind or another, was a fact. It might be hereditary. It was part of its business to promulgate itself, and the pseudo-organism desired, as strongly as the organism of the Church, to have children involved in it by the devotion of their parents. If they were so presented they might grow into it slowly and naturally, but it seems that there, as with all mysteries, a

moment came when they renewed on their own behalf
the vicarious vows. The poor girls, 'ignorant of their
salvation and living like beasts', for whom Mme de
Bourignon established a house at Lille between 1650 and
1660, told her, when it was discovered that a number of
them belonged to the hidden company of witches,[1] that
those who had been offered as children had made their
own promises on coming to the age of reason.

But most children had not been so offered; they grew
up to hear tales of witchcraft at a distance, or indeed in
many towns and villages at not so great a distance. The
minds of some of those developing adolescents played
with the dream. Most children and most youths take
pleasure in fancies; the secrecy of those fancies is sometimes a part of them. That one's parents may be but
foster-parents, that one's blood is particular, that one is
predestined, that a hidden greatness looms in one's heart
—such things are common imaginations. The revolt in
our natures must have its way there, even if those natures
are, in act, subdued to what they work in. Religion is its
opportunity often; to be a child of God and an inheritor
of the kingdom of heaven credits the mind with an
infinite sense of importance—no less dangerous even if
true. But if a religious heart and mind were, for some
reason, oppressed and antagonized by the order of religion in the world, or if greed or curiosity sprang high,
there might be every kind of opportunity to welcome
and enjoy some other fancy, however preposterous,—

[1] Not, perhaps, entirely without Mme de Bourignon's unintentional
assistance. She saw imps hovering over them, and may have encouraged
them to have experiences, as Wesley encouraged the children at Kings-
wood to experience salvation at five years old.

what fancies are not?—of a powerful, satisfying, and secret justification of oneself.

It was at such a moment that the communication was made. No soul was alone; it was watched and accompanied by the invisible lords who desired communion with it, and use of it, and triumph over it; who desired, in their everlasting trouble, a mad union with matter—mad because madness is of their nature, since, by definition, they are opposed to reason and holy intellect, and must infinitely fail from that as from all other good except from what the doctors instruct us is to be regarded as a good—the good of mere being in itself. And even that perhaps they hate more than we ever can. They therefore, alert to do something, slid nearer to the chance that waited for them. They urged within; they provided opportunity without. Often a neighbour was the means. The mind of the girl or the young man received the first whispers of possibility, as when Catherine Delort heard talk of dualism and the coming of Antichrist from her shepherd-lover in Toulouse, or when one of the Discalced Franciscans in Rome found that other mysteries beside the Christian were celebrated among the brethren there, or when James Device in Lancashire heard from his grandmother the first hint of the sacrilegious abstraction of the consecrated Bread. But if no neighbour or lover was at hand it might be that one of the spirits put on the appearance of the incarnation it could not attain, and the black man—which may not mean more than a very dark man or may mean something more like the Ethiopian who waited on the Lady Alice Kyteler—met the restless human soul on the road, or even came to the house at twilight. Sometimes so and sometimes in another shape, as when the tall woman offered to Joan Weir to speak on her behalf to the Queen of Fairie, who was afterwards something more than the Queen of Fairie.

The invited mortal dallied with the thought. It needed but the sinking a little further into illusion than is customary to all sin, for by definition the very essence of sin is a deliberate perversity, and the perversity of the Goetic life was a temptation only to those peculiarly fitted for it —only perhaps to those peculiarly fitted for the religious life. Like Macbeth in the darkness outside the lit hall of Inverness they hesitated, they dallied, they assented. The doctors of the Church through the centuries have not agreed whether that assent was made objectively or subjectively. The images that appeared were certainly images of real states, whether in fact (as was asserted) the assenting witch sat or lay alone and knew her experience only within, or whether the spiritual attraction with which she communed exhibited itself (as was asserted) in shapes and sounds. The agreement was made. The novice of that initiation sometimes, though perhaps rarely, drew up an actual document. Few such remain; one certainly does—the Pact, or the draft of a Pact, made by Urban Grandier, priest of Loudon in the seventeenth century, who was accused and convicted of having bewitched a number of Ursuline nuns. He was condemned to ask their forgiveness and to be burned alive with his magical books and papers. Normally the Pact was supposed to disappear with the spirit to whom it was given, but this —either as a draft only or because it was not used—

escaped both the fire of hell and the Loudon fire. It is headed *Veu de Grandier*, and it runs:

'My lord and master, I take you for my God, and I promise to be your servant while I live, and from this hour I make renunciation of all others and of Jesus Christ and of all saints and of heaven and of the Church Catholic, Apostolic, and Roman, and of all its good, and of all prayers that may be made for me. I promise to adore you and do you homage at least three times a day, and to do the most evil that I can and to draw to do evil as many persons as shall be possible for me; and from my heart I renounce chrism and baptism and all the merits of Jesus Christ; and in case I should wish to change, I give you my body, my soul, and my life as holding it from you, having dedicated it to you for ever without any will to repent. Signed Urbain Grandier in his blood.'

So careful a profession in writing was not always made; other ceremonies were used. There was, sometimes, a parody of baptism and new names—as when Elizabeth How of Salem was baptized by the devil 'in the river by Newbury Falls', or Isobel McNicoll, to whom he came in her own house in the shape of a young man, and baptized her and called her Catherine. More common than all was the sudden pang which meant that the grand spirit had marked the mortal for his own— 'she had great pain thereafter' say the records of the confessions. This was the famous 'witch's mark' which would not bleed and was insensible to pain. Another mark was 'the little teat' where the familiar sucked; it occurred generally in the privy parts, but also on the shoulder or the side. Elizabeth Sawyer of Edmonton had one such; the bottom of it was blue, and the top red.

These initiations were sometimes private and sometimes in the local coven and sometimes in the full Sabbath. Then also the familiar was given, which came in various shapes. An image out of the general place of images attached itself to the witch, seen or unseen; or else an actual animal received the sly spirit into its nature and became magical and was the magical link. Link one way or another there always was—written pact or living familiar or sealed book; and if animal, cat or dog or toad or ferret or rat or even the shape of a child that sat about the house and whispered little blasphemies. The familiar was at once servant and master; it would run about and do mischief but also it would watch and threaten its pretended mistress, whenever that mistress showed signs of failing from her new business.

So initiated, so prepared, the witch came to know her friends and companions. The local groups were as they might be; they had their rulers, like Dr. Fian of North Berwick or George Burroughs in Salem, and it was this ruler who was sometimes called 'the devil' and who directed their activities. It was on this side that witchcraft touched politics, again as in the case of North Berwick where the coven acted on behalf of Francis, Earl of Bothwell, or the priests who assisted Mme de Montespan to enchant King Louis's love. But the great Sabbaths were not generally thought to be ruled by any such mortal masters.

There indeed was the full feast; there the pseudoorganism was in full exhibition. It happened—or it did not happen. But even if it did not happen, if the Canon Episcopi were right, if no meeting ever took place on the German Brocken or the Swedish Blockula, if the place of enchantment and images of enchantment were wholly within—they may have been drawn inwards at once, and the visions to which they assented been common indeed, and those who met only in dream knew certainly that they had met and did not much mind whether in dream or not. But it was supposed to be without. The old notion that witches rode to the place of meeting on a broomstick came from grotesque paintings rather than from the actual confessions, the broomstick being preferably made of hazel. But sometimes the witch acknowledged that she had anointed herself, and, astride a stick, pronounced the incantation that carried her through the air.

Claudine Boban and her mother of Franche-Comté flew in this manner, and are among the very few who spoke of making their departure by the chimney—'sortant le contrement de la cheminée'. In general it was not so; the company went their ways on horse or foot and came together about midnight in the appointed place.

The times of holding the Sabbath differed in various districts; it was not infrequently held on, or almost on, certain feasts of the Church, but there was no general rule. It was held at night, sometimes in an open but secluded place, sometimes in a churchyard, occasionally in a house. The arrangements must have depended on the opportunities of the local coven; the more covens that met together at one time, the more space and seclusion was desirable. The company were sometimes disguised in skins and the heads of animals, or with their faces covered with masks or veils. There was again no definite rule—so that it would seem the disguise was not so much for protection as for fantasy and excitement, the fever of pleasure provoked by all possible means. Even the President did not always, though he did generally, appear as a beast. The President was occasionally the local ruler, but usually he was more; and if he were not more, yet he was felt as more; the lesser ruler was attached to the greater, and the man in the skin, the mask and headdress, and the claws and tail, was identified with the pseudo-God. He was called the Devil; he was adored as the Devil; and, metaphysically, he may have been the Devil.

That, anyhow, was adored. The company wheeled round it in their dances, where it sat, perhaps on a rock or a throne, in their midst. Its most general appearance was in the shape of a great goat. In what is said to be the earliest representation of a witch in cathedral sculpture (at Lyons, of the fourteenth century) a naked woman is riding on a goat, holding to a horn, and with the other hand whirling an animal—possibly a cat—by its tail. Other shapes occur—a cat, a cow, a foal, a dog. Its posterior, or fundament (as it is often called), seemed to be a face also. The grand homage was done by kissing it there, and obscenely. The whole ritual was obscene in its nature, therefore in its details; no kiss there was anything but obscene, and the body that was meant to carry all its members into gay honour and holy joy here reduced all to an indefinable degradation of putrescence. They sidled and slid towards the giant horned thing, and abased themselves under it and thrilled and adored: 'grand seigneur', 'nostre dieu', 'dominus deus'. 'The Devil', said Elizabeth Sawyer, 'taught me this prayer: *Sanctificetur nomen tuum. Amen.*'

Widdershins, they went round. The order of the further Rite varies. But certain things remain, whatever their position: the recital and accounting, the offering of children, the meal, and the promiscuous intercourse. The recital was the statement on the part of the witch of the evil done. Before the swollen bulk that squatted on the throne, the company boasted their malice and their acts of malice. The President approved or disapproved; those who had failed in the ghostly labour were liable to be beaten by their associates or (some said) cruelly tortured by demons. This violence of the Devil towards his servants is asserted everywhere. The Scotch witch, Isobel Gowrie, gave a fantastically realistic account of the Devil's discipline. She said that sometimes, among themselves, the coven would speak of their Master as 'Black John' or what not, and he would come and say to them, 'I ken well enough what ye were saying of me'. 'And then he would beat and buffet us very sore.' She even went into details about the members of the coven under the infliction. Alexander Elder 'was but soft' and used only to weep and cry when he was beaten. 'But Margaret Wilson . . . would defend herself finely and cast up her hands to keep the strokes off from her: and Bessie Wilson would speak crusty with her tongue, and would be belling again to him stoutly. He would be beating and scourging us all up and down with cords, and other sharp scourges, like naked ghosts; and we would still be crying: "Pity! pity! Mercy! mercy! our Lord!" But he would have neither pity nor mercy.' This sounds much more like a scrimmage of combined sadistic and masochistic pleasure than anything more serious; the picture of Isobel Gowrie daringly calling the Devil 'Black John' at the risk of bodily punishment is not in the same class as solemn pacts and angelic treacheries. On the other hand, the coven to which she belonged was mixed up with attempts at murder and with intercourse; it was she who said of the Devil, 'He is abler for us that way than any man can be, he was heavy like a malt-sack, a huge nature, very cold, as ice', or again, 'his nature cold within me as spring-well-water'.

The meal, or banquet, was held after the homage, the recital, and the offerings. In the ordinary meetings of the covens the food served seems to have been of the usual kind, varying only according to the social rank of the persons concerned. At the high feasts of the Sabbath, dishes of a special kind appeared. Here there is again one chief distinction in the confessions: at some Sabbaths the food was said to be delectable, at others intolerable. It is difficult to see any reason for this difference, except that of the taste of the witches—and even that, one would think, would be rather a mental than a physical choice. Dr. Montague Summers says: 'There is even mention of putrefying garbage and carrion being placed before his evil worshippers by their Master. Such would appear to have been the case at those darker orgies when there was a manifestation of supernatural intelligences from the pit.' It is, of course, a possible explanation, if we take the full objective view of the banquet. But if we consider those cases in which the subject remained in the full view of the spectators, rigid and unconscious of calls and blows, or sleeping quietly in bed, it seems as if the difference in the attributed food might be rather due to varying imaginations, corresponding to different tastes; as between caresses and ill treatment. Those who wished for good food dreamed they had it, 'delicious and delicate'; those who yielded themselves to the infinity of hell dreamed of obscenity in their food also. It is a kind of parody of what happened when the High Prince came to Camelot, and 'all had what food they desired'. The best choice there was perhaps not to change the immediate food on the table but to enjoy it in the power and goodness of the High Prince; and so at the tables of hell it may have been ordinary food which was eaten with every intense consciousness of decay. The serving up of the dead children is another thing. Cannibalism of that kind was the answer of the pseudo-organism to the mysterious communion of the Eucharist.

A ritual equivalent to the Black Mass is also said to have taken place. The Eucharist had, for centuries, been employed for purposes of separation and tyranny—for the opposite of all ends to which it was designed. There had been amatory Masses and mortuary Masses. There was abstraction of the consecrated Host. This was one of the easiest things to do, since the Host could be secretly removed from the mouth immediately after reception, and taken away to serve for any wished purpose. Familiars—dogs or toads—were fed with It; It was carried to the Sabbath and pierced and defiled; It was used for love charms, being kneaded into paste and made into confectionery. It was peculiarly at the disposal of the priest, if the priest were of the company: as was Urban Grandier or Louis Gaufridi, who claimed in 1611—probably falsely—to have been the first to say the Black Mass at the Sabbath, and to sprinkle the gathering with the Divine Blood, while they cried out '*Sanguis ejus super nos et filios nostros*'.[1]

The Mass at the Sabbath was sometimes said to be celebrated by the Devil himself, which would presumably be impossible if it were to be a true Mass, unless the Devil in that case were a masquerading priest. The Devil himself cannot say a valid Mass. Often it was a priest of the company who officiated. He wore a black cope, without a cross. The altar was a rock or a stone laid on stones. He used, sometimes at any rate, a book of the Rite. He said neither *Confiteor* nor *Alleluya*. He turned his back on the altar, muttering the incantation. He used a black Host—or sometimes a slice of a turnip also black. He consecrated, and if he wore a horned headdress he sometimes elevated It by thrusting It on a horn; the assembly crying out meanwhile. They communicated in order, a mite of the Host to each, and to each a taste of the consecrated drink. The wine of this chalice was a brew 'of such foul taste and smell, that they sweated to swallow it, and so cold that it froze their bodies'. After the Reformation the Sacrament was administered after some such manner through the Protestant countries as well as the Roman—in Sweden, in Scotland, in New England.

---

[1] It was held by some doctors that the aim at the Sabbath was to gratify Satan by making sacrifices to him with the same ceremonies as those by priests to God: the pseudo-organism in ritual.

The celebration and the banquet were followed by the promiscuous intercourse. The demons took part, and the President himself. This, like the banquet and the wine of the celebration, was in many cases intensely disagreeable: one said it was as agonizing as travail; another that his member being scaly, she suffered 'une extreme douleur', others that they had great pain. On the other hand the girls of Mme de Bourignon, for example, spoke with pleasure of their caresses. One said of them: 'I will not be other than I am; I find too much content in my condition; I am always caressed.' The contrast seems again to be partly due to the way in which it was imagined. It is generally agreed that, as far as the general meetings were concerned, an artificial phallus must have been used, though for those who hold that the Devil himself was concerned, the explanation seems unnecessary. The Devil presumably, by one means or another, could do his own work. Dead bodies were sometimes said to be used, though they were made to appear fresh and lively. The incubi and succubi were not, of course, confined to the Sabbaths; they came to the homes of the witches, and even married them. Rebecca West, an Essex witch, confessed that the Devil came to her 'as she was going to bed and told her, he would marry her, and that she could not deny him; she said he kissed her, but was as cold as clay, and married her that night in this manner: he took her by the hand and led her about the chamber, and promised to be her loving husband till death, and to avenge her of her enemies; and that then she promised him to be his obedient wife till death, and to deny God and Christ Jesus'. This is obviously one of the early meetings, and the time of the verbal pact, but the marriage apparently continued.

The Sabbath broke up. The assembly scattered and went to their homes. Those who had all this while lain rigid in trance stirred. Those who had gone from their husbands' or their wives' side returned and the spirit who had lain there instead disappeared, or else they themselves moved whatever they had left in a magical substitution—a pillow or a stick. The morning came; they went out into the lanes and streets, upon their business and upon their own very special business. For there had been one more concern at the great meeting, and that had been the harm that could be done against others. This was generally a matter of exhortation at the grand Sabbaths, when the Devil or the priest in his stead preached at the Mass; but at the lesser meetings it was often plotted and arranged—as when the North Berwick covens conspired against King James, or the Auldearne witches charmed the minister of the parish from recovering from his sickness, or Alexander Hamilton of Edinburgh entreated the Devil for revenge against Lady Ormestoun the younger. Storms were raised at these meetings; the covens beat a river with rods or threw bodies of animals into the sea; the crops of their enemies were destroyed either by those storms or by other magical means or by merely trampling them down. These were the group movements, but the encouragement of malicious acts against neighbours was solitary as well as communal, and it was these which were to be always pursued. It was this consciousness which was abroad, and this panic.

The malice had many ways of working. Image-murder or plain poison was common enough; so was the 'ligature', the interference with the sexual relations of men or women, or indeed with any of the entrails and tubes of the human body, which were twisted and impeded by the twisting of the magical link. The learned judge Jean Bodin had had it explained to him fully. He says he had been told 'that there were more than fifty ways of knotting the *aiguillette*, whether to impede the man or the woman only, so that one, disgusted with the other, would pollute him or herself with adultery; but that it was mostly the man and rarely the woman who was tied. It could be for one day, for a year, for eternity unless the knot was loosened. There was a knot by which one would love the other desperately and not be loved, but be vehemently hated; there was one by which they would love each other ardently, but when they came to congress they would tear each other shamefully with their nails. And what amazed me more was that while the knot remained there would appear lumps on the strap like warts, showing the number of children that would have been born but for it. The knot can be made not to prevent congress, but procreation. There were men who could not be ligatured; others whom the knot would impede before marriage; others who could be impeded after marriage, but with more difficulty. Also that urination could be impeded, and many died of it. Thus I found a wretched boy nearly dead from this, until the impediment was removed by him who had made it—a sorcerer who died insane a few months later. The woman also repeated various phrases appertaining to the various kinds of knots, which were neither Greek, Latin, Hebrew, French, Spanish, nor Italian, nor I think belonging to any other tongue. She also told of what leather and what colour the ligature should be made. When this evil was increasing in Poitou, in 1560, a bride accused a woman neighbour of ligating her husband, and the magistrate threw her into prison, threatening that she should never leave it until the impediment was removed; in two days she ordered the spouses to copulate; they did so and she was discharged. Words and the strap have really nothing to do, but only the malice of the Devil aiding the evil will of men.'

Such were the details. The account of them, without the human prisoner, is bound to appear cold and even silly. But only in the studies of the theologians and jurists were the details given without the human prisoner. It was precisely the prisoner or the suspect, he or she, who gave form and validity to the imagination. It was the pretty young woman in the next house, the ascetic priest of the parish, the dignified wife of the town-councillor, the idiot son of the poor couple in the hovel, the old market-woman with the power of invective, the wandering pedlar, the learned scholar, at whom men and women looked; whom they saw, whom they heard, whom (once the *fama* had begun) they imagined doing this and the other—talking to the tall black, running upstairs to a materializing lover, dancing, kissing, blaspheming. They felt the sudden unexpected moments when anything or anyone—one's wife, one's friend, one's neighbour—*might* be something else, disguised and malicious. Nowadays we do not, at those times, habitually think of sorcery and the hidden coven. They did. It needs but for a moment to contemplate another human being with that possibility in mind, in the street or in the train or the house, to understand what happened. Add the temptation, the fever, the panic fear; add the longing—so universal though so generally denied nowadays—for hate, for anger, for destruction. The moment of doubt, of horror, of enjoyment of the thrill, resolved itself into belief instead of into disbelief—precisely as in more ordinary cases of jealousy or pride we now resolve our doubts into belief instead of disbelief; and that resolution provokes us to action. It was in that conviction that there was drawn up, as action, a form of sentence which may be given here because it recounts almost the whole story. It comes from Avignon and dates from 1582. It runs:[1]

'Considering the processes against N.N.N. etc., accused before us, in which, as well as by the relations and confessions judicially made by you and each of you before us, repeated often under oath, as by the accusations and depositions of witnesses and other lawful proofs, from which acts and processes it has been and is lawfully established that you and each of you have renounced the one and triune God, the creator of us all, and have worshipped the merciless Devil, the old enemy of the human race, and have devoted yourselves to him forever and have renounced before the same cacodemon your most sacred baptism and your god-parents in it and your share of paradise and the eternal inheritance which our Lord Jesus Christ by his death acquired for you and for the

[1] Lea, *Materials.*

whole human race, that roaring Devil himself pouring
the water which you accepted; changing the true name
received in the baptismal font, you have allowed a false
one to be imposed on you in that fictitious baptism; in
pledge of the faith professed in the demon you have
given him a fragment of your garments; and in order
that your name should be removed and obliterated from
the Book of Life, by command of the Father of Lies,
with your own hand you have placed your sign in the
black book of perpetual death and of the reproved and
damned; and, in order that he might bind you more
firmly to such great infidelity and impiety, he branded
each of you with his mark or stigma, as being his own
property; and upon a circle, which is the symbol of
divinity, traced upon the earth, which is the footstool of
God, you and each of you have bound yourselves by
oath to obey his orders and commands, trampling upon
the cross and the sign of the Lord; and in obedience to
him, mounted on a staff and with your thighs anointed
with a certain most execrable unguent prescribed to you
by the said Devil, you have been carried through the air
by the said tempter, in an unseasonable hour of the night
fitting for malefactors, to the appointed spot on certain
days, and there, in the synagogue common to other
witches, sorcerers, heretical enchanters and worshippers
of demons, by the light of a noisome fire, after many
jubilations, dancings, feastings, drinkings and games in
honour of the presiding Beelzebub, prince of demons, in
the form and appearance of a most black and filthy goat,
you have adored him as God, by acts and words, ap-
proaching him suppliantly on your knees, offering him

lighted candles of pitch, kissing with the utmost reverence and a sacrilegious mouth his most stinking and nasty anus, invoking him by the name of the true God, asking his aid to punish all your enemies and those who refuse you anything, and, taught by him, inflicting revenge, injuries and enchantments on men and beasts; with the aid of Satan you have thus committed many homicides of children, have deprived mothers of milk, have caused wasting sickness and other most severe disease and, with the knowledge and assent of many, you have exhumed children, killed by your malefic art and buried in the church-yards, and have taken them to the above described synagogue of your accomplice witches, offering them to the demon presiding on his throne, where, after keeping the fat and cutting off the head, the hands and the feet, you have cooked the trunk and by command of your said *fattur* you have damnably devoured them; then, adding evil to evil, you men have fornicated with succubi, you women with incubi, committing the execrable crime of sodomy with them in spite of their freezing coldness. And what is the most detestable of all, when you receive the most august sacrament of the Eucharist in the church, by instruction of the said serpent, ejected from paradise, you have retained it in your mouths and nefariously spit it out on the ground so as to insult our true and holy God with the greatest show of contempt, contumely and impiety, thus promoting the glory, honor, triumph and kingdom of the Devil, whom you have adorned with all honor, praise, dignity, authority and adoration, all of which most grievous, horrid and abominable acts are

171

directly insulting and contumelious to the omnipotent God, the Creator of all things. Wherefore we, Friar Florus, Provincial of the Order of Preaching Friars, Doctor of Holy Theology and Inquisitor-general of the Holy Faith in all this Legation of Avignon, having the fear of God before our eyes, sitting as a tribunal, by this our definitive sentence, which, by the custom of our predecessors, we render in writing with the advice of theologians and jurists; piously invoking the names of our Lord Jesus Christ and the Blessed Virgin Mary, we declare and pronounce and definitively sentence all you the above-named and each one of you to have been and to be true apostates, idolators, rebels to the most holy faith, deniers and contemners of Omnipotent God, sodomites guilty of the unspeakable crime, adulterers, fornicators, sorcerers, witches, sacrilegious heretics, enchanters, homicides, infanticides, worshippers of demons, assertors of the satanic, diabolic and infernal science and of the damnable and condemned faith, blasphemers, perjurers, infamous, and to have been convicted of all evil witchcraft and crimes. Therefore we remit you all and each one of you, really and effectively, by this our sentence to the secular court, to be punished by its judgment with condign and lawful penalties.'

Chapter Eight

THE GRAND WAR

Honorius VIII had issued in 1484 a Bull against sorcery. Kramer, afterwards to be the principal of the two authors of the *Malleus*, proceeded into the Tyrol, to the diocese of Brixen, where he put himself in communication with the bishop and with the Archduke Sigismund and caused the Bull to be published. But the bishop seems to have been one of those half-hearted ecclesiastics against whom various comments in the *Malleus* were aimed. The Inquisitor allowed himself to become involved in a court intrigue centring round the archduchess. She was accused of attempting to enchant and envenom her husband, and a voice was heard to denounce a number of other ladies her friends. It was said by critics that, far from being the voice of a spirit, this was in fact the speech of someone concealed in the palace oven. The Inquisitor, however, had some of these ladies arrested and, in due sequence of law, put to the torture. The archduke permitted it. But the bishop energetically intervened. He wrote to the Inquisitor commanding him to leave the district; when Kramer took no notice, he wrote again, hinting, if not threatening, the vengeance of the male kinsfolk of the ladies who had been accused. He also wrote stiffly to all the clergy of the diocese. The Landtag of the Tyrol protested against the action of the archduke and at the usage applied to the ladies. The archduke sent presents to Kramer, but he could not or would not do more. Kramer was compelled to withdraw. It is supposed to be then that he settled down to compose the *Malleus*.

So tiny a defeat, though it stood for something, stood for what was not to become effective for two hundred years. From the publication of the *Malleus* about 1490 to the publication in 1693 of the Retraction of the Salem jurymen in New England—undiscovered in 1484—is a convenient reckoning for the time of the frenzied and frenzying attack. There was at last provided a full codification of the great offence; it had been done before, but never so fully; nor had it before corresponded with a general willingness to take every advantage of the formulation. In the best days of the Middle Ages trials might take place and tortures be both threatened and applied— more often perhaps threatened than applied. But the cases of acquittal were fairly frequent, and such cases as that of Saint Joan show that the ecclesiastical courts were sometimes indisposed to push the torture to its extreme. She was shown the instruments; they were not used. They might have been used on Gilles de Rais, had he not confessed. But even with Gilles de Rais, the spectacular scene of the Bishop of Nantes embracing the convicted prisoner shows that something of the sense of Christendom remained vital and active. If it was melodrama, it was proper melodrama. If it was insincere (which there is no reason to suppose) it was yet an insincerity which pretended the right things and which did not involve the prisoner in much worse things. But now all was changed. The Middle Ages had, as it were, abandoned that effort and dream of sanctity. The awful strain had been too much for them. They had learnt the great fundamental lesson, produced by all individual and social experience, that it is much easier, and in a general way as profitable, to blame someone else rather than to blame oneself. They had discovered that it is always agreeable to hold someone responsible. They had discovered of what their doctrines and legal codes were capable. And they proceeded to use them. Contrition for sin had largely vanished from Christendom; conflict about sin took its place.

It is always to be remembered, as one looks sideways —one hardly dare look direct—at the horror that now spread that two things—three things—were true. The power of invisible malice against which the full new attack was aimed was a very old thing. Through Middle Ages and Dark Ages, through falling Empire and standing Empire, the great tradition went. As difficult as it is for us, after some two centuries' more or less relief from the nightmare, to believe in pack and coven, in Sabbath and sacrifice, so difficult was it for them, after fifteen centuries' exhibition of it, to be even a little uncertain of those things. Second, it is as certain as can be that some had been practised. It is most unlikely that no bodies had been found in the castle of Gilles de Rais; it is certain that, of all those waxen images of which we hear, not all can have been put into the chests and cupboards of their reputed owners merely to cause them to be found guilty. The Duchess of Gloucester had certainly tried to do something. When all is said, malice existed, and malice that would make use of any supernatural power. Thirdly, a great effort towards explanation and education and all the rest had been genuinely made. It was perhaps unfortunate that in the end Aquinas had been quite so logical. The Angelic Doctor was, no doubt, right; but his exactness of intellect, as it turned out, was in this respect something of a misfortune to the Church. Yet the logical decisions of all the schoolmen would have achieved nothing had not the official mind become inflamed. 'The quality of disbelief' which in the Middle Ages was still allowed (outside formal dogma) to be part of the general air was now, in this respect, more and more expelled from it. Where suspicion had been, at first and on the whole, discouraged, it was now encouraged.

The full development of the horror came in the second of the two centuries. The sixteenth century produced many executions; the seventeenth many more. Little distinction seems to have existed between the Roman and the Reformed Churches; on hardly any other point were they in such hot agreement. The fires of the Tyrol were answered by the fires of Geneva. It has been argued that the greater destructiveness of the seventeenth century on both sides was due to the success of the Counter-Reformation. It would perhaps be true to say that the preoccupation of the sixteenth century with the direct religious quarrel partly distracted men's minds from the subject. But the records are incomplete and deductions unsafe. On this subject it is clear that if our fathers erred, they erred all together. Catholic and Reformed disputed about heaven; they almost made a pact over hell.

No certainly accurate statement can be made about the number who suffered death. It has been reckoned in millions, which is unlikely, and in hundreds of thousands which is not so unlikely. A certain witch-finder named Balthasar Ross in Fulda claimed that he had been the cause of putting some 700 men and women to death, and hoped to reach a total of one thousand. In Geneva, between 1542 and 1546, there were a large number of executions out of 700 arrests after a plague. In Berne during ten years 900 executions. In Werdenfels among the Alps, from 1590 to 1591, fifty executions; in the whole of Alsace, between 1615 and 1635, it has been estimated that five thousand were burnt. In three parishes in Sweden, during two years, seventy executions. In districts around Trier, between 1587–93, three hundred and sixty executions. In Würzburg, a list made out in 1629 of the executions showed a hundred and sixty burned; a number which included five canons, a theologian, a provost of the cathedral, the governor of the hospital, and other priests. And so on.

Like the tales of the witches themselves, the tales of the witch-trials have a hideous similarity. So have the executions. The executions were, generally, of three kinds. There were those who were beheaded or strangled before being burnt; there were those who were burnt; and there were those who were mutilated before being burnt. The use of the red-hot pincers spread. A woman of Zeil in 1629 was convicted of having four times desecrated the Host and of having murdered her child. She was therefore, on her way to be burned alive, torn six times by the glowing iron—four times to avenge our sacred Lord and twice to avenge her human child. It would be bad enough if she were innocent; it is worse if she was guilty. For then the horror of the whole thing becomes unbearable: the screams of the sacrilegious murderess, as she is stopped for the fourth, for the fifth, for the sixth tearing, ascend like an epitome of the nature of man.

The rules about the use of torture seem in most places to have been abandoned: especially in Germany. But even where they were a little kept, they became a formality. The trials became, especially under the secular governments, a pageant of torture. In the Tyrol, in 1505, a woman was tortured eighteen times 'to the confusion of the diabolical arts'. In Nördlingeen, in 1589, Maria Holl, the wife of an innkeeper, was said to have been tortured fifty-six times. Special torments were invented. The witch-chair was an iron chair, with blunt studs all over it, in which the accused was fastened, while fire was lit below the seat. This was frequently used, sometimes after earlier tortures of the more general kinds—the thumb-screwing, the leg-crushing, the scourging, the hoisting with weights. The idea of torture had been that it helped the truth. Pain brought the human spirit to its last point of mortal existence; there, in its nakedness, it was asked and answered the question. Torture was precisely, in that sense, the question. But now the idea of the solemn rarity of the agony was lost; the pain became popular, and monotonous, and irrelevant.

At Bamberg a special witch-prison was built. It was a large building, having a central passage with cells on each side. At the back was an open space, beyond which was the chamber for torture; under it ran a brook. There was also a chapel. Over the main door was a statue of Justice, and a line from Virgil: 'Discite justitiam moniti et non temnere divos'. The text from I Kings (ix. 8-9) was also there:

'And at this house, which is high, every one that passeth by it shall be astonished, and shall hiss; and they shall say, Why hath the Lord done thus unto this land, and to this house?

'And they shall answer, Because they forsook the Lord their God, who brought forth their fathers out of the land of Egypt, and have taken hold upon other gods, and have worshipped them, and served them: therefore hath the Lord brought upon them all this evil.'

Bamberg, in central Germany, achieved a great reputation for the suppression of witchcraft. Between 1609 and 1633 it is reported that it saw 900 executions. The chancellor of the diocese, his wife and his son, five burgomasters, and a number of town councillors were burnt. There were accusations against the judges and the chief persecutors themselves, but these were suppressed. A letter still exists, written by one of the accused privately to his daughter, showing how the confessions in some cases were obtained. Johannes Junius, a councillor and burgomaster, was arrested in 1628. The witnesses against him were the chancellor Dr. Georg Haan, and his son, and a woman, all of whom were then under arrest, and all of whom deposed to seeing Junius at the Sabbath. He denied it and was tortured by thumbscrews and by hoisting eight times. He was then removed from the pulleys and warned that he would be tortured till he confessed. He proceeded therefore to relate something which he hoped would sound convincing, though he wrote to his daughter that it was all false. He had been once in a meadow (he said) when a girl came to him who after some interchange of talk turned herself suddenly into a goat. The goat attacked his throat, saying, 'You shall be mine'; presently others were there—men and women—who urged him to renounce God. He consented and was baptized infernally. He had been to the Sabbaths, but he had not recognized anyone. The Court threatened the torture and asked him if he had not seen the chancellor: he agreed. He had had a succubus. They asked him for more names; he said he knew none. They threatened the torture; he named some thirty. He said he had been given a grey powder to kill his son, but he had used it on his horse instead. They asked what more; he knew of nothing. They threatened the torture; he said he had abstracted and buried a consecrated Host. His succubus had told him he would be arrested but would afterwards be set free. He ratified the confession; he wrote to his daughter: 'It is all falsehood and invention . . . They never cease the torture until one says something.' We do not definitely know what happened to him, but he was no doubt burnt—probably after having been torn with pincers to gratify the insulted jealousy of our sacred Lord in His sacrament.

Such tales are frequent. A terrible case is that of a man who was put to death in 1645 in Meran in the Tyrol, and whose name has since accumulated stories about itself. Michael Perger was a wandering fellow who lived by his wits. He was almost sixty when he was arrested in May. He was asked about his beliefs; he said he believed what the Church believed, though he was careless in his religious duties. He admitted he had talked charms and astrology in many places, and gossiped superstition, as that a man should not wash on Friday, or even wear a shirt washed on Fridays.[1] Witnesses were examined in various places. They related how he foretold storms, and made butter come; how he read the stars, told fortunes, was knowledgeable with herbs, could read many books, and sometimes stole one; how he uttered threats and then misfortunes happened; how he made indecent jokes with the serving women. All this gathering of idle chit-chat took until June, when he was examined for the witch-mark, and one was found on his tongue. He was prepared for the torture, but he still denied sorcery except that he had once 'conjured a little book out of a chest'. In July he was hoisted several times, once with a weight of two hundred pounds on his feet; after this, he admitted that he once met a woman who solicited him; he lay with her; she, perhaps, was a demon. In August the torture was seriously applied. After hoisting with weights he was tied to a trestle, his legs pressed together in irons, and he was beaten whenever he tried to sleep. After thirty-six hours of this he gave way. He acknowledged that the woman of whom he had spoken was an evil spirit; her name was Belial. The details followed; how he had

[1] On the other side it was maintained that an arrested witch ought to be clothed in a new chemise which had been washed on an Ember Sunday in holy water and blessed salt.

renounced holy things, had seen a book written in red, had written a pact in his blood, had been to the Sabbath, had raised storms, and had had intercourse. 'He was released from the trestle at 6.30 in the morning.'

He was not released from confessions, and they continued recklessly. Belial and he had done many things— raising storms, stealing the Host (which he sold 'for six kreutzer to a black merchant'), damaging vines, ill-wishing neighbours, and so on. He began to name others, and the naming continued during the August examinations. In September they wanted to examine his foot for the mark where (he had said) Belial had drawn blood for his signature, but so swollen was the foot, from the torture presumably, that they could not find it. He confirmed all his confession—on being threatened with red-hot iron plates.

In October those involved, with other witnesses, were examined. There was a good deal of talk about the well-to-do farmers who had been accused by Perger, and obviously a good deal of ill feeling. But nothing much is on record about them. On the 11th October Perger revoked his confession, and so on the 12th October; he said he had had nothing to do with evil spirits. They threatened to set him on the fiery iron plates, and brought them out ready. He confirmed his confession—and tried to stifle himself with straw, but the gaoler stopped him. On the 26th October the sentence was delivered; it does not remain in the records, but he is generally reputed to have been burnt.

The decisions, even had what must be called the madness not arisen, would not have been made easier by the self-accusations and obstinacies which arose. A young man in Würzburg, related to the bishop, was accused and convicted. Both Jesuits and Franciscans endeavoured to bring him to repentance and failed. At last he was brought to the castle for private execution, but he wept and begged for mercy so that fresh efforts were made to convert him and he was even promised his pardon on that condition. He only said: 'If you had seen what I have seen you would become what I am, and if I were not so I would become so.' He was taken back to the room of execution, but there he shrieked and struggled, refusing to repent and refusing to die, until the executioner managed to strike off his head.

An odd case at Stablo seems to show that the ecclesiastical authorities were sometimes slow to act. A certain Jean del Vaux, priest and monk of the abbey, having been under suspicion, said that he was tired of the Devil's tyranny, and wished to free himself by confession. He had met, at the age of fourteen, 'an old man in a religious habit' in a wood, who made him many promises, and advised him to enter the priesthood. He had committed many murders with diabolic poison. He detailed the Sabbath, and named many accomplices.

The ecclesiastical examiners were very slow to accept his professions. The vicar-general and the chancellor of the diocese were on the commission and no question of torture was raised for a very long while. They repeatedly exhorted him to beware of false accusations, and they tried by mixing up the names to get him to contradict himself. This, however, he failed to do. They suggested that it might be illusion; he denied it. They warned him again not to risk his soul by perjury. It was at last demanded by the prosecution that he should be tortured, in order that 'his evidence could be better and against his accomplices'. It had been reported that he was insane, but the Court, having caused him to be confronted with a number of outsiders and heard his answers, decided that he was too lucid and consistent for this suggestion to be sustained. He was then lightly tortured, while the improbability of his story was urged on him. He remained steadfast in the assertion of his guilt. Eventually he was convicted and beheaded. Some of his reputed accomplices were examined, but otherwise the accusations were allowed to drop.

It is clear that, at least in some places, the proceedings were used to cover personal hate. The confiscation of the property of those accused was a contributory cause among the prosecutors; among the accused, a determination not to die alone, and sometimes to take their enemies or even their judges with them. Accusations against judges were generally ignored—at the time. But at a future day the accusation could easily give rise to what the *Malleus* called 'suspicion'. At Offenburg, a family feud worked itself out in charges and counter-charges. In the same town, in 1627, the wife of Stattmeister Philipp Beck was arrested. 'She was a young, beautiful, and attractive woman. Beck asked for permission to write to his wife, saying she might confess to unfaithfulness, and she should be tortured about young Hauser.'[1] She was executed nine days later.

Children, of course, were prominent. The school-

[1] Lea, *Materials*.

children were sometimes taken to executions; at one ceremony in North Germany two witches were beheaded and one strangled, while the clergy, the schoolchildren, and the crowd all sang hymns loudly. It is not surprising therefore that children played with the tales. In Szegedin, in Hungary, a cobbler's son bragged one morning to a playfellow that he would raise storms and teach him to do so. At dinner-time there was, in fact, a storm; the other boy told his father of the talk, the father told the officers; the cobbler's son was arrested, and presently six men and seven women were burnt. In 1694 a schoolgirl of ten bragged to her companions in the schoolroom that she could make mice, and was said to have done so out of a handkerchief. There was immediate arrest, both of the girl and of the woman from whom she said she had learnt the sorcery. Torture by rods was demanded by the prosecution, but there was a university decision that the acts in question were not sorcery, and the accused escaped. The cessation of the madness saved them; at Würzburg, seventy years before, in 1628, the schoolchildren came under suspicion; two girls, of eleven and twelve, were put to death in January; in October a boy who was brought to confess only after more than a hundred stripes; in November another boy of twelve, after heavy scourging.

Monotonous repetition of the miserable tales serves no purpose. The evil things of the Sabbath, by all these ways, reproduced themselves everywhere. That is not to say that the Sabbath did not exist. But the idea of the Sabbath had become an obsession to all alike, to the witches and the witch-hunters. Almighty God was denied on the one hand and defended on the other. Our Lord in his Sacrament was subjected to the intention of defilement on the one hand and to the intention of vengeance upon the other. The blasphemies of the Sabbath were answered by the hymns around the fires. The diabolic familiars were invisible on the one hand, and visible on the other; toads and cats, judges and torturers. The use of excruciating pain had become automatic, and had become so in order to produce the right kind of detail. 'Children of two', said one prosecutor, 'can be interrogated in cases of witchcraft'. It was not the witch-midwives alone who sacrificed their children to their god. The Holy Innocents must have received many into their company during those awful centuries.

At this time also the grand attack produced, after its own kind, what all such attacks do produce—the informer. The casual, the gossiping, the terrified, the malicious informer had, of course, been there from the beginning; it was in them that the *fama* or suspicion began. But what had been amateur became professional. Most of the serious writers on the subject, on whichever side, had declared the difficulty of discovery, though indeed in practice the difficulty seemed small enough. But the notion of the difficulty added to the general pious fear, and (to be just) one must add that the hypothesis—it was part of its horror—did precisely involve the unknown and unsuspected witch beside the suspected or known. *Someone* was; *anyone* might be; neither a show of devotion nor a strength of worldly reputation were a guarantee of innocence. To discover the guilty, as the Court of the Inquisition in Spain presently said, was a business almost beyond human power to decide. The Inquisition in Spain, however, as will be seen, tended to take the view that human power had better not attempt the task, and informers there were generally discouraged. Over the rest of Europe—especially in the Germanies—they throve. Courts began to make use of the travelling witch-finder and presently even to call him in. In the countries which, after the Reformation, remained in communion with the Roman See the witch-finder not infrequently took the form of a wandering exorcist, who went about the country, often in state, sometimes cursing and some-times denouncing. The ecclesiastical authorities did not much approve; they tried to insist that such men must have licences from the bishop; they drew up regulations; they discouraged irregular beatings and fumigations of the suspect or the possessed. Some doctors of the subject held that such things were always improper; some, how-ever, held that though they were useless and even pro-fane if intended directly for the expulsion of the demon, yet they were permissible if meant only to show con-tempt for it, and thus indirectly lead it to depart.

It is hardly necessary to add that presently the exor-cists themselves came under suspicion; the Devil was said to be in agreement with them, and to pretend to be cast out in order to deceive others. The horrid word *Pact* was pronounced, especially about the unlicenced exorcizer. He who was not commissioned by heaven was suspected to be directed by hell—and perhaps with more justice than was usually shown in these matters.

The abominable name of Matthew Hopkins belongs to the group of informers. He was certainly no exorcizer—only a finder of witches; he operated in Essex and the adjoining counties during the seventeenth century. He began his work at Manningtree, where in 1644 he asserted that a number of witches came to hold their meetings close by his house, and there offered sacrifices. They were seized, vulgarly ill-used, and hanged. His discovery settled his vocation; he pursued it jealously, and it is computed that he managed to put more than two hundred to death from 1645 to 1647. He was assisted by the Government of the Interregnum, which took witchcraft as seriously in theory and more seriously in practice than the Stuarts; and until it was forbidden he made a habit of 'swimming' witches, though he claimed that he only did so when they themselves desired it. Local authorities were very grateful to him; he throve on their thanks and payment, and so successful was he that it was reported that he had secured one of the Devil's lists of witches. He was, however, not a continuous success; there grew up some feeling against him, and he was compelled to defend himself in a pamphlet. It pleased God to let him die 'peaceably' in his house at Manningtree in 1647, after a long consumption, thus cutting short his activities against the presumed enemies of God.

Chapter Nine

IN ENGLAND

The two centuries of war took on in England a different shape from that they endured on the Continent. The evil (on both sides) may have been as high, but it was English; it was, that is to say, rather brutal than cruel, rather local than organized, rather sensitive than theoretical. There were many executions. But there does not seem to have been the same effort to force everything into a pattern; the accused were not compelled to recollect all the things that the schoolmen had laid down as possible to them. Torture was not formally and legally applied, though there was a good deal of barbarous usage of prisoners. Torture-chambers were not blessed with holy water and holy herbs, nor were the instruments of pain solemnly exhibited. The guilty were hanged and not burned. And it looks (as far as one can see) as if there was a greater likelihood of acquittal.

To say so much is not to underrate the agony. A woman tied cross-legged or in some other uncomfortable position and kept for days and nights without sleep suffered as much perhaps—if one can imagine degrees in

189

such misery of pain—as one manacled in the slowly
heating iron chair of the Bamberg Court. But at least
the one was not intellectually and formally complicated
with the Christian idea; it was but dubiously legal; and it
was rather stupidly horrid than ingeniously horrible.
The Christian doctrine of pure love was hardly more
obvious in England than anywhere else. But, whether
from a lack of intelligence or a lack of cruelty, the Christian doctrine of pure love was not so neatly intertwined
with what came to be much like an officially Christian
doctrine of pure vengeance.

This may, certainly, have had something to do with
the Reformation. The exclusion of the grand Roman
pattern, and the uncertainty in the minds of almost
everyone what religious pattern exactly was in the mind
of the Government in London, the prevention of the
full Calvinist doctrine, the check (as it were) on all ex-
tremism, and the very great determination that there
must not be any *trouble* anywhere—all this must have
acted against a complete acceptance of the pattern of
sorcery. It was not to anyone's interest, certainly not to
that of the authorities, to encourage, after the manner of
the authors of the *Malleus*, an imagination of a great re-
bellion against the Crown and the Church. Even on the
Continent that imagination had taken place before the
violent Reforming movements began, and had they
begun earlier there might have been no time or room for
concern with it. If Luther had been born thirty years
sooner, the lives of thousands of reputed witches might
have been saved.

Certainly, that general attack of 1484 and onwards

operated in England also, to the extent that the comparatively placid earlier consciousness of sorcery became increased and excited. Almost the last of the Noble Trials took place at the end of the fifteenth century. In 1470 the Duchess of Bedford protested to the Privy Council that she had been slandered by accusations of image-witchcraft brought against her by a certain Thomas Wake. He had pretended that she had brought about the marriage of King Edward IV and Elizabeth Grey by these means. The case against her broke down. King Richard III, however, revived the claim that the two had been brought together 'by sorcery and witchcraft', though he attributed the operation not to the Duchess of Bedford but to Elizabeth Grey herself. It was also Richard, then Protector, who in the Privy Council in 1483 denounced Jane Shore and the Queen for witchcraft worked on his person, showing his arm supposed to be withered. But 'every man's mind misgave him, well perceiving that the queen was too wise to go about any such folly'.

With a few minor exceptions, accusations against certain lords, this fashion of attack began to disappear from high circles, though any report of divination continued to be dangerous, as when Sir William Neville was arrested in 1532 on such grounds. Henry Neville, son of the Earl of Westmorland, was a subject of investigation in 1546, but he had been engaged in a complication of magical operations—a ring for finding hidden treasure, a raising of the spirit Orpheus to cause him to play on the virginals, and suspicion of magical murder of his wife. He was, however, released. Thereafter divination lingered, but image-sorcery, either for love or hate, was neglected until in 1617 occurred the famous discovery of the Countess of Somerset and Dr. Simon Forman. The laws against witchcraft, however, began to be tightened.

In 1542 the first Tudor Act against witchcraft was passed; among the practices charged as criminal was the 'digging up and pulling down an infinite number of Crosses in this realm'. This, however, is not the dark blasphemy one might suppose, as we know from the case of Henry Neville above; the reason for overthrowing crosses was that treasure was often said to be buried beneath them. The Act was aimed against the use of sorcery for the discovery of such treasure as well as for the 'wasting, consuming, or destroying any person in body, members or goods or to provoke any person to unlawful use'. This Act, however, was repealed in the first year of Edward VI, among a number of others which had created new felonies during the reign of Henry VIII, and the next passed was in 1563 under Elizabeth, followed by a like one under James I in 1604. Of the Act of 1542 Dr. Kittredge says: 'It is true to English tradition. It penalizes incantation and conjuring, witchcraft that kills or maims a person, and destroys or impairs his goods and chattels, and other offences of like nature. It does not in the remotest way recognize the existence of Satanic assemblies or of demon-worship *en masse*. Elizabeth's law of 1563 is little more than a preciser enactment with a modification of penalties, and the law of James I is a mere revision of Elizabeth's.'[1]

The abstracts of indictments for the Home Counties in

[1] *Witchcraft in Old and New England.*

Elizabeth's reign confirm this.[1] There are a number of accusations of the bewitching of 'a black cow', 'eight pigs', 'thirteen turkey-cocks', 'a bull', 'one horse, one cow and one hog', 'two sows', etc., etc. The rest are accusations of personal harm, even to death, done by witchcraft. Most of the sufferers are said to have 'languished' until death or until 'the taking of this inquisition'. The list is occasionally varied by a different charge; thus Robert Browning of Aldam in Essex, 'labourer, defrauded the King's subjects, persuading them that by conjuration and invocation of evil spirits they might discover hidden hoards of gold and silver, and regain lost goods.' Typical confessions were those of the Chelmsford witches in 1566. The confessions of the group so arrested were published with two preliminary poems by John Phillips, which are more like the *Midsummer Night's Dream* than would be expected.

> Draw near, you patrons with your babes,
>   come, view this hapless hap;
> In flushing floods of coming tears
>   your tender beauties lap . . .
> Three feminine dames attached were
>   whom Sathan had infect
> With Belial's spirit whose sorcery did
>   the simple so molest . . .
> Which thing when thou hast viewed well,
>   good Reader, do thou pray
> To God the Lord that he from us
>   would witches take away.

[1] C. L'Estrange Ewen, *Witch-Hunting and Witch-Trials*, 1559–1736.

Elizabeth Francis, the first to be examined, deposed as follows:

'First she learned this art of witchcraft at the age of twelve years of her grandmother, whose name was Mother Eve of Hatfield Peverell, deceased. Item when she taught it her, she counselled her to renounce God and his word and to give of her blood to Satan (as she termed it), which she delivered her in the likeness of a white spotted cat, and taught her to feed the said cat with bread and milk, and she did so, also she taught her to call it by the name of Satan and to keep it in a basket.

'When this Mother Eve had given her the Cat Satan, then this Elizabeth desired first of the said Cat (calling it Satan) that she might be rich and to have goods, and he promised her she should—asking her what she would have, and she said sheep (for this Cat spake to her as she confessed in a strange hollow voice, but such as she understood by use) and this Cat forthwith brought sheep into her pasture to the number of eighteen, black and white, which continued with her for a time, but in the end did all wear away she knew not how.

'Item, when she had gotten these sheep, she desired to have one Andrew Byles to her husband, which was a man of some wealth, and the Cat did promise she should, but that he said she must first consent that this Andrew should abuse her, and she so did.

'And after when this Andrew had thus abused her he would not marry her, wherefore she willed Satan to waste his goods, which he forthwith did, and yet not being contented with this, she willed him to touch his body which he forthwith did whereof he died.

'Item, that every time that he did anything for her, she said that he required a drop of blood, which she gave him by pricking herself, sometime in one place and then in another, and where she pricked herself there remained a red spot which was still to be seen.

'Item, when this Andrew was dead, she doubting herself with child, willed Satan to destroy it, and he bade her take a certain herb and drink it, which she did, and destroyed the child forthwith.

'Item, when she desired another husband he promised her another, naming this Francis whom she now hath, but said he is not so rich as the other, willing her to consent unto that Francis in fornication which she did, and thereof conceived a daughter that was born within a quarter of a year after they were married.

'After they were married they lived not so quietly as she desired, being stirred (as she said) to much unquietness and moved to swearing and cursing, wherefore she willed Satan her Cat to kill the child, being about the age of half a year old, and he did so, and when she yet found not the quietness that she desired, she willed it to lay a lameness in the leg of this Francis her husband, and it did in this manner. It came in a morning to this Francis' shoe, lying in it like a toad, and when he perceived it putting on his shoe, and had touched it with his foot, he being suddenly amazed asked of her what it was, and she bad him kill it and he was forthwith taken with a lameness whereof he cannot be healed.

'After all this when she had kept this Cat by the space of fifteen or sixteen years, and as some say (though untruly) being weary of it, she came to one Mother Waterhouse her neighbour (a poor woman) when she was going to the oven and desired her to give her a cake, and she would give her a thing that she should be the better for so long as she lived, and this Mother Waterhouse gave her a cake, whereupon she brought her this cat in her apron and taught her as she was instructed before by her grandmother Eve, telling her that she must call him Satan and give him of her blood and bread and milk as before, and at this examination would confess no more.'

Agnes Waterhouse, who was said to have received the cat, was presently examined 'before Justice Southcote and M. Gerard the Queen's attorney'. She was a woman of sixty-four; her daughter Joan was examined also, and the chief evidence against them was that of a child of twelve. The account is as follows:

The Confession of Agnes Waterhouse the xxvii day of July in Anno 1566 at Chelmsford before Justice Southcote and M. Gerard the queen's attorney.

'First being demanded whether that she were guilty or not guilty upon her arraignment of the murdering of a man, she confessed that she was guilty, and then upon the evidence given against her daughter Joan Waterhouse, she said that she had a white Cat, and willed her Cat that he should destroy many of her neighbours' cattle, and also that he should kill a man, and so he did, and then after she must go two or three miles from her house, and then she took thought how to keep her Cat, then she and her Cat concluded that he the said Cat would become a Toad, and then she should keep him in a close house, and give him milk, and so he would continue till she came home again, and then being gone forth, her daughter having been at a neighbour's house there by, required of one Agnes Brown, of the age of twelve years or more, a piece of bread and cheese, and the said Agnes said that she had none, and that she had not the key of the milkhouse door, and then the said Joan went home and was angry with the said Agnes Brown and she said that she remembered that her mother was wont to go up and down in her house and to call Satan Satan she said she would prove the like, and then she went up and down the house and called Satan, and then there came a black Dog to her and asked her what she would have, and then she said she was afraid and said, I would have thee to make one Agnes Brown afraid, and then he asked her what she would give him and she said she would give him a red cock, and he said he would have none of that, and she asked him what he would have then, and he said he would have her body and soul, and so upon request and fear together she gave him her body and soul (and then said the queen's attorney *How wilt thou do before God?* O my Lord, I trust God will have mercy upon me, and then he said *thou sayest well*), and then he departed from her, and then she said that she heard that he made the said Agnes Brown afraid.

'The said Agnes Brown was then demanded and called for, and then she came in, and being asked what age she was of she said she thought she was twelve years old, and then the queen's attorney asked her what she could say, and then she said that at such a day, naming the day certain, she was churning of butter and there came to her a thing like a black Dog with a face like an ape, a short tail, a chain and a silver whistle (to her thinking) about his neck, and a pair of horns on his head, and brought in his mouth the key of the milkhouse door, and then my lord she said, I was afraid, for he skipped and leaped to and fro, and sat on the top of a nettle, and then I asked him what he would have, and he said he would have butter, and I said I had none for him and then he said he would have some or he went, and then he did run to put the key into the lock of the milkhouse door, and I said he should have none, and he said he would have some, and then he opened the door and went upon the shelf, and there upon a new cheese laid down the key, and being a while within he came out again, and locked the door and said that he had made flap butter for me, and so departed, and then she said she told her aunt of it, and then she sent for the priest, and when he came he bade her to pray to God, and call on the name of Jesus, and so the next day my lord he came again to me with the key of our milkhouse door in his mouth, and then I said in the name of Jesus what hast thou there, and then he laid down the key and said that I spake evil words in speaking of that name, and then he departed, and so my aunt took up the key, for he had kept it from us two days and a night, and then we went into the milkhouse and there we did see the print of butter upon the cheese, and then within a few days after he came again with a bean pod in his mouth, and then the queen's attorney asked what that was, and so the other Justices declared, and then she said my lord I said in the name of Jesus what hast thou there, and so then he laid it down and said I spake evil words and departed and came again by and by with a piece of bread in his mouth, and I asked him what he would have, and he said butter it was that he would have, and so he departed, and my lord I did not see him no more till Wednesday last, which was the 28th day of July, why said the queen's attorney was he with thee on Wednesday last, yes she said, what did he then to thee said he, my lord said she he came with a knife in his mouth and asked me if I were not dead, and I said No I thanked God, and then he said if I would not die that he would thrust his knife to my heart but he would make me to die, and then I said in the name of Jesus lay down thy knife, and he said he would not depart from his sweet dame's knife as yet, and then I asked of him who was his dame, and then he nodded and wagged his head to your house Mother Waterhouse, then the queen's attorney asked of the said Agnes Waterhouse what she said to it, then she demanded what manner knife that it was and Agnes Brown said that it was a dagger knife, there thou liest said Agnes Waterhouse, why, quoth the queen's attorney, marry my lord (quoth she) she saith it is a dagger knife and I have none such in my house, but a great knife, and therein she lieth, yea yea, my lord quoth Joan Waterhouse she lieth in that she saith it had a face like an ape, for this that came to me was like a dog, well said the queen's attorney, well, can you make it come before us now, if ye can we will dispatch you out of prison by and by, no faith said Agnes Waterhouse I cannot, for in faith if I had let him go as my daughter did I could make him come by and by, but now I have no more power over him, then said the queen's attorney, Agnes Waterhouse when did thy Cat suck of thy blood never said

she, no said he, let me see, and then the jailer lifted up
her kerchief on her head, and there was divers spots in
her face and one on her nose, then said the queen's attorney, in good faith Agnes when did he suck of thy blood
last, by my faith my lord said she, not this fortnight, and
so the jury went together for that matter.'

*The end and last confession of mother Waterhouse at her
death, which was the 29th day of July, Anno 1566.*

'First (being ready prepared to receive her death) she
confessed earnestly that she had been a witch and used
such execrable sorcery the space of fifteen years, and had
done many abominable deeds, the which she repented
earnestly and unfeignedly, and desired almighty God's
forgiveness in that she had abused his most holy name by
her devilish practises, and trusted to be saved by his most
unspeakable mercy. And being demanded of the by-
standers, she confessed that she sent her Satan to one
Wardol, a neighbour of hers, being a tailor (with whom
she was offended) to hurt and destroy him and his goods.
And this her Satan went thereabout for to have done her
will, but in the end he returned to her again, and was not
able to do this mischief, she asked the cause, and he
answered because the said Wardol was so strong in faith
that he had no power to hurt him, yet she sent him
divers and sundry times (but all in vain) to have
mischieved him. And being demanded whether she was
accustomed to go to church to the common prayer or
divine service, she said yea, and being required what she
did there she said she did as other women do, and prayed
right heartily there, and when she was demanded what

prayer she said, she answered the Lord's prayer, the Ave Maria, and the Belief, and then they demanded whether in Latin or in English, and she said in Latin, and they demanded why she said it not in English but in Latin, seeing that it was set out by public authority and according to God's word that all men should pray in the English and mother tongue that they best understand, and she said that Satan would at no time suffer her to say it in English, but at all times in Latin: for these and many other offences which she hath committed, done and confessed, she bewailed, repented, and asked mercy of God, and all the world forgiveness, and thus she yielded up her soul, trusting to be in joy with Christ her Saviour, which dearly had bought her with his most precious blood. Amen.'

It is an example of the trials of the period. The last years of Elizabeth were full of them, as they were, but with hoistings and chairs and red-hot pincers and burning plates, through most of the rest of Europe. The coming of King James did not at first make much difference. It was not until the king's own particular enjoyment of his own intelligence began to work that any change was observable. The king came certainly from a country where the attitude towards witches was more consistently stern than in England. The ministers of the Kirk were far more like the ideal Inquisitors of the *Malleus* than were most of the English bishops. Inquisitors, bishops, and ministers, all believed that witches existed. But the bishops were a little more inclined to allow that hysteria and fraud might play a part in the accusations. As indeed was King James, whose sympathy with the bishops was as much intellectual as ecclesiastical. He had grown up amid trials and denunciations. In the year 1590 he had found himself the personal object of attack by the North Berwick witches, the account of whom forms one of the most famous cases in witch history. The moving influence seems to have been that of Francis, Earl of Bothwell, the king's enemy, and it is even probable that he acted as the devil in the meetings of the witches. The whole conspiracy came to light (according to the pamphlet *News from Scotland*) accidentally. A certain Gilly Duncan, maidservant to David Seaton the Deputy Bailiff of her town, began suddenly to acquire a reputation for magical cures, and to be absent by night from her master's house. Suspicion being thus aroused, Seaton examined her, and on her remaining obstinately silent, proceeded to torture. But it was not until the Devil's mark was found 'in the forepart of her throat' that she was able to confess, which she then did, accusing many others, both men and women.

David Seaton, however, did not know what he had been instrumental in disclosing. The prisoners were sent to the king and the Council for examination. The two chief prisoners were Agnes Sampson of Haddington and Dr. Fian, a schoolmaster, of Lothian. The usual process of shaving, torture, and examination for the Devil's mark having been gone through, Agnes Sampson spoke of a gathering of two hundred witches on All Hallow E'en, who went by sea in sieves, drinking wine as they floated, to the church of North Berwick, where they sang and danced. The King's Majesty, with that lively curiosity which distinguished him, sent for Gilly Duncan, who had played the dance, and caused her to play it again in his presence—upon a small trump, called a Jew's trump. The song of the dance was

> Cummer, go ye before; Cummer, go ye;
> If ye will not go before, cummer, let me.

Within the church the Devil appeared in the likeness of a man, and after obscene genuflections, delivered an oration against the king.

James, however, having listened to the various confessions, said in some impatience that 'they were all extreme liars'. Confronted with this unbelief on the king's part, Agnes Sampson, instead of taking advantage of it, did a remarkable thing. She was 'matron-like, grave, and settled in her answers'. She said that 'she would not wish his Majesty to suppose her words to be false, but rather to believe them. . . . And thereupon taking his Majesty a little aside, she declared unto him the very words which passed between the King's Majesty and his Queen at Oslo in Norway, the first night of their marriage, with their answer each to other: whereat the King's Majesty wondered greatly, and swore by the living God that he believed that all the Devils in hell could not have discovered the same: acknowledging her words to be most true, and therefore gave the more credit to the rest'.

'The rest' was the manner in which the death of the king had been planned. One method was to have been to spread the venom of a toad (hung for three days) on any linen which the king had worn; another was to christen a cat, and having bound to each part of the cat

'the chiefest parts of a dead man', to throw it into the
sea in order to destroy the king's ship as it sailed from
Denmark. All this the Devil vehemently encouraged
them to do. For when an image was made of the king it
was delivered to the Devil, who said certain words over
it and returned it; it was passed from hand to hand, and
they all said, one to the other: 'This is King James the
Sixth, ordained to be consumed at the instance of a noble
man, Francis, Earl Bothwell.' It is commonly now held
that the black man was Francis, Earl Bothwell, himself.
But if that were so, then he must himself have believed
very strongly in magical murder, for beyond that there
was nothing he could achieve by means of those covens,
the seven score who danced after the schoolmaster John
Fian round the church of North Berwick. They could
not help him to seize or slay the person of the king; they
could not plan court conspiracies or correspond with
powers beyond the frontiers. The only power they could
bring to bear was the occult power of Goetia. If the
'Devil' were Bothwell, he must have believed in the
Devil as firmly as them all; if it were not . . . it was whom
you please. The image seems to have disappeared, much
to the disappointment of some of the sorcerers: 'four
honest-like women were very earnest and instant to have
it.' And the plot failed; the royal fleet reached Scotland;
the venom did not work. And presently Gilly Duncan
was arrested and questioned by her master.

One odd incident marked the trial. John Fian had been
tortured and had confessed; he was thrown into solitary
prison for the night. The next day he was full of a tale
that the Devil had appeared to him to tempt him—

clothed in black, carrying a white wand. Fian renounced: 'I have listened too much unto thee.' The Devil answered: 'Once ere thou die thou shalt be mine,' snapped his white stick, and vanished. All that day Fian was left in solitude to recover from the torment, and called much on God with great penitence and prayers. The darkness of the night came down on his cell, and in the morning when the guard came to him—in the morning of the Holy Innocents—he was gone. James heard the news, and ordered 'a hot and hard pursuit', by which, in due course, the fugitive was discovered and brought in. But he had changed. In the king's presence he was examined touching his escape; he would say nothing. He was re-examined concerning points in his earlier signed confession; he utterly denied and renounced it. 'Everything he had said was false, and now he would say nothing.' The King, sitting there with the lords of the Council about him, looked on the wretch and thought he knew what had happened; in that supernatural absence he had met again the supernatural Prince of the abyss and made new covenants. The supernatural evil that James feared and defied lifted itself in that moment in his own soul; vividly it lived in the chamber, no more about John Fian, broken schoolmaster, but in the hearts and faces of his judges, achieving its end (as the habit of supernatural things, good or evil, is) by the apparent rejection of itself. The king called for more torments. In that presence they brought them, they pierced and twisted and rent him, 'and notwithstanding all these grievous pains and cruel torments, he would not confess anything'.

It is not perhaps surprising that King James, who had

been the very object of all this malicious art, found himself inclined to believe that there was such an art in active practice; more especially as soon another magician was found who had made another image of the king 'in magical ceremonies between the body of a fox and the head of a young calf'. The king tried to seize Bothwell. Six years afterwards, in 1597, he wrote *Demonologie*, a dialogue upon witchcraft. It is not particularly original, but then it would have been very difficult indeed for anyone, at this date, to be original on witchcraft. It has the directness, the sincerity, the colloquialism, of most of James Stuart's writing. Apparently it was provoked by two sceptical—or at least doubting—books which had appeared; the one was by an Englishman, Reginald Scot, author, in 1594, of *The Discoverie of Witchcraft*; the other was by Johannes Wierus, or John Weyer, author of *De Prestigiis* and *De Lamiis*.

The king analysed the whole Goetic kingdom in the approved manner; he distinguished between great necromancers and ordinary witches; he even admitted that 'many honest and merry men and women have publicly practised [charms], that I think if ye would accuse them all of witchcraft ye would affirm more nor ye will be believed in'. He came back to the old business of the pact. Necromancers begin by commanding devils but sooner or later 'they begin to be weary of the raising of their Master by conjured circles, being both so difficile and perilous, and so cometh plainly to a contract with him, wherein is specially contained forms and effects'. This is much like the declension which has been remarked before, in the matter of the Duchess of Gloucester. To command the Devil is one thing; to continue to command the Devil is quite another. 'The ninth step is nine times as difficult as the first', and the patience of that strange control did not belong to 'circles and conjurations'. It was the Devil himself, King James said, who made them glory in 'the empiring over him'. That remark was truer than King James altogether thought. All over Europe the Devil was engaged in causing men to glory in the empiring over him.

To be fair, however, to King James, he was not anxious to take part in that diabolical empiring. He had investigated the witches of North Berwick; there was in his nature a streak of that dallying with cruelty. He had written his book on demonology; he was always acutely interested in the ways of the supernatural. But it had been Agnes Sampson, that matron-like woman, who had (if the record is true) almost forced him into belief. He had said at first, impatiently incredulous (perhaps of the sieves on the sea), that 'they were all extreme liars', and though he was theoretically opposed to the scepticism of Weyer and Scot, he was practically opposed to the credulity of the crowd. It may have been partly conceit; he liked finding things out—even more, he liked being known to have found things out. But even in that case his conceit overrode his credulity. When he came into England there was talk enough of witches. He himself talked to Sir John Harington, who despised him with insufficient cause, of witches and second sight and divination, but as a man curious rather than a man fearful. He wrote to his son Prince Henry warning him 'how wary judges should be in trusting accusations without an exact trial'. He assented indeed—he does not seem to have done more—to the new Act. But he allowed popular (and unpopular) reputed magicians to work in London—such as Simon Forman; he did not interfere with Dee; he sent pardons in all doubtful cases; he set himself to discover impostors. The cases in which he is known to have been concerned were all of that kind.

There were at least three—and probably several more —of these; the most famous is the case of a boy at Leicester. He had fits; he was reported bewitched; nine persons were found guilty of his sufferings and hanged; another six were in prison when the King's Majesty reached the town. He heard of the prosecution, sent for the boy, and questioned him. The boy made a slip; the king ordered him to be sent to Lambeth, to the Archbishop, where he was examined again at more leisure. Before the king had finished the progress, the boy had been sent back to him, with the fraud confessed. The king forgave him, but he showed his displeasure to those concerned with the executions. In the last nine years of his reign there were five executed for witchcraft. Given the ideas of the time, one could hardly wish for a more intelligent view than the king's.

The difference between the king's intellectual acceptance of the idea together with his continual hesitation in practice, and a really full-blooded belief, can be seen if he is contrasted with Sir Edward Coke, Lord Chief Justice of England at the time of the Somerset trial. The Countess of Somerset had previously been married to the Earl of Essex; she had brought a suit for nullity of marriage, which after long discussion had been decreed. But afterwards, by the chance confession of a boy dying in Flushing, there crept gradually into light a much more horrid past. It seemed that the nullity had been not natural, but 'procured'. The countess had been active with that same Simon Forman, who professed and practised magic. She had initiated efforts to devitalize Essex and to vitalize Somerset in their relations to herself. Images had been made—'a naked woman spreading and laying forth her hair in a looking-glass', and another woman (or rather another image of the same woman) 'sumptuously apparelled in silks and satins'. She had had philtres brewed either way. But even this was not enough. There was a certain friend of Somerset's, Sir Thomas Overbury, who on some offence given to the king had been sent to the Tower. The countess conceived the belief that he was her enemy and the intention of doing away with him. She practised *maleficium*. But it seems that there Forman was not enough. There was another, a procuress, a friend of Forman's, Anne Turner. Either Forman or she, but more probably she, supplied other philtres, to undo not masculinity but life, venomous. It is the old story; there is no staying on the path to hell but by abandonment. In 1613 the countess was married to her desired Somerset (all in white, as a virginal innocent), and Sir Thomas Overbury died in agony in the Tower.

There is nothing particularly different about the case, except that it became spectacular, and except for Sir Edward Coke's capacity for belief. 'My lord Coke', said Francis Bacon, 'hath filled this part with many frivolous things.' The Chief Justice was concerned rather with the poison than the witchcraft. He seized on a confession by one of the hired go-betweens to develop the fancy of a venomous philtre which, like a delayed time-bomb, might lie innocuously in the body for months before it acted. He expanded the suspicion of poisoning from the death of Overbury to the death of the king's son, 'that sweet babe, Prince Henry', who had died in 1612. He stretched it further: 'if this plot had not been found out, neither Court, City, nor many particular houses had escaped the malice of that wicked crew'. Had the king had the same kind of mind, then or ever, England would have been continuously full of gallows all his reign. Fortunately for many lives, he had not. 'They are all extreme liars' was a phrase natural to him and very unnatural to Coke, who much preferred 'they' should not be. 'Our deliverance', he cried out in full court, 'was as great as any that happened to the children of Israel.' The king and Francis Bacon took the management of the trial away from him. The countess—and Somerset himself (probably unjustly)—were tried, found guilty, imprisoned, pardoned, and left to die in obscurity.

Christ had long since warned his Church against an over-attention to miracles; Sir Edward Coke, among the law-books of England, had forgotten his New Testament. At the same time the malice had existed; the images, the consultations, the love-philtres had existed; and beside the figure of the ceremonial sorcerer Forman there had existed the other figure of Mrs. Turner, who had introduced starch into England. Like Margery Jourdemayne centuries before, like La Voisin in Paris in the same century, something more adequate than divination lurks in the circle of the diviners. The only difference between those workers of *maleficium* and such others in later times as Crippen and Armstrong is that the earlier poisoners may have thought they were in pact with diabolic spirits, or at least in operation with them. The later, almost certainly, did not. But if there are indeed spirits fallen from good, and if sin consists in the decision of the will, there is not so very much difference between the formal and the informal Pact. Except (which is enough) in the panic-fear the thought of the Pact and the ensuing power is likely to arouse in those around.

Another famous case which seems to have created something of the same panic, but this time in another locality, was that of the Lancashire witches. The trial of the Countess of Somerset took place in 1616. Four years before there had lived in a barren district of Lancashire two poor old women, between whom and their families a general feud existed. One of them, Elizabeth Demdike, was the oldest witch of the district; from her the others derived or swore they did, even including her rival Anne Chattox. Anne at her own trial swore that she had been induced by the Demdike to make a profession of witch-craft, after which the Devil one night appeared to them both in the likeness of a man, to meet whom they went out of the house, and there in the open air concluded the rustic equivalent of the solemn Pact of other places. There were also connected with old Demdike her daughter Elizabeth and her husband John Device, and their children James, Alizon, and Jennet, the last being about nine years old. Anne Chattox had her own daughter Anne, also accused of witchcraft, married to Thomas Redferne. There was, however, conflict between the

families, and John Device was said to have been bewitched to death by Anne Chattox for not paying his
yearly dole. There seems to have been a kind of reign of
terror maintained over the district, and other neighbours
had been bewitched or were fearful of bewitching.

The authorities at last took action and the old women
were arrested, with their daughters, and committed to
Lancaster Jail for trial. A kind of demonstration was
made, directly after this, by the witches (male and
female) of the neighbourhood. A number of them met
at Malking Tower, Demdike's house, on Good Friday,
1612. The conspiracy there was said to have intended to
do three things: (i) to name Alizon Device's familiar,
which they could not do, she being in prison; (ii) to free
the prisoners by killing the jailer at Lancaster and blow-
ing up the castle where the prison was; and (iii) at the
request of one of their number to lend her their power
for the destruction of another enemy of her own. The
whole affair caused some stir; further arrests were made,
and new evidence procured.

The chief of the fresh witnesses was little Jennet
Device. Unlike some other children in other trials, she did
not claim to have been personally bewitched.[1] But she
said she had seen everything that had been going on. She
was first introduced into the court in order to give evidence against her mother Elizabeth Device. The woman
broke into screams and shrieks, cursing and crying out

[1] Perhaps the most dreadful example in England was the case of the
Witches of Warboys, where an old woman, Mother Samuel, was
begged by the 'afflicted children' to confess in a particular formula. She
refused for a long time; when, however, she did at last speak the words
they proposed, they recovered and she was hanged.

against the child, 'as all the court did not a little wonder at her, and so amazed the child, as with weeping tears she cried out unto my lord the judge and told him she was not able to speak in the presence of her mother'. The statement is by Thomas Potts, Esquire, Clerk to the Court. The mother was removed. The nine-year-old child was set upon a table in the middle of the court, and there proceeded to deliver her evidence. She said that she knew her mother was a witch for she had seen her spirit sundry times come unto her said mother in the likeness of a brown dog, which she called Ball; she recounted how her mother and Ball had destroyed a neighbour, John Robinson of Barley, by witchcraft, and afterwards John's brother James, and afterwards again one Humphrey Mitton, who (as James Device swore) had once refused to give the mother a penny.

This was the beginning of Jennet's evidence. But as more prisoners were brought up at different times, she provided more and more testimony. She swore to the meeting at Malking Tower; she swore to those present whom she knew, and that others were there whom she did not then know. She testified how they had to their dinners 'beef, bacon and roasted mutton' (the mutton being of a wether belonging to the bewitched Robinsons). It is an English meal, and very different from the noisome dishes of the usual Sabbath. She proceeded to give detailed evidence against her brother James; 'it was wonderful to the court, in so great a presence and audience, with what modesty, government, and understanding, she delivered this evidence against the Prisoner at the bar, being her own natural brother, which he himself could not deny, but there acknowledged in every particular to be just and true'.

The examinations continued to involve others; most remarkably a woman of a quite different social class called Alice Nutter. She belonged to a yeoman's family, and both Jennet Device and James Device swore she had been at the great meeting at Malking Tower, and had taken an active part in the bewitching of Humphrey Mitton. If there were any more evidence to suggest that she had been connected with the other accused women at other times than at the grand meeting, it would not be impossible to imagine that she was the leader of the coven. Certain of her family were reported to be among those done to death by sorcery. On the other hand, it is by no means impossible that advantage was taken of the trials to include her by the evidence of the nine-years-old child. The evidence succeeded in this case against all the prisoners; they were convicted and hanged.

It is of some interest to note that apparently Jennet Device, years afterwards, was herself in the same danger of death from the same cause—witness borne against her by a child; this time a boy who had seen greyhounds turn into women, and had seen a meeting of witches. He reported one adventure which still retains a kind of thrill. His father had sent him to fetch home the cows; on the way he had met with another boy in a lane, with whom he had fought till 'looking down he saw the boy had a cloven foot, at which sight he was afraid and ran away from him to seek the kine. And in the way he saw a light like a lanthorn, towards which he made haste, supposing it to be carried by some of Mr. Robinson's (his father's) people. But when he came to the place, he only found a woman standing on a bridge, whom when he saw her he knew to be Loynd's wife (by whom he had already been followed that afternoon), and knowing her, he turned back again, and immediately he met with the aforesaid boy, from whom he offered to run, which boy gave him a blow on the back which caused him to cry.'[1]

So admirable a moment might have produced conviction in the modern reader, were it not that precisely the event which has most terror about it—the evening, the boy with the cloven foot, and the waiting woman on the bridge—was told by one of those rare things, a really discredited witness. For in this case seventeen persons having been arrested, sent for trial, and found guilty by the jury, the judge, instead of sentencing them, referred the matter to take the king's pleasure. Four of those convicted were sent to London, and the boy and his father after them. The king's physicians were sent to them, and they were afterwards examined by King Charles I in person. The witnesses were kept in custody and examined separately, and the case broke down. The boy confessed that his father and others had set him on, through 'envy, revenge, and hope of gain'. The accused were pardoned and dismissed, and the Stuarts had another gem to their honour.

The Lancashire trials preserve two charms, used (according to his sister Jennet's evidence) by James Device. The matter of charms of this kind had always been a difficulty. The dilemma was that a mere prayer as such could hardly be regarded as wrong, whereas any alter-

[1] *Discovery of Witches in the County of Lancaster* (1845).

ation might make it diabolical, and an evil intention might suppress or mumble the Divine Names. Saint Thomas had brooded over the problem, and the *Malleus* had formulated it. It had laid down seven conditions by the observation of which charms might be reckoned lawful and the users of them might be called 'exorcists or lawful enchanters'. The conditions were as follows: (i) there must be nothing in the words which hints at any expressed or tacit invocation of devils—and this depends not only on the words but also on the intentions, of which 'not only physicians and astronomers but also theologians must be the judges'; (ii) they must contain no unknown names, which might conceal something undesirable; (iii) there must be nothing untrue—and here the *Malleus* fell into its only quotation of light verse, quoting as untruth

> Blessed Mary went a-walking
> Over Jordan River.
> Stephen met her, and fell a-talking;

(iv) there must be no vanities or characters except for the sign of the Cross; (v) no faith must be put in the method of writing, reading, or fastening on the charm, since that has nothing to do with reverence to God; (vi) if divine words are used they must be used only with regard to their proper meaning and to the reverence to God; (vii) all result must be submitted to the Divine Will, which only knows what is best. The *Malleus* concluded therefore that the wise thing to do was to make use of the Lord's Prayer, the Angelic Salutation, of His Birth and Passion, His Five Wounds, the Seven Words, and such other verbal invocations. But it would have been likely to condemn the charms of Lancashire as expressly as did the English justices. A Roman writer in 1651 warned his readers against using a charm (a verse from the one-hundred-and-seventh psalm) to ensure waking at the desired time; it had been found that if, before use, a protest were made that worship was meant for God, the charm did not work; it was therefore clearly diabolical.

The first charm or prayer of the Devices was to get drink. It ran: 'Crucifixus hoc signum vitam Eternam. Amen.' James Device (his sister swore) said 'that he by this prayer hath gotten drink; and that within an hour after the saying the said prayer, drink hath come into the house after a very strange manner. And the other prayer, the said James Device affirmed, would cure one bewitched, which she recited as follows:

> Upon Good Friday, I will fast while I may
> Until I hear them knell
> Our Lord's own bell,
> Lord in his mess
> With his twelve Apostles good,
> What hath he in his hand
> Lie in leath wand:
> What hath he in his other hand?
> Heaven's door key,
> Open, open Heaven door key,
> Steck, steck, hell door.
> Let Christ child
> Go to its Mother mild;

What is yonder that casts a light so farrandly?
My own dear Son that's nailed to the Tree.
He is nailed sore by the heart and hand,
And holy harne Panne,
Well is that man
That Friday spell can,
His Child to learn;
A Cross of Blue, and another of Red,
As good Lord was to the Rood
Gabriel laid him down to sleep
Upon the ground of holy weep:
Good Lord came walking by,
Sleepest thou, wakest thou Gabriel?
No Lord I am sted with stick and stake,
That I can neither sleep nor wake:
Rise up Gabriel and go with me,
The stick nor the stake shall never deere thee.
Sweet Jesus our Lord. Amen.'

The saying of the prayers in Latin by the Chelmsford witch and the ancient recollections in James Device's charm can be paralleled by other instances of the old Rites lingering. Thus, in 1665, one Mrs. Pepper, a midwife, was indicted at York for using charms. Her particular method was to declare that any sick person was bewitched, and to draw the evil spirit out of him, as she did with Robert Pyle, a pitman, who was 'in a very sad condition, looking with a distracted look, every part of his body shaking and trembling, being deprived of the use of his body and senses'. Mrs. Pepper tried several remedies; she sprinkled with holy water his face and 'a red hot spot on the back of his right hand', and she 'did take a silver crucifix out of her breast, and laid it upon the said spot. And did then say that she knew by the said spot what his disease was, and did take the said crucifix and put it in his mouth.' Either after or before, she took his child 'and another sucking child, and laid them to his mouth'.[1]

Without the *Malleus* it would be tempting to assume that this was the superstition of a Protestant country, but with the *Malleus* it is clear that such habits might as well be also the superstition of a Catholic. 'Superstition', says the *Malleus*, quoting the Gloss on the *Epistle to the Colossians*, 'is undisciplined religion, that is, religion observed with defective methods in evil circumstances.' The use of charms, the use of the sucking child, the use of the crucifix, might not unfairly be so described. They are in the tradition of the English countryside, and so are less suitable things. In Northumberland wise women used ducks and drakes to draw out the evil spirit; they were 'presented' for pretending to be 'common charmers'. What happened to them or to Mrs. Pepper we do not know. They seem harmless enough workers. But in fact there lay behind that mumbling over crucifixes and children the reliance on the dim power which had lain about the world in the days of the high Roman Empire. Mrs. Pepper was, no doubt, kind. But Mother Demdike, it seems probable, was not so kind; the terror of Malking Tower threatened as much of her world as she could reach, and high beyond her was the Countess of Somerset

---

[1] *Depositions from the Castle of York relating to offences committed in the Northern Counties in the seventeenth century* (1861).

involved in magical operations against her first husband. The crucifix laid to the mouth of Robert Pyle, pitman, was answered at a great distance by the crucifix veiled at the trial of Gilles de Rais, Marshal of France. Mrs. Pepper had said that Robert Pyle was bewitched. James Device had (he said) been bidden by his grandmother Demdike to bring away the Sacred Bread of the Eucharist and deliver it to 'such a thing as should meet him on the way'. A thing like a hare did meet him, and was very fierce with anger when it heard that James had disobeyed and had consumed the Divine Element. And beyond James Device, some half a century later in Paris, was the valid and heart-breaking consecration by an apostate priest of the elements over the naked altar-body of a woman.

There are but three methods by which both sorcery and slander of sorcery can be defeated, and the whole dangerous imagination purified and hallowed. They are devotion, the quality of disbelief, and the armed energy of the law.

Chapter Ten

THE PHILOSOPHICAL AND LITERARY MOVEMENT

In the year 1650 there were published in London, 'printed by T. W. for H. Blunden at the Castle in Cornhill', two small volumes containing five tracts. They were the work of Thomas Vaughan, the brother of Henry Vaughan the poet, and they were concerned, under a different terminology, with the same preoccupations as occupied most of the poems. Thomas wrote under the name of Eugenius Philalethes, and the tract which is here of most interest is that called *Magia Adamica; Or the Antiquity of Magic and the Descent thereof from Adam downward proved*. The word is returned, in very different surroundings, to that operation which Apuleius meant when he spoke of magic as being 'high priestess of the mysteries of heaven'. While Matthew Hopkins, the detestable witch-finder, was busy in the eastern counties of England with his search after the lowest forms of sorcery, Thomas Vaughan had become an Anglican priest and rector of a Welsh living till he was ejected by the Parliament for supporting the Royalist

Cause. He went to Oxford in 1649 and there pursued his studies 'in a manner valued to him'. That manner, or some part of it, he described in the first sentences of the *Magia Adamica*. 'That I should profess magic in this discourse and justify the professors of it withal is impiety with many but religion with me. It is a conscience that I have learned from authors greater than myself and scriptures greater than both. Magic is nothing but the wisdom of the Creator revealed and planted in the creature. It is a name—as Agrippa saith—'not distasteful to the very Gospel itself'. Magicians were the first attendants our Saviour met withal in this world, and the only philosophers who acknowledged Him in the flesh before that He Himself discovered it.'

Vaughan proceeds to assert that this high art has always been in the world, and that it was this of which wise men in all generations had been aware. 'The magicians had a maxim among themselves "that no word is efficacious in magic unless it be first animated with the Word of God".' This profound sentence, a proposal of the union of all great formulae, was misunderstood and debased by 'the common man'. Hence 'lawyers and common divines who knew not these secrets, perusing the ceremonial superstitious trash of some scribblers who pretended to magic, prescribed against the art itself as impious and anti-Christian, so that it was a capital sin to profess it, and the punishment no less than death'. In this confusion therefore the great magicians for long buried their knowledge in silence. The foolish imitated their knowledge, on a lower level, by charms, characters, circles, triangles, and fantastic vocabularies, 'but knowing not what spirit that was which the magicians did bind he (the common man) laboured and studied to bind the Devil'. And the great persecutors, also ignorant of the truth of the age-long operations, denounced and destroyed all alike. Until indeed God deigned to excite certain great spirits to rediscover the hidden treasure.

The spirits so inspired whom Vaughan here named were 'Cornelius Agrippa, Libanius Gallus, the philosopher Johannes Trithemius, Georgius Venutus, Johannes Reuchlin'—after whom he named himself as 'usher to the train'. The best known of all these was Cornelius Agrippa. Trithemius was his teacher, and Abbot of Würzburg, but the pupil's reputation, anyhow in the general world, went beyond the master's, as that of Paracelsus, also his pupil, has done. All these occult students—whatever they called themselves or were called, philosophers, alchemists, magicians—were concerned to discover a principle of operation in the universe. On the one hand, the search for that principle touched the methods of the spiritual Way and all that has been called mysticism; on the other, it was concerned with transmutation of metals and prolongation of life. Between the two lay every kind of real or debased science—astrology, anatomy, biology, medicine, metallurgy. Much of what we now know concerning those things has been helped by the incitement felt by these scholars. The central passion, however, has been—like witchcraft itself—not so much disbelieved as dismissed and not so much dismissed as despised. Yet that principle had, in its day, a great imaginative appeal. It could be more or less summed up in the old maxim: 'as above, so below'. In the days before the Fall, wrote Vaughan, 'there was a more plentiful and large communion between heaven and earth, God and the elements, than there is now in our days'. But afterwards the direct light was separated from the reflected; 'the Divine Cohabitation ceased, and the society was divided'.

The formal teaching of the Christian Church was no other. But, according to that teaching, the effectual restoration and closing of the breach was found by the practice of religious rites and duties. The occult philosophers dreamed also of another means, a means not necessarily opposed, nor even alternative, but perhaps complementary or only auxiliary, but certainly practical, could the *praxis* be discovered. The desire and the design spread widely, and while the Wars of Religion devastated Europe, the intellectuals, in their own intellectual way, sought the Union, and (according to their capacity and interest) the various corollaries of the Union.

This is not the place to discuss that particular theme; it has been done enough, and there are schools to-day engaged in more or less the same work. The very language they used needs an encyclopedia to explain it—the Salts and the Vitriols, the Sulphurs and the Stones, the Eagles and the Dragons, the Ternary and the Septenary, the Dissolutions and the Coagulations, the Males and the Females. It was a specialized, and in the end an almost meaningless, language. But it would be a mistake to suppose that the language never sprang from any living heart. They were as specialized in their speech as any modern scientist, but they were nothing like so specialized in their subjects—they, like that different man,

Francis Bacon, 'took all knowledge for their province'. Bacon was born in 1561 and died in 1626. In 1527 there had been born in England a great student of the other way, Dr. John Dee, who died in 1608, at the age of eighty-one. At the age of twenty, he said, he had begun to study 'the heavenly influences and operations actual in the elemental portion of the world', and in 1594-5, when he was almost seventy, he defined his life's activities even more closely. The definition was in a letter to Archbishop Whitgift, so little did Dee suppose his activities anti-Christian, any more than, fifty years after his death, the Anglican rector Vaughan. In this letter—it was called *A Letter containing a most brief Discourse Apologetical*—he said that he had written it ' . . . not so much, to stop the mouths, and at length to stay the impudent attempts, of the rash and malicious devisers, and contrivers of most untrue, foolish, and wicked reports and fables of and concerning my foresaid studious exercises, passed over, with my great (yes incredible) pains, travels, cares, and costs, in the search and learning of true philosophy; as, therein, so to certify and satisfy the godly and unpartial Christian hearer or reader hereof; that, by his own judgement (upon his due consideration, and examination of this, no little parcel of the particulars of my foresaid studies and exercises philosophical annexed), he will, or may, be sufficiently informed and persuaded; that I have wonderfully laboured, to find, follow, use, and haunt the true, straight, and most narrow path, leading all true, devout, zealous, faithful, and constant Christian students, *ex valle hac miseriae, et miseria istius vallis: et tenebrarum Regno; et tenebris istius Regni, ad montem sanctum Syon, et ad coelestia tabernacula.* All thanks are most due, therefore, unto the Almighty; seeing it so pleased him (even from my youth, by his divine favour, grace, and help) to insinuate into my heart an insatiable zeal and desire to know his truth: and in him, and by him, incessantly to seek and listen after the same; by the true philosophical method and harmony: proceeding and ascending (as it were), gradatim, from things visible, to consider of things invisible; from things bodily, to conceive of things spiritual; from things transitory and momentary, to meditate of things permanent: by things mortal (visible and invisible) to have some perseverance of immortality, and to conclude, most briefly, by the most marvellous frame of the *whole World*, philosophically viewed, and circumspectly weighed, numbered, and measured (according to the talent and gift of God, from above allotted, for his divine purposes effecting) most faithfully to love, honour, and glorify always, the *Framer*, and *Creator* thereof.'

Dee had certainly had difficulty enough in his life, both in and because of the studies he had determined to pursue. He had concerned himself as much with the invisible world as with the visible; he had endeavoured after 'commerce with angels', and had communed with spirits in crystals. He was much given to what were untruly called 'lewd and vain practices', and in 1555, when he was only twenty-eight, he had been up before the Privy Council on a charge of killing and blinding children by magic, and of carrying out magical operations against the life of Queen Mary. He was examined and discharged on his own recognizances. Later on, under

Mary's sister Elizabeth, he became a client of the Earl of Leicester, as afterwards the equally notorious, but less reputable, Dr. John Lambe of the Duke of Buckingham. Lambe was mobbed and killed by a London crowd. Dee was not injured in person, though in 1583, while he was on the Continent, his house at Mortlake was sacked by a crowd, and his library destroyed. The stories that were about concerning him were sinister. He was said to be an arch-conjurer, invocator of devils. In 1581 a certain Edward Kelley had come to him at Mortlake, claiming to be able to commune 'with spiritual creatures'. Kelley seems to have been a very dubious character; he was then twenty-six and he put himself at Dee's disposal. There is a story relating to his past which was published in 1631 and relates how in the churchyard of Wootton-in-the-Dale he had necromantically evoked the spirit of a dead man. It was said that this was done for the purpose of discovering hidden treasure. Dr. Dee himself had trouble with him; in 1583 Kelley confessed that he had been in relation with evil spirits, which was utterly alien from Dee's wishes. But Kelley's desire was for immediate profit; it was why he was attracted to alchemy. He had some sort of hieroglyphical manuscript upon which Dee presently spent time, but without results. There was indeed little in common between the two: a great sincerity is predicable of Dee; of Kelley we may think what we will.

In 1584 the two of them, however, went together with a royal visitor, the Prince of Poland, to his castle at Cracow. They resumed both the effort to communicate with spirits and the effort to perform the alchemical work in a house there. Dee was bidden by the Angel

Uriel go to the Emperor and call on him to repent—and apparently went. According to his own account, the alchemical work was here achieved; in 1587 Dee was passionately grateful to Kelley for communicating to him 'the Great Secret'. But in spite of this they had parted in 1588 and Dee returned to England, while Kelley was first knighted and afterwards imprisoned by the Emperor, and seems to have died in attempting escape.

Dee in England was protected by his own sovereign. On the 16th December 1590 'Mr. Candish received from the Queen's Majesty warrant by word of mouth to assure me to do what I would in philosophy and alchemy, and none should check, control or molest me; and she said that she would ere long send me £50 more to make up the hundred pound', and when he came to his death he was still communing with spirits and angels, though he does not seem ever to have fallen back on the ceremonial method, which Vaughan was later to denounce, of 'conjurations and circles'. The angels misled him to the last, though perhaps with a holy misleading: he was promised health, a journey 'beyond seas', and knowledge; and all these he soon had, or so the promises may be interpreted in his death.

In the historical sense of the word neither Dee's concern with spiritual creatures nor Vaughan's with alchemical works, nor that of any of their contemporaries, corresponded to Magic, of whatever kind. Yet both, and perhaps all, might have claimed that this was what lay behind the old kind, and was the only valuable thing in it, as Vaughan clearly did. They would have assented, in faith and hope, if not in knowledge and experience, to

Pico della Mirandola's saying that 'No science gives greater proof of the divinity of Christ than magic and the Kabbala'. This is no place to search into that tradition of Jewish theosophy. Magical dreams and decorations had accumulated there, as everywhere. One example may perhaps be given from the *Zohar*, because it refers to one of the better-known tales of the Bible— the story of Balak and Balaam—and shows how these had been enlarged in the meditations of centuries.

Balak was not only a king; he was also a sorcerer, while Balaam was the greatest of diviners. Balak was called 'the son of the Bird', because he had mastered all the twenty-eight degrees of enchantment by birds. He became afraid of Israel because of what was told him by an image called 'the Image of the Bird', made of gold and silver and polished brass, and having its mouth furnished with the tongue of an actual bird. It was set in a window facing the sun or moon, and after incantations had been performed before it for seven days the tongue began to quiver; then, being pricked by a needle, it spoke strange things. Balak sent for Balaam to divine the hour and method of attack on Israel. Balaam had learnt his magic from two of the fallen Watchers. He was supreme among the Lower Crowns as Moses among the Upper Crowns; it was he who afterwards gave the book of Asmodai to King Solomon. He practised sorcery in the night at the head of his company, and by these he gained access to 'the Supreme Chieftain of the side of the Left'. It is from the Left that those things come which are meant by the saying—'At night many dogs are loosened from their chains and go wandering about the world, and many chieftains guide them'. It was these also for whom Balaam used to prepare a table with food and drink, 'as is the custom of those who practise magic, in order to bring together the evil spirits'. On this occasion however, he was defeated by 'the Tent of Assembly', which is a reference to the children of the mystical Israel in a withdrawn state. He tried to make divinations of the proper hour and could not, 'for there was no great wrath in the world'. 'When burning wrath is rife the Left is aroused, and the wicked Balaam knew how to take hold of the left side so as to curse; but on this occasion he looked and saw that the wrath was not there.' The holy unity of the Tent of Assembly in the heavens and the earth prevented it. After he was slain his bones became serpents; anyone who can find those serpents can learn enchantment. But it is to be remembered, concerning that Way of Perversity, that 'such is the way of that side that he who follows it is killed by it, and it is with his soul when it departs from him'. This is the fate of Goetia.

This is not entirely a lesser fancy of magic; it has a great moral. So (to return to the Christian students) it is suggested, here and there in the works they produced— suggested rather by the phrases they use than by any certain statements—that the old search into the relation of body and spirit was what partly preoccupied them. The mingling of fancies which had produced the obscene horrors of incubi and succubi is here for a moment reversed and becomes vivid in a nobler manner. Vaughan himself was preoccupied—at least occasionally—with the thought of the body of the Resurrection, 'the body of adeptship', the body of energy and light, and yet a real body, as real as and related to that which is all we know at present. All, that is, but for the accounts of something other, the prophecies of something other, and the vision of something other. The tale of Moses coming from Sinai, of Moses and Elijah on Tabor; the continual Christian doctrine of the heightening and englorying of the present flesh; the illumination of that flesh seen in certain states of love—these are the justification of the dream and even (could Vaughan's tracts be understood, and could the operation be so consummated) of the experiment. The divine Milton had said something very much like it in *Comus*, but to him then in his youth the process was one of high chastity.

> So dear to heaven is saintly chastity,
> That when a soul is found sincerely so,
> A thousand liveried angels lackey her,
> Driving far off each thing of sin and guilt,
> And in clear dream and solemn vision
> Tell her of things that no gross ear can hear;
> Till oft converse with heavenly habitants
> Begins to cast a beam on th' outward shape,
> The unpolluted temple of the mind,
> And turns it by degrees to the soul's essence,
> Till all be made immortal.

It is at least arguable that Vaughan thought he was talking about that in all his complicated terminology, though not, of course, only about that. The movement of the sex energy, the very flow of the semen itself, was to be turned, purified, divinitized, in Christ. Through the spirit and the soul, the Divine Grace was to descend upon that Matter. It was certainly a speculative and no practical imagination, but it was not Manichean; it did not despise the body or the operations of the body. It rooted the Cross in the place of generation, and it proposed to itself the discovery of a method by which, through the Divine Salvation, the glory of the Resurrection should be known in the flesh. Chastity (whether virginal or marital) was a necessity; so was belief; so was devotion; so was charity.

The high transmutations had their lower correspondences, and to these alchemy belonged. The more universal souls, like the notorious Cornelius Agrippa himself, aimed at all knowledge; leaning sometimes to believe that there was one general principle, one equation, one epigram, as it were, which would resolve all; in such power as in ancient times had been attributed to the pronunciation of the Tetragrammaton. They moved through Europe seeking hints of it, founding companies or gathering scholars to help in the search, or perhaps remaining still and pensive in their cells or chambers, like Vaughan in his Rectory, 'in the obscurity necessary to adepts'. Whether they moved or stayed, they came under deep suspicion. Agrippa was the centre of tales, like his contemporary Paracelsus; he was said to have been accompanied by the Devil in the shape of a black dog and to have possessed a great book of magical spells. He did indeed produce three books *De Arte Occulta*, and a forged fourth book was afterwards added to them dealing explicitly with the more ordinary Magic, because the ascription was credible. It was he whose disciple once called up a devil and was killed by that devil. And it was

he who was brought by Marlowe into his *Dr. Faustus* as
a high master of that magic with which Faustus was concerned. It is worth quoting some lines not only for the
poetry, but because the poetry is the shape of that
intellectual-sensual exaltation which must have lain behind many of the minds of that time. Cornelius Agrippa
and Valdes come to Faustus.

> *Faustus.* Come, German Valdes and Cornelius,
> And make me blest with your sage conference.
> Valdes, sweet Valdes, and Cornelius,
> Know that your words have won me at the last
> To practise magic and concealed arts:
> Yet not your words only, but mine own fantasy,
> That will receive no object; for my head
> But ruminates on necromantic skill.
> Philosophy is odious and obscure,
> Both law and physic are for petty wits,
> Divinity is basest of the three,
> Unpleasant, harsh, contemptible, and vile:
> 'Tis magic, magic, that hath ravish'd me.
> Then, gentle friends, aid me in this attempt;
> And I, that have with concise syllogisms
> Gravell'd the pastors of the German church,
> And made the flowering pride of Wertenberg
> Swarm to my problems, as the infernal spirits
> On sweet Musæus when he came to hell,
> Will be as cunning as Agrippa was
> Whose shadow made all Europe honour him.
> *Valdes.* Faustus,
> These books, thy wit, and our experience

Shall make all nations to canonize us.
As Indian Moors obey their Spanish lords,
So shall the spirits of every element
Be always serviceable to us three;
Like lions shall they guard us when we please;
Like Almain rutters with their horsemen's staves,
Or Lapland giants, trotting by our sides;
Sometimes like women, or unwedded maids,
Shadowing more beauty in their airy brows
Than have the white breasts of the queen of love:
From Venice shall they drag huge argosies,
And from America the golden fleece
That yearly stuffs old Philip's treasury;
If learned Faustus will be resolute.

    Faustus. Valdes, as resolute am I in this
As thou to live: therefore object it not.

    Cornelius. The miracles that magic will perform
Will make thee vow to study nothing else.
He that is grounded in astrology,
Enrich'd with tongues, well seen in minerals,
Hath all the principles magic doth require:
Then doubt not, Faustus, but to be renown'd,
And more frequented for this mystery
Than heretofore the Delphian oracle.
The spirits tell me they can dry the sea,
And fetch the treasure of all foreign wrecks,
Ay, all the wealth that our forefathers hid
Within the massy entrails of the earth:
Then tell me, Faustus, what shall we three want?

    Faustus. Nothing, Cornelius. O, this cheers my
       soul!

Come, show me some demonstrations magical,
That I may conjure in some lusty grove,
And have these joys in full possession.

It is about this time that the historical Faust makes
his first appearance.[1] In a letter to a professor of Heidelberg, the Abbot of Würzburg, Johannes Trithemius,
writes indignantly of a certain George Sabellicus, who
(he says) has arrogated to himself unbecoming titles such
as 'Faustus junior, fons necromanticorum, astrologus,
magus secundus, chiromanticus, agromanticus, pyro-
manticus, in hydra arte secundus': that is, 'the younger
Faust (but why younger we do not know), the fountain
of all necromancy, astrologer, the second magus, diviner
by palms, diviner by earth, diviner by fire, second in the
art of divination by water'. Once the Abbot had almost
met him at an inn, and had heard of him from other
sources. He was reported to have said that Christ's
miracles were nothing so amazing, and that he could do as
much himself whenever he chose; he also claimed to be
a master of alchemy. The Abbot went on to report that
Faust had been a schoolmaster at Kreuznach, through
the influence of Franz Von Sickengen, but had fled after
accusations of misbehaviour with the boys. It seems that
Professor Virdung was expecting him at Heidelberg, and
it seems also that he came there and matriculated with
some increase of reputation, for he is presently known as
'the demigod of Heidelberg'. But then he is found on his
travels again; boasting at inns, casting horoscopes for the

[1] The references are taken from *Sources of the Faust Tradition*, by
P. M. Palmer and R. P. More.

Bishop of Bamberg, claiming himself to be born under the conjunction of the Sun and Jupiter (favourable for grand workers such as prophets and magicians), refused entry to Nuremberg as a 'sodomite and necromancer', and ordered away from Ingolstadt by the City Council. In 1535 he joined the army of the Empire that was besieging the Anabaptist stronghold of Münster and prophesied its capture that night; another letter shows that a few years afterwards he was also foretelling the bad fortune of an expedition to Venezuela; 'the philosopher Faust', wrote one of the sufferers, 'hit the nail on the head'.

This is the total record of the living Faust; after 1540 he disappears. But his reputation as a diviner and necromancer was high enough to cause legends to collect round his name. Luther had heard of him and been scornful; he had heard that he called the Devil his brother-in-law. 'He would have destroyed me if I had given him my hand', said Luther, 'but I would not have been afraid of him; God protecting me, I should have given him my hand in the name of the Lord'. He was reported to have possessed two familiars, a horse and a dog, to have destroyed another magician at Venice, to have caused an inhospitable monastery to be haunted by an evil spirit, to have made plugs in a table from which he produced four kinds of wine, and so on. What afterwards gave rise to one of the most thrilling scenes of English drama—the calling up of Helen—derives first from a tale that he was once lecturing at Erfurt on Homer, where he was so detailed in his description of the heroes that his hearers asked him by his art to cause them to appear. 'When the hour had come and more students than ever had appeared before him, he said in the midst of his lecture that they should now get to see the ancient Greek heroes. And immediately he called in one after the other, and as soon as one had gone another came in to them, looked at them and shook his head as though he were still in action on the field before Troy. The last of them all was the giant Polyphemus, who had only a single terrible big eye in the middle of his forehead. He wore a fiery red beard and was devouring a fellow, one of whose legs was dangling out of his mouth. The sight of him scared them so that their hair stood on end, and when Dr. Faust motioned him to go out, he acted as though he did not understand but wanted to grasp a couple of them too with his teeth. And he hammered on the floor with his great iron spear so that the whole Collegium shook, and then he went away.'[1]

Stories of efforts to convert Faust and of his miserable death were also frequent—he was choked to death in a village of Würtemberg by the Devil, as was becoming to a student of the black art. By 1587 the first book on Faust had appeared, and the wandering boasting astrologer had become a fixed star of legend. There was a free English rendering of this, 'translated by P. F., Gent.', of which the earliest extant edition appeared in 1592; it served as the basis for Marlowe. It is in this that there appears that superb description of the kingdoms of hell which was afterwards used by Sheridan Le Fanu in *The House by the Churchyard*, and it is not out of accord with

[1] From a chronicle of Erfurt of the seventeenth century, based on one of the middle of the sixteenth.

the rest of the book, which has in it here and there a touch of greatness. Mephistopheles, speaking to Faustus, describes how God made light: 'and the light was on God's right hand and God praised the light. . . . God stood in the middle, the darkness was on his left hand, in the which my lord was bound in chains until the day of judgement: in this confused hell is nought to find but a filthy, sulphurish, fiery, stinking mist or fog. Further we devils know not what substance it is of, but a confused thing. For as a bubble of water flieth before the wind, so doth hell before the breath of God. . . . Know that hell is as thou wouldst think with thy self another world, in the which we have our being, under the earth, and above the earth, even to the heavens; within the circumference thereof are contained ten kingdoms, namely: (1) Lacus mortis; (2) Stagnum ignis; (3) Terra tenebrosa; (4) Tartarus; (5) Terra oblivionis; (6) Gehenna; (7) Herebus; (8) Barathrum; (9) Styx; (10) Acheron. The which kingdoms are governed by five kings, that is, Lucifer in the Orient, Beelzebub in Septentrio, Belial in Meridie, Astaroth in Occidente, and Phlegeton in the middest of them all; whose rule and dominions have none end until the day of Doom.'

The invention of printing enabled the publication not only of such tales but also of another kind of work—the rituals and incantations of control and command over spirits. These of course were supposed to be of the higher kind; there was no black man, no Sabbath. On the other hand there was a great deal of information on the hierarchies of hell and the various vocations of the princely demons. Most of these efforts, whether they were intended seriously or whether they were the work of leisured ingenuity, safeguarded themselves by pretending to be composed on the side of devotion and White Magic. But the purpose bewrayed them; they were mostly aimed at immediate profit—to discover treasure, to ensure protection, to achieve love. The confusion of this double effort is contained in a particular evocation: 'I conjure you, ministers of love and incontinence, by Him who hath condemned you to hell.' So, for the purpose of causing invisibility, a ring is to be fashioned on which is to be inscribed: 'Jesus, passing through the midst of them, disappeared.'

A number of these books were, after the not unusual custom, ascribed to writers or other great men of the past: thus one was declared to be the *Enchiridion of Pope Leo III*; others were ascribed originally to King Solomon; and yet another was said to be derived from Pope Honorius III. The *Enchiridion* was supposed to consist of a collection of prayers which the Pope gave to Charlemagne when he left Rome. It is, of course, not only possible but likely that the Pope did give Charlemagne such a volume of prayers. But it is extraordinarily unlikely that there were mixed up with them devotional charms and magical secrets: 'a kind of royal road to the chief ends of Magic, without apparently exceeding the devotional discipline of the Church'.[1]

But if the *Enchiridion* allows itself some latitude in this respect, the *Constitution of Pope Honorius* entirely boxes the compass. It is supposed to have been published in

[1] *Book of Ceremonial Magic*, A. E. Waite: from which the quotations are taken.

1629, Honorius III having occupied the Apostolic Chair from 1216 to 1227. He was a great preacher and director of the affairs of the Church. But this concern of his the *Constitution* enlarges as follows, in what is supposed to be a papal communication to all clerics.

'The Holy Apostolic Chair, unto which the keys of the Kingdom of Heaven were given by those words that Christ Jesus addressed to Saint Peter: I give unto thee the Keys of the Kingdom of Heaven, and unto thee alone the power of commanding the Prince of Darkness and his angels, who, as slaves of their Master, do owe him honour, glory and obedience, by those other words of Christ Jesus: Thou shalt worship the Lord thy God, and Him only shalt thou serve—hence by the power of these Keys the Head of the Church has been made the Lord of Hell. But seeing that until this present the Sovereign Pontiffs have alone possessed the power of using invocations and commanding Spirits, His Holiness Honorius the Third, being moved by his pastoral care, has benignly desired to communicate the methods and faculty of invoking and controlling Spirits to his venerable Brethren in Jesus Christ, adding the Conjurations which must be used in such cases, the whole being contained in the Bull which here follows.

HONORIUS

'Servant of the Servants of God, unto all and each of our venerable Brethren of the Holy Roman Church, Cardinals, Archbishops, Bishops, Abbots; unto all and each of our sons in Jesus Christ, Priests, Deacons, Subdeacons, Acolytes, Exorcists, Cantors, Pastors, Clerks both Secular and Regular, Health and Apostolic Benediction. In those days when the Son of God, Saviour of the World, generated in the fulness of time, and born according to the flesh, of the Race of David, did live on this earth, Whose Most Holy Name is Jesus, before which the heavens, earth and hell do bend the knee; we have seen with what power He commanded demons, which power was also transmitted to Saint Peter by that utterance: Upon this rock I will build my Church, and the Gates of Hell shall not prevail against it. These words were addressed to Saint Peter as the Head and Foundation of the Church. We then, who, by the mercy of God, and despite the poverty of our merit, have succeeded to the Sovereign Apostolate, and, as lawful successor of Saint Peter, have the Keys of the Kingdom of Heaven committed to our hands, desiring to communicate the power of invoking and commanding Spirits, which hath been reserved unto us alone, and our predecessors did alone enjoy; wishing, we repeat, by Divine inspiration, to share it with our venerable Brethren and dear sons in Jesus Christ, and fearing lest in the exorcism of the possessed, they might otherwise be appalled at the frightful figures of those rebellious angels who in sin were cast into the abyss, lest also they should be insufficiently learned in those things which must be performed and observed, and that those who have been redeemed by the blood of Jesus Christ may not be tormented by any witchcraft or possessed by the demon, we have included in this Bull the manner of their invocation, which same must be observed inviolably. And because it is meet that the ministers of the Altar should have authority over the rebellious Spirits, we hereby depute unto them all powers which we possess, in virtue of the Holy Apostolic Chair, and we require them, by our Apostolic authority, to observe what follows inviolably, lest by some negligence unworthy of their character they should draw down on themselves the wrath of the Most High.'

The information which the pseudo-Pope proceeded to convey to the Cardinals, Archbishops, etc., down to Exorcists, Cantors, and Clerks both Secular and Regular involves the most curious and dreadful combination of the Sacrifice of the Mass with sacrifices of animals, with recitation of sacred Names and markings of occult signs; it consists of the highest possible operations aimed at the lowest possible ends. The operator should be a priest; before the commencement of the work he should confess, fast, and say a Mass of the Holy Ghost. This is on a Monday. He must proceed then to kill a black cock,[1] tearing out the eyes, tongue, and heart (reducing them to a powder), and a feather from the left wing. This feather he lays on the altar, with a new pen-knife, on the Tuesday, while he says a Mass of the Angels. He is to write on a clean sheet of paper, with the Consecrated Wine, certain signs, and to wrap it in a veil of violet silk with a fragment of the Consecrated Host. On the Thursday evening he says the Office of the Dead, with special prayers for protection when he invokes the demons; he then sacrifices a male lamb of nine days, preserving the skin 'in the middle of a field' for another nine days and sprinkling it

[1] *The Book of True Black Magic*, another of these volumes, substitutes a male goose.

with the powder obtained from the cock, when after additional ceremonies he buries it secretly. On the last day of the month he says a Mass for the Dead, including a recitation of the seventy-two Sacred Names of God, as follows:

'In Honour of the Most Holy and August Trinity, the Father, the Son, and the Holy Ghost. Amen. Trinitas, Sother, Messias, Emmanuel, Sabahot, Adonay, Athanatos, Jesu, Pentagna, Agragon, Ischiros, Eleyson, Otheos, Tetragrammaton, Ely, Saday, Aquila, Magnus Homo, Visio, Flos, Origo, Salvator, Alpha and Omega, Primus, Novissimus, Principium et Finis, Primogenitus, Sapientia, Virtus, Paraclitus, Veritas, Via, Mediator, Medicus, Salus, Agnus, Ovis, Vitulus, Spes, Aries, Leo, Lux, Imago, Panis, Janua, Petra, Sponsa, Pastor, Propheta, Sacerdos, Sanctus, Immortalitas, Jesus, Christus, Pater, Filius Hominis, Sanctus, Pater Omnipotens, Deus, Agios, Resurrectio, Mischiros, Charitas, Aeternas, Creator, Redemptor, Unitas, Summum Bonum, Infinitas. Amen.'

The circles having been drawn, he pronounces the conjurations, having in his possession a book in which all the names of the demons—or at least of their princes —have been written, and their powers. In some cases this book was to be presented and the evil spirits were to be compelled to seal it, each separately. The conjurations are by every detail of the Gospel—'by the Child in swaddling clothes, by the crying Child, borne by the Mother in her most pure and virginal womb'—and of the Faith—'by the Church Militant, by the Holy Trinity, by all other mysteries'. Various spirits must be invoked on various days of the week, and various offerings made; thus Lucifer is invoked on Monday, preferably between the hours of eleven and twelve or three and four, and a mouse is to be tossed to him. Other spirits preferred bread, a nut, or a hair of the magician's head. The last, on the general principles of the art, one would have thought dangerous. To dismiss the spirits the Pentacle of King Solomon must be exhibited to them.

A few other matters may be remarked. At one point in the ceremony the evil spirit is invoked not only by the Divine Names previously given, but also 'by the ineffable Names of God, Gog and Magog.' At another the Rite requires the circle to be sprinkled with holy water by means of 'the wood of the blessed Cross'. If the actual Cross itself is meant, then most of the lesser orders of the hierarchy for whom the pseudo-Pope wrote would have had some difficulty in fulfilling the Rite, and the Bull would have been nullified. But it is possible that the word is used generically, and that any cross would have served the purpose. Finally, there is included in the book a 'very powerful Conjuration', for all times and over all spirits, by which hidden treasure may be obtained—'by the power of God the Father, by the wisdom of God the Son, by the virtue of the Holy Ghost, by the authority I derive from our Saviour Jesus Christ, the only Son of the Almighty and the Creator. . . . Who ordains that you do hereby abdicate all power to guard, habit, and abide in this place'. Such was the command, and such the intention, of the Rite, and all these Rites are like it.

The energy required for them, if they were to be taken seriously—the care, patience, and even courage—

would be very great. It has been well said that one could become a saint with less expenditure of devoted skill than was required, on the showing of the books, to make one an adept of magic. The process of becoming a saint is perhaps duller; it consists so often in doing or not doing such ordinary things. Yet the process of this kind of magic would have been as dull—the learning and the writing and the watching. The great distinction between the Way and the Perverted Way was in the self-concentration of perversion. The great aim of the Ritual was to intensify the magician's power; that is, to intensify his self. It was for this that he was bidden tear the bird and sacrifice the lamb; the Sacred Mysteries were obviously recited for his own increase, and all the divine Names were a litany of his greatness.

It would be rash to say that the end was never achieved. Anyone who could bring himself, after saying a Mass of the Holy Ghost, to tear the eyes from a black cock as a part of the same operation, might, by pursuing that way, bring himself to a state where, fortified within his circle of charcoal and chanting the barbarous speech of Goetia, he might very well suppose he saw—or indeed see—the shape of some being to whom he must throw a mouse for the fulfilment of the Ritual. There certainly such beings could be seen as lords and gods, defiantly controlled by the great adept. But the Dominical saying was greater: 'I saw Satan as lightning fall from heaven', and the old tradition which decreed that it was as false and dangerous to believe such things as to do them. 'I am very much in the mind, and abundantly persuaded', wrote the minister of Salem Village in New England, in 1694, 'that God has suffered the evil angels to delude us on both hands; but how far on the one side, or the other, is much above me to say.'

The Grimoires may, indeed, have been but ingenuities —the ghost-stories, the literary fancies, of their day. The novel, as a fashionable form of activity, had hardly come into existence, and the whole arrangement of the *Constitution of Pope Honorius* disposes one to think that some leisured cleric took his intellectual recreation in this form. It can be traced through the centuries—consciously or unconsciously; the composed books about Faust or the uncomposed fables about the Borgias. The fourth and forged book of Cornelius Agrippa is of a similar kind. Agrippa had not formally dealt with magic, and so someone else would. It is to be admitted, even so, that the literature is of the lowest kind. But the direct harm it did was probably not very large. The conditions of activity were too difficult, too devious, and too dangerous. The indirect harm may have been considerable. It is possible even now to feel a slight movement of the blood in reading the Ritual for Necromancy—of the spell 'by the power of the East and the silence of the night, by the holy rites of Hecate', of the mastic and gum-aromatic, of the striking the body, of its rising and standing, and of its faint responses to the questions asked. So Edward Kelley was said to have raised the dead in Wootton-in-the-Dale, and so the stories, at least, had gone abroad in the days of Virgil and Apuleius. The dialogue of the Church is more tender, more human, and operative over all: 'Rest eternal grant unto them, O Lord.' 'And let light perpetual shine upon them.'

Chapter Eleven

THE SUSPENSION OF BELIEF

The Stuarts, while allowing the real existence of witches, had by their insistence on clear proof done as much against allowing the belief to produce its ordinary results. There was, in all Europe, one other country where similar action took place, where cool intellect considered not only the theory but the incidents, and that—a little surprisingly—was Spain. There were, certainly, writers elsewhere—scattered over Europe—but the one official body that appears to have deprecated the general belief and to have taken trouble to check, if not wholly to suppress, the clamour of accusation, was the Spanish Inquisition. The Roman Inquisition followed suit, a little later. But the Spaniards were the first and firmest.

In this general attitude the Supreme Court of the Inquisition and its representatives had no encouragement from the secular courts or from the secular world as such. The suspicion of sorcery and witchcraft was as general in Spain as anywhere, and the grand attack, with its questionings, its tortures, and its fires, looked like coming to operation there in the opening of the sixteenth century as much as in Central Europe. There were persecutions in Saragossa, in Biscay, in Catalonia. But in 1526 the Supreme Court, instead of following the *Malleus* and the Bull of Innocent VIII, began an inquiry of its own. The inquiry was made by ten inquisitors, and of these ten a majority of two only—six to four—decided that witchcraft was real and not a delusion. It determined also that witches, if they were reconciled to the Church, were not to be passed over to the secular authorities— not even if they accused themselves of murder, for such confessions might be delusions. If the secular courts chose to indict for murder on other evidence it could not be prevented. The inquisitorial court, however, must not refer publicly to such crimes, for it must not assist the secular judge; its business had been quite other. It was determined that confessions were possibly enough to justify conviction, but not to involve any other parties. It was also determined that general instruction for the common people was desirable, and so also a general reformation of the clergy. It was even proposed that very poor people under suspicion should be financially helped, so that they should not be exposed to temptation.

It seems to have been some years before the Inquisition took action on these lines, but by the middle of the century it had moved. It insisted that all witchcraft cases belonged to its own jurisdiction; it compelled all sentences to be submitted to the Supreme Court for confirmation; it limited the use of torture; and like King James it insisted, in its instructions, on the exercise of the greatest care in cases, which, it said, were almost beyond human power to decide. No-one was to be arrested on suspicion nor on the accusation of reputed or confessed accomplices; all self-accusations were to be very carefully compared with the ascertainable facts. If anyone confessed to doing injury to human beings or crops, it was to be discovered whether in fact those human beings or crops had been injured. The *Malleus*, it added, was not always to be believed; its authors were human and might be mistaken.

All this was in complete contrast to what was happening almost everywhere else. It is true that the Inquisition had its own particular enemies, the heretics, Jews, and Moriscoes, and it pursued them with perhaps a fiercer determination. Men can be cool on subjects other than their manias. But whatever the cause, in spite of all protests and shocked complaints, 'the imperturbable Suprema maintained its temperate wisdom'.[1] It struck at precisely the methods which had been, almost everywhere else, adopted. It forbade judges to ask leading questions, it forbade threats and hints of what confessions were wanted; it forbade—what the *Malleus* had encouraged—false promises; it commanded that sermons should explain how the destruction of crops was due to the weather, and not to witches; it continually imposed as sentence only the most formal abjuration; and, finally, it even trained its courts so well that before 1600 a woman who twice accused herself of having carnal relations with an incubus was discharged each time. Another accuser of herself and others only succeeded in getting herself flogged, not for witchcraft but for slander and defama-

[1] H. C. Lea, *History of the Inquisition in Spain*.

tion. Others were formally reconciled to the Church and condemned to penance, but not to any temporal punishment, though it seems that in those cases some formally heretical element had entered in.

In such conditions it seems that no fresh details of witchcraft were added to the disastrous chronicles. Where there was any question of pact the inquisitorial courts could be severe enough. But at least pact had to be admitted, and it came under the head of heresy. Even then, however, abjuration and a hundred lashes might reconcile the apostate—perhaps with some years' exile. On the other hand the Inquisition seems, in general, to have been much more severe against astrology; presumably because of the danger of heresy and denial of the Faith in the matter of free-will. Thus in 1582 the Supreme Court took strong action against the University of Salamanca, where astrology was notably taught. Even in this dangerous subject, however, it allowed 'astrology which pertained to the weather and the general events of the world, agriculture, navigation, and medicine, and also that which indicated at birth the inclinations and bodily qualities of the infant.'[1]

The event of most importance was the visitation to Navarre of the Inquisitor Alonzo Salazar de Frias in 1611. What King James of England was doing spasmodically Salazar did carefully and formally. There had been an outbreak of fear, suspicion, and action in Navarre. The secular authorities acted, and the inquisitorial authorities in this case supported them. The Supreme Court for once assented. A grand auto-da-fé was held, at which

[1] H. C. Lea, *History of the Inquisition in Spain.*

twenty-nine of the fifty-three victims were guilty of sorcery—and five of the twenty-nine were but bodies, they having died in prison. Of the twenty-four remaining, five were flogged and six burned; the rest apparently were but exhibited as part of their penance. This was in November 1610. By the next March the Supreme Court had taken alarm at even so comparatively mild a display. They published what was known as an Edict of Grace, and sent Salazar with it on a visitation of the district. He was there from May 1611 to January 1612; his report was delivered in March.

It must be considered one of the great documents of the Church—not perhaps in regard to witchcraft alone. Salazar was an inquisitor and a judge; he was sent by his brothers of the Holy Office, with complete trust reposed in him. He admitted what Father Herbert Thurston has said, that 'in the face of Holy Scripture and the teaching of the Fathers and theologians the abstract possibility of a pact with the Devil and of a diabolical interference in human affairs can hardly be denied'. But he was also intelligent and good. He had already been connected with the examinations, and had been made uneasy by the kind of evidence presented, but he had been overruled by his colleagues.

'Salazar received eighteen hundred and two applicants (under the Edict of Grace), of whom thirteen hundred and eighty-four were children of from twelve to fourteen years of age and, besides these, there were eighty-one who revoked confessions previously made.'[1] He examined, he cross-questioned, he counterchecked.

[1] H. C. Lea, *History of the Inquisition in Spain.*

He found, by one means and another, that some sixteen hundred persons had been falsely accused. At one place he found tales of a Sabbath held at the very place where his own secretaries had been harmlessly on the night named. He had women who confessed to carnal intercourse physically examined by women; they were found to be virgin. He received various ointments stated to be magical; the chemists found them frauds. He investigated the methods used to collect evidence and confessions, and recorded his horror. He hunted down the rumours and searched out the children who, here as elsewhere, were often responsible. And finally he wrote:

'Considering the above with all the Christian attention in my power, I have not found even indications from which to infer that a single act of witchcraft has really occurred, whether as to going to aquelarres,[1] being present at them, inflicting injuries, or other of the asserted facts. This enlightenment has greatly strengthened my former suspicions that the evidence of accomplices, without external proof from other parties, is insufficient to justify even arrest. Moreover, my experience leads to the conviction that, of those availing themselves of the Edict of Grace, three-quarters and more have accused themselves and their accomplices falsely. I further believe that they would freely come to the Inquisition to revoke their confessions, if they thought that they would be received kindly without punishment, for I fear that my efforts to induce this have not been properly made known, and I further fear that, in my

[1] The Spanish equivalent of the Sabbath.

absence, the commissioners whom, by your command, I have ordered to do the same, do not act with due fidelity, but, with increasing zeal are discovering every hour more witches and aquelarres, in the same way as before.

'I also feel certain that, under present conditions, there is no need of fresh edicts or the prolongation of those existing, but rather that, in the diseased state of the public mind, every agitation of the matter is harmful and increases the evil. I deduce the importance of silence and reserve from the experience that there were neither witches nor bewitched until they were talked and written about. This impressed me recently at Olague, near Pampeluna, where those who confessed stated that the matter started there after Fray Domingo de Sardo came there to preach about these things. So, when I went to Valderro, near Roncesvalles, to reconcile some who had confessed, when about to return the alcaldes begged me to go to the Valle de Ahescoa, two leagues distant, not that any witchcraft had been discovered there, but only that it might be honored equally with the other. I only sent there the Edict of Grace and, eight days after its publication, I learned that already there were boys confessing.'

The Supreme Court, having received the report, issued new instructions. It was the year 1614, and the attack on the invisible malice of the Devil was, visibly and often maliciously, increasing everywhere—except, thanks to King James, in England. The Court no more denied witchcraft than the king. But it put every possible difficulty in the way of proof. And it went as far as the

Supreme Court, which was not primarily responsible, could go in expressing regret and making reparation for the affair of Navarre. Three times only has the Holy Spirit deigned to allow such repentance in such matters to be publicly recorded and known to the future. This was the first occasion; another was when a Bishop of Würzburg instituted with the Augustinians of the city a commemoration of the victims—presumably a yearly Mass; another was in the village of Salem, New England, eighty years later. It is odd to think what the Supreme Court of the Holy Office in Spain and the Calvinist jury of New England would have said of each other, and yet how forward they both were to Christian righteousness.

The actual regulations were of the usual kind. There was never any difficulty in knowing what ought to be done; the difficulty was to get it done. All that was needed was to get the mass of people to pay attention to all the evidence, and to refrain from putting other people to very intense pain in order to make them say certain things. That the same principle might have been with advantage applied to the cases of other kinds of which the Inquisition took cognizance may be true. It was, nevertheless, applied to this kind; we may be grateful for it. The effect was marked, all over Spain. Accusations of witchcraft were simply not brought, or only a few were brought. Rumour might exist, but there was no haste to bring rumour to the attention of the cool intellectual tribunals who, under orders of the Supreme Court, would examine, criticize, and might punish, the informer. Sometimes a wretched creature would accuse herself, as has been said, and, as has been said, she was usually pitied and discharged. From 1614 onwards witchcraft practically disappears from the formal religious courts of Spain.

In other parts of Europe, though no such practical effect was achieved, there yet arose more and more controversy. The quarrel between the two schools of delusion and actuality which had been present, though subdued in the Middle Ages, produced now a great number of books. One group of these—and much the larger —was produced by theologians and judges; the other— and smaller—by those who, whether from intellectual judgement or from sheer revolt, opposed the dominating idea. The *Malleus* itself began to be regarded as out of date. Its place was taken by two other books, the *Daemonolatreia* of Nicholas Remy (1595), and the *Disquisitiones Magicae* of Martin Del Rio (1599–1601). Both these were the work of men of high culture. Remy had been privy councillor to the Duke of Lorraine and had acted as judge in the witch-trials for some fifteen years. In his later retirement he composed his book, which had the great advantage over the *Malleus* that it gave particulars for every statement made. He drew on his own experience of confessions. He had fought, he maintained, in those trials with the very powers of hell, who were continually about the arrested witch, threatening and persuading her. Thus, on one occasion, he was examining a witch who was on the point of confession when she stared and stopped. Remy asked what ailed her. She answered that in a corner of the room she saw her familiar spirit, clutching at her with great hooked pincers, like a crab's, and again in another corner butting at her with horns. Remy encouraged the accused to despise the demon, and himself courageously mocked at it—the invisible thing which at that moment the whole Court felt to be leaping, madly and fiercely, in the room, terrifying its old mistress and snarling at the officers of the Faith. He succeeded; the demon disappeared. The witch confessed and was burnt, but on her own word when she was taken to the stake she saw the spirit no more.

Such labours had convinced Remy. The chief thing that he regretted as, in his country retirement, he wrote what were, in effect, his *Memoirs*, was that he had been too tender to children. Witches were always pressed by the devils to make their children members of their own order; most did; a few refused—or said they had refused. Remy, whenever he came across a case (and there were, he said, many) in which a child under about fourteen years had been so initiated, had always been merciful; as he now, the old man looking back, repentantly thought, he had been unwise. He had been in the habit of having the child stripped naked and flogged three times round the place where its parent had been burnt. Sometimes when the child confessed to any participation it was shut up in a convent; as had happened to the seven-years-old boy Laurent of Arselai, who said he had turned a spit at the Sabbath, and had been furnished with a familiar and a powder to kill cattle. Remy felt that the tenderness had been misplaced. Scourging three times naked round the stake where one's mother had been burnt did not root out the evil: death, and only death, could do that.

The book went through a number of editions. It gave all judges exact information as to what they might expect witches to confess, and what indeed they ought to see that witches did confess. The items were all substantiated. Only the inquisitorial courts of Spain, at almost exactly the same date, were suspending similar cases right and left, and releasing suspects merely after abjuration.

Remy's book held its place until Del Rio's appeared, though his book was rather that of a theologian than of a judge. He concentrated great attention on refuting the Canon Episcopi, which was still proving something of a trouble to thinkers of his own kind. It had certainly been largely nullified by the theological discovery that, though the carrying through the air, the Sabbath, and so on, might be a delusion instilled by the Devil, yet if, after waking, the victim recollected the dream—if dream it were—with pleasure, mentally consented to it, or wished for it, he or she became at once as guilty of it as if it had been carried out in action. Thus the question became not so much *did it happen?* as *did you approve of its happening?* Act or dream, it was all the same if consent were yielded. But this distinction in identity was largely a matter of abstract thought; in the trials the act was assumed.

Other books supported the same side; they provided little new. Jean Bodin in *De Magorum Daemonomania* (1581) lamented the hesitation of the courts in France and the spread of disbelief. He too looked to the children, but for a different reason; he had found that older criminals could resist torture better, and he therefore preferred to use the inexorable engines on more delicate frames. He insisted on all children involved being executed, though he was prepared to allow strangulation before burning. He was also much more inclined than were the clerical authors to see witchcraft among the clergy; he said he had observed that nearly all witches had priests as their accomplices. Again, unlike the Spanish courts, he thought the evidence of accomplices indispensable; he referred to the *Malleus* to prove it. It was apparently the hesitation of the French courts in accepting this which caused him to feel that they were not making use of all opportunities.

Another Frenchman, Henri Boguet, also a chief judge, produced about the same time, 1590–1601, his *Discours des Sorciers*. He too wrote from experience, and at the end of the book he drew up seventy rules for judges, which were taken as a code. It is, in some ways, a more terrible book than the intellectual arguments of Del Rio or his peers. A certain man named Guillaume Vuillermoz had been accused by three convicted witches, by a girl of twelve, and by his own son who was then fourteen. He was confronted with his son, whom at first he either did not, or pretended he did not, recognize. At last he gave way and admitted that it was his son Pierre. The boy declared that his father had taken him to the Sabbath, and so on. The father cried out: 'Ah son, you will ruin us both!', and with 'execrable imprecations' denied it. At another confrontation Pierre swore that his father had urged him to give himself to the Devil, but that he had always refused. Boguet proceeds:

'It was a strange and harrowing experience to witness

these confrontations. For the father was emaciated through his imprisonment, he had fetters on his hands and feet, he wailed and shouted and threw himself to the ground. I remember too that, when he became calmer, he sometimes spoke kindly to his son, saying that whatever he did he would always own him as his child. And all the time the son never trembled in any way, but seemed as one insensible, so that it appeared that Nature had furnished him with weapons against herself, seeing that his own blood was in a way to bring to an ignominious death the man who had given him life. But assuredly I believe that in this was manifested a just and secret judgement of God, who would not allow so detestable a crime as witchcraft to remain hidden and not be brought to light. Also it is reasonable to believe that the son was not at that time pierced by the pangs of Nature, because his father had openly leagued himself against God and Nature.'[1]

The father died in prison. The boy was kept for some days in prison, and released to be instructed in the Faith. The girl who had also borne witness against Vuillermoz and others was commanded to be present at the executions, and was then banished. She was treated thus leniently because as soon as the suspects had been arrested she had immediately 'spread the report that she had been taken by them to the Sabbath' and because, as soon as she herself was arrested, she accused her accomplices. In this connection it is perhaps worth summarizing the grounds on which, according to Boguet himself, Vuillermoz was

[1] Henri Boguet, *An Examen of Witches*. Translated by Montagu Summers.

condemned. They were seven: (i) statements by other suspects; (ii) common repute of witchcraft; (iii) suspicion of his mother; (iv) incapacity to weep; (v) his volunteering to be examined for the witch's mark; (vi) his cursings; (vii) his confrontations with his son. On the other hand, it may be put to Boguet's credit that, except for very unusual cases, he disapproved of promises being made to the accused which would not be fulfilled, and even of sending apparently friendly persons into the cells of prisoners in order to extort confessions.

Such were the labours and such the divisions of the judges, as the seventeenth century proceeded. Against them there appeared a few sceptical or passionate volumes. One of the most important was by that John Weyer, who has been mentioned as helping to provoke the *Demonologie* of King James. He had been a pupil of the famous Agrippa, and it may have been from his master that he learned his scepticism. Agrippa by now was becoming almost as fabulous a figure as Faustus, though he was not taken up by the poets. His reputation, however, was not wholly evil, for his pupil became court physician to the Duke of Cleves. He was a Protestant, but that is of small importance to this particular controversy, since the division between the believers and the agnostics corresponded with no division between the Churches; the second name among the agnostics is that of a Jesuit. Weyer did not, of course, deny witchcraft; he took the more usual line of delusion, whether it existed in the minds of the self-styled witches or of their prosecutors. Also he urged that the whole subject belonged more properly to the domain of medicine than of theology—at least as far as the usual victims were concerned. He distinguished these from the great and dangerous magicians whom he believed to derive from Ham, son of Noah. He identified Ham with Zoroaster, and he believed the art to have been introduced into Europe during the invasion of Xerxes. Thence it descended through such figures as Hermes Trismegistus, Simon Magus, Apollonius of Tyana, Porphyry and the rest, Julian the Apostate, Roger Bacon, and so on. He denounced the Abbot Trithemius but defended Cornelius Agrippa, demanding that the forged Fourth Book of Occult Philosophy should be burnt, both as a slander and as a danger. He divides and defines all the modes of the art—of which now the very names are forgotten: thyromancy (divination by cheese), daphnemancy (by the burning of laurel), alectriomancy (by a cock pecking at grains of corn laid with letters in a circle), and others. All this Weyer thought might well be diabolic—the investigation of forbidden things in forbidden ways. But for the rest, it was imposture or it was delusion.

His book appeared in 1563. There were, it seems, not many to support him, though a few lawyers and theologians cried out for more care, until the year 1631 when there appeared a book by Friedrich von Spee, *Cautio Criminalis*. Spee was a Jesuit and had been confessor to the Bishop of Würzburg during the persecution there. He had left in 1629; he was himself already half-suspect, and it was reported that his hair had turned white before its time owing to the horrors he had seen, and still more to the fact that from his personal conversation with the condemned he had believed them all to be innocent. He was even reported to have been imprisoned for his protests and to have escaped.

He too wrote out of his experience—as much as Remy or Boguet. If his accounts are even partly true, the persecutions were even darker than they seemed. He declared that some judges and inquisitors made money out of the trials, and that the phrase 'without torture' might mean that the victim's legs had been pressed in an iron cage, which was not technically regarded as torture. Once, he wrote, he had no doubt that there were witches in the world; the more he studied the cases, the more he doubted. Torture had filled Germany with so-called witches. The agony of thousands cried out, and the only answer was more and repeated agony.

Spee said practically the same as Salazar: 'there were neither witches nor bewitched until they were talked and written about'. By about half-way through the century the Roman Inquisition began to take the same line. In 1623 and in 1631 the Popes Gregory XV and Urban VIII had issued fresh Bulls against the evil. The Bull of Urban was especially aimed at divination, and again especially at divination concerning the life of the Pope. In 1634 a conspiracy against Urban involving both divination and an attempt on his life by melting images was discovered, all but in the Sacred College itself. The nephew of one of the Cardinals was beheaded and his accomplices hanged or sent to the galleys. In spite of this, however, the Holy Office at Rome in the same year was ordering that sermons should be preached to the common people on the delusions of the witch-idea, and soon afterwards interfering to prevent any popular attack on reputed witches. In 1657 it issued a series of Instructions. These, like the Spanish Instructions, were aimed at the two worst features of the business, (i) the arrest on common suspicion, (ii) the indiscriminate use of torture. It defined, as the error most prevalent among judges, the haste to arrest, examine, and torture a reputed witch before the actual *maleficium* had been established. The Spanish Inquisition had proceeded along the same lines. The problem of delusion or actuality in the abstract was left undecided, or at least as it might be held to have been decided by the Bulls of the Holy See. But the problem of the actuality of a crime was quite another matter. It was the growing demand for exact proof which was to affect the whole legal system of Europe, but it must be admitted that, on matters of witchcraft, the directors of the Inquisition were the leaders of that demand.

At a time, however, when the ecclesiastical courts began to fall into this habit, and the whole persecution, if it could not be said to be flagging, was at least not increasing—when the exhausted spirit of Europe was turning altogether from religion and finding in this world a relief from the wars which were all that the thought of the other seemed to involve—at that moment there was exhibited in France one of the most appalling spectacles of the whole history. It was the thing in action that was seen, and is seen even more clearly by us than by its contemporaries—the thing free from fabulous trappings and pious myths—the thing cruelly evil and malevolent, and by its nature obviously instructed by a tradition. Whatever then in Paris appeared above ground was certainly a continuation of something that had been happening underground; it was the justification of the avenging horrors, or would have been if anything could be: disgusting, vulgar, obscene.

In the year 1679 a number of arrests were made in Paris, on suspicion of murder by poison. It was soon after the notorious Mme de Brinvilliers case, and the king's administration were particularly attentive to such things. They had in fact laid a trap for the woman first accused, and it was in the process of the criminal investigation that the greater offence came to light. In March 1679 the police arrested among those others a woman named Catherine Deshayes. She was the wife of a small jeweller, Antoine Monvoisin, whose shop had failed and who had been forced to become a pedlar of his wares. She was a small, stout, pretty woman, commonly called La Voisin, and under this name, after her husband's failure, she had made her house a centre of Paris and especially of the high society of Paris. She professed, openly, physiognomy and palmistry, clairvoyancy and occult science; she helped beauty and soothed the mind. It was all a common affair. But, as with the diviners of old, she had soon consented to encourage the future to hurry: love-charms and death-charms were her trade. She made great profit, and (having supported her old mother out of her takings) dressed up to her profit and her reputation; her robe and cloak cost 15,000 livres. In these she made known the mysteries, and everyone consulted her. She had her lovers—nobles and artists, the executioner of Paris, and magical workers like herself. Her arrest startled society.

The examination of the prisoners led to more arrests. A man named Lesage, a priest named Mariette, another priest named Guibourg, the sacristan of a Paris church, were seized; La Voisin's friends and her daughter Margaret. The investigation was conducted by a court specially instituted by the king, Louis XIV. It was called *La Chambre Ardente*, from the candles that lit the black-hung room in which it met. The court numbered twelve Commissioners, among whose names that of Nicholas de La Reynie is now most remembered. He was a man of very high character, incorrupt, courageous, intelligent, and devoted to the king and to France. He was a man of principle and care, checking and counter-checking, and it is to his notes that we owe the inner history of the whole matter. But he was no credulous pain-maker; he was alert, like Salazar, to the principle of disbelief and its usefulness in such matters. At the same time that he was, in 1679, tracing out the actual occult evil, he encouraged laughter. He gave to a dramatist of the day, Donneau de Visé, as a subject for a comedy, the popular belief in magic. Visé collaborated with Thomas Corneille, and on the 19th November 1679 there was produced in Paris by the king's company a new play, *La Devineresse ou les Faux Enchantements*. La Voisin was still in prison, the full darkness of her work was not yet known, or La Reynie might have found it more difficult to laugh. But he was right, and again right. La Voisin was represented as Madame Jobin, laughing at her own supernatural pretences and the gullibility of the world. An engraving, advertising the play, showed 'a monstrous satanic figure'; a devil in the play cried out: 'Mercy, sir! I am a good devil.' The play ran for forty-seven nights, and was repeated over five months.

Meanwhile La Reynie and the other Commissioners were conducting the investigation. One of the first persons in society to be involved was the wife of a fashionable musician, flautist to the king, who was convicted of poisoning her first husband, and was executed in May. Another young wife, similarly convicted—though in this case the poison failed—was banished; so were the wives of two distinguished lawyers. All these had applied either to La Voisin or to some other of the group. The Marshal de Luxembourg had gone, with a list of his wishes, to Lesage, who posed as a magician. The Duchess de Bouillon had gone to La Voisin and to others for poison; the Countess de Soissons also. The great Racine was accused, by more than one of the prisoners, of poisoning his mistress, the actress Marguerite Thérèse du Parc; he seems only to have escaped arrest by the reluctance of a fellow academician in the court to issue the warrant.

Thus by the end of the year the affair was spreading in all directions. The king personally commanded the investigation to be pressed to the utmost. He gave a few of the nobility the chance to flee from Paris and escape arrest, but he told La Reynie that he was to 'penetrate as deeply as possible into the abominable traffic . . . to do strict justice, without distinction of person, rank, or sex; and this his Majesty told us clearly and emphatically'. This was on the 27th December 1679. But by the next October the king had had certain evidence removed from the records, had suspended the sittings of the court,

and had reduced all the affair to the most private—
though still persistent—inquiry by La Reynie and one
companion. Louis had been caught in the trap of his own
nature; his sensuality had given rise to the thing with
which his justice was at war. It was one of the most
appalling moments of his life.

La Voisin, after the ordinary and extraordinary torture, had been burned alive in February 1680. After her
death her daughter and other confederates began to give
evidence more freely; this was in July. In September
Lesage was examined; in the same month more evidence
came—under torture—from a condemned woman, one
of the worst of the company, Françoise Filastre. On
October 1st these latest testimonies were presented to the
king; on October 1st he suspended the *Chambre Ardente*.
Why? 'The answer is that the evidence . . . contained
overwhelming proof that of all the ladies of the court
and the city who had been convicted of intercourse with
the atrocious wretches awaiting the penalty of their
crimes in the dungeons of the Bastille and Vincennes
none had been more guilty, in intention if not in deed,
than the woman who had been for twelve years the
mistress of the king, the woman whose children had been
made sons and daughters of France'[1]—Françoise Athenais
de Rochechouart, Marquise de Montespan. She had
had, by 1680, three children by the king—the Duc de
Maine, a boy of ten; the Comte de Vexin, a boy of eight;
Mademoiselle de Nantes, a girl of seven. It was now to
be seen what had lain behind the relations of their mother
and the king.

[1] H. Noel Williams, *Mme de Montespan*.

The beginnings were thirteen years old. In 1667 Mme de Montespan had been one of the queen's ladies; the royal mistress then had been the Duchesse de la Vallière. It had, however, already begun to appear that the Montespan was rising into favour. She had intended it—how firmly only became evident in 1680. She had been brought into touch with Lesage and with Mariette. In a house in Paris an altar was set up. There a certain Rite was gone through; probably an amatory Mass. Mariette, properly vested, sang the Rite. Lesage invoked the Holy Ghost by the *Veni Creator*. Mme de Montespan knelt before the celebrant, who read the Gospel over her head; invocations were made and incantations uttered against La Vallière and the queen; 'that the queen may be barren, that the king leave her bed and table for me, that I obtain from him all that I ask for myself and my relatives; that my servants and domestics may be pleasing to him; that, beloved and respected by great nobles, I may be called to the councils of the king and know what passes there; and that, this affection being redoubled on what has existed in the past, the king may leave La Vallière and look no more upon her; and that, the queen being repudiated, I may espouse the king.'[1]

This Rite was repeated in Saint-Germain, in Mme de Montespan's sister's lodgings. It was repeated at the Church of Saint Severin; there were used as a magical link the hearts of two pigeons, solemnly consecrated to the names of the king and de Montespan, and laid before the supernatural power in the Mass itself. It was the lesser bloody sacrifice; the other was to come.

[1] F. Funck Brentano, *Princes and Poisoners*.

It seemed to the ambitious heart of the Montespan that the Rite achieved its end. The king increased his favour to her. La Vallière was abandoned; and if the queen still remained in the kingdom, yet the new favourite had all the power and the glory. She had one time of fright—there were rumours abroad, and Mariette and Lesage were arrested, examined and sentenced. Mme de Montespan left Paris. But the two, by artifice or by influence, regained their freedom, and she returned. She continued, of course, to have difficulties with the king's other amours. What was gained by the Rite, if it were gained by the Rite, was not finally gained. Something more had continually to be done. She had to return continually to her helpers—the priest, the magical charlatan, and the lady of them all, Catherine La Voisin. The formal invocation of the Holy Spirit to achieve the desires of her heart had in fact, by very necessity, addressed itself to quite another spirit. The supernatural never stands still; it increases or it decreases. It increased—after its own kind. 'Every time', said Margaret Monvoisin, 'that anything fresh happened to Madame de Montespan and she feared some diminution in the favour of the king, she told my mother, so that she might provide some remedy; and my mother at once had recourse to priests, whom she instructed to say Masses, and she gave her powders to be administered to the king'. The confection of powders was placed, as was the tradition, under the chalice during the amatory Mass. The paste was then sent to the favourite, and by contrivance mixed with the king's food. Up to 1672, and the birth of the boy who was to be the Comte de Vexin, these served. By 1673 the favourite was with La Voisin again, and a stronger enchantment was tried.

Lesage was half a charlatan; Mariette was a priest. But now La Voisin, appealed to by the Montespan in a state of jealousy and fear, introduced to her another priest, the Abbé Guibourg. He was an old man of seventy; he had a bloated face, with prominent blue veins, and a squint. He was promised, if he would help, a sum of money, about £40, and an ecclesiastical living. He agreed. Mme de Montespan and her lady in waiting came to the Castle of Villebousin at Mesnil; two or three others were with them. Francoise Athenais disrobed, went into the chapel of the château, and lay across the altar. Guibourg vested and entered. He set the chalice on the belly of the favourite. He proceeded to say Mass. At the Offering of the Elements a small child was produced and stabbed in the throat. The blood was caught in the chalice; flour was added and a wafer made. The Mass proceeded. At the consecration, Guibourg on behalf of Françoise Athenais—or perhaps she herself—recited the incantation: 'Ashtaroth, Asmodeus, Princes of Affection, I conjure you to accept the sacrifice I present to you of this child for the things I ask of you: which are that the affection of the king and my lord the Dauphin for me may be continued; and that, honoured by the princes and princesses of the court, nothing may be denied me of all that I shall ask the king, as well for my relatives as my servitors.'[1] Some of the blood, with the conse-crated Host, was put into a glass vessel, which the favourite took away. The secret tradition prescribed the

[1] F. Funck Brentano, *Princes and Poisoners.*

saying of the Mass three times. It was done again, two or three weeks afterwards, in a hut; and again, a little later, in a house in Paris.

The Rite seemed successful; the king remained attached, though he was very ill that year, perhaps from the confections. But crises continually recurred. In 1676 the Abbé was again called in. This time, according to the evidence, the celebration did not take place in a chapel but in La Voisin's house. Margaret Monvoisin 'helped her mother to get things ready'. A mattress was laid on seats, 'two stools at the sides on which were candlesticks with candles'. Guibourg came in from an adjoining room, vested in a white chasuble embroidered with fir-cones. La Voisin brought in the favourite, naked. She lay on the mattress; it was too short; they turned a chair over, put a pillow on it, and set it as a support to her head. Her lower legs dangled. A napkin covered her belly; a cross was set on it. The chalice was on the belly. The child was offered, and the blood. The Mass was concluded. 'My mother next day carried the blood and wafer to Dumesnil to be distilled, in a glass vessel which Madame de Montespan took away.'

It had to be done three times. But Mme de Montespan could not or dared not be absent so long; the whole business had taken two hours, from ten to twelve at night. She insisted that La Voisin should act for her, and so it was done; substitution ruled in hell as in heaven. Twice La Voisin lay naked in her house and the Mass was said over her on behalf of Françoise Athenais.

The children were obtained in various ways. There were those who were prematurely born, those who were bought—for something like a pound in present-day reckoning; those who were stolen. Guibourg is said to have stabbed his own; Margaret Monvoisin saved hers from her mother by taking it away and keeping it secretly. In 1676 there had been a riot in Paris over the disappearance of children, though it was not then attributed by the mob to the true cause, and the trouble was suppressed. During the inquiry of the *Chambre Ardente*, three hundred and sixty seven persons were arrested, and two hundred and eighteen kept in custody. Of these seventy-four were sentenced; others died or killed themselves in prison. The number of priests among the accused was high.

It was in 1677 apparently that Mme de Montespan began to grow determined that 'where she could not govern she would destroy'; it was in 1679 that she renewed the determination. The king's amours frenzied her. She turned from the amatory Mass to the mortuary Mass. Guibourg was made to say this Mass of Death, where there was no bloody sacrifice, and indeed no consecration but the solemn recitation of enchantments against the king's life. The last stage of the Way was in 1679. The king in February fell in love with Mlle de Fontanges. The first arrests in the matter of suspicion of poison had been made in January. The investigation was beginning, but neither Montespan nor La Voisin knew that. Montespan wanted 'to go to extremities . . . against the king'. La Voisin hesitated, and agreed. There was a meeting between La Voisin and a partner of hers called La Trianon, and two men called Romani and Bertrand. The two witches were to deal with the king by means of a poisoned petition; the two men with the Fontanges by means of poisoned gloves and poisoned silks. The petition was prepared and La Voisin took it to Saint Germains on the 5th March. She failed to give the petition into the king's own hand, and determined to go on the 13th March. On Sunday, the 12th March, she was arrested as she left the Church of Notre Dame de Bonne Nouvelle after Mass. On the 15th March Mme de Montespan left the Court for Paris. La Voisin said: 'God has protected the king.'

It was when these facts had been laid before the king that he finally crushed the inquiry. It was impossible for him publicly to recognize the horrible crimes in which the favourite, the mother of the children of France, had been involved. In the middle of August 1780 he had an interview with Mme de Montespan; she was removed from his intimacy, but the real nature of the breach was concealed. The king received and visited her courteously for some ten years; then in 1791 she retired from the Court. She lived for another sixteen years, her religious devotion, her humility, her repentance increasing. She wore rough linen and a body belt of steel. She gave away her money. Yet—till the last—she feared death, and even the darkness and solitude of night. At the end she seems to have been at peace.

And the accomplices? The king had wished their trials to proceed, the facts about Mme de Montespan only being withheld. But La Reynie could not see his way to this. He continually appealed to the king and to the king's ministers to permit the revelation, so that the other criminals might be brought to sentence. The evidence was there. The king refused. La Reynie also remained obdurate. 'The affair in question', he wrote, 'is in the nature of things, not susceptible of the proposed expedient'. Either Mme de Montespan must be exposed or the other criminals would escape—including Guibourg: 'Guibourg!' wrote La Reynie, 'this man, who cannot be compared to any other in regard to the number of his poisonings, his dealings with poison and sorcery, his sacrilege and impiety, knowing and known by every notorious criminal, convicted of a great number of horrible crimes—this man, who has mutilated and sacrificed several children; who, apart from the sacrilege of which he is convicted, confesses to inconceivable abominations; who says he has practised by diabolical means against the life of the king; of whom we hear every day new and execrable things, and who is loaded with accusations of crimes against God and king—he, too, will assure impunity to other criminals.'

Eventually the matter was settled by *lettres de cachet*. The prisoners were carried away to fortresses and there chained to the wall in their cells. A typical order to the governors of the fortresses ran—'The king having thought fit to send to the château of Saint André de Salins some of the people who were arrested in virtue of warrants of the court that dealt with the matter of the poisons, his Majesty has commanded me to inform you that his intention is that you prepare two rooms in the said château, so that six of these prisoners may be kept safely in each of them, the which prisoners are to have each a mattress in the place arranged for them, and to be fastened either by a hand or a foot to a chain which shall be fastened to the wall, the said chain however to be long enough not to prevent them from lying down. As these people are criminals who deserve extreme penalties, the intention of the king is that they be thus fastened for fear they should injure the people set to guard them, who will go in and out to bring them food and attend to them generally. His Majesty's intention is that you prepare two similar rooms in the citadel of Besançon, so that twelve of the prisoners may be kept securely there. You will observe that these rooms are to be so situated that no-one can hear what these people say.'

It was in Besançon that Guibourg was chained; he lived three years. Others lived longer; it was in 1724—forty years later—that the last chained witch of Paris died.

Chapter Twelve

SALEM

The history of the Salem witches deserves to be noticed
separately, not so much because of its process as because of its end. It was not altogether a coincidence that
the end of the trial came so near the pacification in the
whole general war; men's beliefs were already shaken,
and the Salem conclusion is likely to have affected minds
in England at least. It is a smaller coincidence, but one
that should not be forgotten, that this particular end
should come at a place called Salem.

The facts themselves are nothing new. One of the
most horrible themes of the whole history is the conflict, as it were, between children and the accused. Children had been supposed to be a particular prey. In a book
by a certain Ignatius Lupo published at Bergamo in 1648,
or a little earlier, the question was raised why God
allowed the deaths of so many children at the hands of
witches. Lupo fell back on His inscrutable wisdom and
goodness. But the answer was only pious and the problem
oppressed many. All over Europe the attack of Goetia
had been felt to be aimed at children, either to pervert

or to kill. The authors of the *Malleus* had imagined a kind of destruction of all Christendom by such means; with the dwindling of the generations, and with the increase of the abhorred conventicles in every generation, the number of the faithful would diminish and perhaps disappear. But also, imaginatively, there was that old junction of opposites—the supreme supernatural malice and the semblance at least of natural innocence. The very appearance of a natural child was clearly the thing in all the world most unlike the body of evil, especially of aged evil, which was a witch, and most provocative to it. Was it wonderful that the witch should desire to destroy it?

As it were by diabolical intervention, the children retaliated. In England, in France, in Germany, in Spain, in New England, the clear voices of children gave evidence against their neighbours, their friends, their kindred, their parents. Yes, those small voices said, they had been at the Sabbath; yes, they had helped to cook the food; yes, they had seen so-and-so there and so-and-so and such-a-one; yes, they had given themselves to the devil, or had not; yes, father or mother or brother had said or done this or the other. And then mostly they vanish—scourged three times naked round the stake, or shut up in a convent, or driven away from their homes, or even, like Jennet Device, living a quite ordinary life after their month of exhibition, until, in turn, a boy's voice pipes up with the same accusation against them which had come against others from their own younger lips.

Such had been the history, but the war was, at least for a while, to cease; the children of Salem were to be among the last who had the opportunity to testify: Elizabeth Parris, nine years old, daughter of the Reverend Samuel Parris, minister of Salem, and Abigail Williams, eleven years old, her cousin; Anne Putnam, twelve years old, daughter of Thomas Putnam, the parish clerk, and others, but it was those three with whom the thing began, for they were seen 'to creep into holes and under chairs, put themselves into odd postures, make antic gestures, and utter loud outcries'. It was a land where everything was immediately translated into terms of God; that is, no doubt, proper, but then they must be His terms and not ours—the terms He deigns to apply, not the terms we force on Him. And this, it seems, is the use of all science —to discover His own terms. The minister and the family prayed and asked serious questions; the children responded. Names were heard—Tituba, the old Indian servant of the minister; Sarah Good, Sarah Osburn, two very old, very poor members of the congregation. Warrants were issued, and the three were arrested.

It is more than possible that the whole thing had be-gun with Tituba, that it was she whose tales, or other than tales, had thrilled, excited, and provoked the chil-dren. If so, the reveries of her race returned on her from her pupils. When the three prisoners were examined in turn Tituba was quicker than the other two to see what was expected or to confess what had happened. She put all the blame on the other women; there had been four of them and a man; they had said to her: 'Hurt the chil-dren or we will do worse to you'. She added: 'Last night there was an appearance that said: "Hurt the children."' What was it like? 'Like a hog, and sometimes like a great dog.' She said they had all gone to the meeting: 'We see nothing but are there presently.' She told of the familiars the other women had. Sarah Good had a little yellow bird, which was seen afterwards by the afflicted children. 'What hath Sarah Osburn?' 'Yesterday she had a thing like a woman with two legs and wings.' This also the afflicted Abigail found that she had seen. 'What else have you seen with Osburn?' 'Another thing, hairy; it goes upright like a man; it hath only two legs.' The man with the four women went, she thought, in black clothes; he was a tall man with white hair.

Sarah Good at first refused to admit any guilt. The children were ordered to look at her, when they all found themselves tormented. This was the great dramatic thrill of the examinations. There stood the children, and if any of the prisoners moved a limb they cried out accordingly: if a hand, they were pinched; if a foot, they were stamped on; if the body, they were crushed. 'Why do you torment them?' the court asked Good. She denied it; she said: 'What do I know? You bring others here, and now you charge me with it.'

'Why, who was it?'

'I do not know, but it was some you brought into the meeting-house with you.'

'We brought you into the meeting-house.'

'But you brought in two more.'

At last she said yes; Osburn had done it. All three were remitted to prison. Sarah Osburn died there. The others in due course were put to death.

It appeared, however, that there were more. Two more certainly; Good and Tituba had both testified to it.

There were, walking about the meeting-house, two beings, either the hairy winged things going on legs that Tituba had seen, familiars of witches, or perhaps the witches themselves. Here again is that curious horror in which it can be believed that a man or a woman can be in one place and yet in another place. Two women might be in their own houses, at their own work, and yet walking also in the meeting-house; or they might even be sitting in that very meeting-house, orthodox, pious, attentive, shocked, and yet they might be walking about in it, tormenting the children, evil and restless, like the Devil, in dry places. There were, though the Salem magistrates may not have known it, thousands of stories —of how a woman would be seemingly asleep by her husband's side, and yet it was but a shape that slept there, for the woman herself was away at the Sabbath. Crudely, it was said to be the familiar or some other devil who put on the identity, but it seems sometimes as if this were but a manner of speech; as if the witch body shed itself or multiplied itself,[1] and went as it would and stayed as it would; so that no-one could know to whom they spoke, whether to the witch or her shape; and in those places and times no-one could know, till confession, who was the witch. Who, of all the women in Salem, were the two? Everyone looked and shrank and wondered. And the afflicted children were still afflicted before them all.

From that moment the panic spread. More were arrested, and more in danger. Sarah Good was hanged:

---

[1] Golden-thighed Pythagoras is said to have lectured in two cities at the same time; it is an ancient dream of power.

when she came to the scaffold, one of the ministers, Mr. Nicholas Noyes, of First Church, Salem, urged her to confess, and she refused. He said: 'I know you are a witch'; she answered: 'I am no more a witch than you are a wizard, and if you take away my life, God will give you blood to drink.'

The afflicted children continued to testify; there entered into the cases what was called 'spectral evidence', a declaration by the witness that he or she could see that else invisible shape before them, perhaps hurting them. It was a very ancient tendency of witnesses, and it had occurred in a number of trials in Europe. 'Many a man hath verily believed he hath seen a spirit externally before him when it hath been only an internal image dancing in his own brain,' wrote Francis Hutchinson in 1720 in the chapter of his *Historical Essay concerning Witchcraft* which deals with the Salem trials; and to the objection that 'God would not allow such horrors' he answers, in a sentence worthy to be recollected continually: 'Hath God anywhere promised that he will save credulous men from being deceived because otherwise the blood of the innocent man will be in danger?' The children at Salem supplied all that credulity needed. At the trial of Martha Carrier they declared that 'the black man' was present in the court. Martha Carrier was another of those parents who were convicted on the evidence of her own children. Four of them were taken to prison, and Sarah Carrier, a child of seven, was examined.

'How long hast thou been a witch?'

'Ever since I was six years old.'

'How old are you now?'

'Near eight years old; brother Richard says I shall be eight years old in November next.'

'Who made you a witch?'

'My mother; she made me set my hand to a book.'

'How did you set your hand to it?'

'I touched it with my fingers, and the book was red; the paper of it was white.'

She went on to say that her mother had 'baptized' her with the words: 'Thou art mine for ever and ever, Amen'; and had sent her to afflict folks by pinching them. She added that her mother, while confined, had come to her in the shape of a black cat. 'The cat told me so, that she was my mother.' And the cat carried the child 'in her spirit' to afflict. She confirmed other testimony that Martha was she to whom the Devil had promised that she should be Queen of Hell.

The black man was also seen to be spectrally present at the execution of the Reverend George Burroughs. Burroughs had been a minister in Salem, but had left the village for another pastorate. He was, however, arrested on a warrant from Boston and on the 4th May brought back to Salem to be tried. At the trial Ann Putnam (it may be remembered that she was twelve years old) testified as follows:

'On the 8th day of May, at evening, I saw the apparition of Mr. George Burroughs, who grievously tortured me, and urged me to write in his book, which I refused. He then told me that his two first wives would appear to me presently, and tell me a great many lies, but I should not believe them.

'Then immediately appeared to me the forms of two

women in winding sheets, and napkins about their heads, at which I was greatly affrighted; and they turned their faces towards Mr. Burroughs, and looked very red and angry, and told him that he had been a cruel man to them, and that their blood did cry for vengeance against him; and also told him that they should be clothed with white robes in heaven, when he should be cast into hell; and immediately he vanished away. And, as soon as he was gone, the two women turned their heads toward me, and looked as pale as a white wall; and told me that they were Mr. Burroughs' two first wives, and that he had murdered them. And one of them told me that she was his first wife, and he stabbed her under the left arm and put a piece of sealing-wax on the wound. And she pulled aside the winding-sheet and showed me the place; and also told me that she was in the house where Mr. Parris now lives, when it was done.

'And the other told me that Mr. Burroughs and that wife which he hath now, killed her in the vessel, as she was coming to see her friends, because they would have one another. And they both charged me that I should tell these things to the magistrates before Mr. Burroughs' face; and, if he did not own them, they did not know but they should appear there. This morning, also, Mrs. Lawson and her daughter Ann appeared to me, whom I knew, and told me Mr. Burroughs murdered them. This morning also appeared to me another woman in a winding-sheet, and told me that she was Goodman Fuller's first wife, and Mr. Burroughs killed her because there was some difference between her husband and him.'

Other evidence proved that he was the 'devil' of the coven; it was he who had seduced many to join, and who summoned the witches to their meeting with the sound of a trumpet. He preached at the meetings and was present when they 'had a Sacrament at a house in the village, and they had Red Bread and Red Drink'. One of the witnesses said she had been taken up by Burroughs 'into a very high mountain, where he showed her mighty and glorious kingdoms'. These however, like her great Exemplar, she refused. During the examinations the sufferers cried out that he was biting them, and there were seen on their flesh the prints of teeth, 'just such a set of teeth as G.B.'s . . . which could be distinguished from those of other men'. His unusual strength was also brought in evidence against him. Eventually he was found guilty. At his execution he made a prayer and made an address to the crowd of such ardent devotion that it seems to have shaken many. But 'the accusers said the black man stood and dictated to him. As soon as he was turned off, Mr. Cotton Mather, being mounted upon a horse, addressed himself to the people, partly to declare that he (Mr. Burroughs) was no ordained minister, and partly to possess the people of his guilt, saying that the Devil had often been transformed into an angel of light; and this somewhat appeased the people, and the executions went on.'

By now the whole tale had been reaffirmed: the coven, the meeting, the infernal sacrament, the book of signatures, the devil-master and his deputy, familiars, charms, deaths, and destructions. By now also the usual witnesses appeared. The general informer was in this case a man called Joseph Ring, and he was the subject of much admiration on the part of the great Mr. Cotton Mather when he wrote of the affair in his *Wonders of the Invisible World*. 'This man has been strangely carried about, by demons, from one witch-meeting to another, for near two years together.' He was visited by unknown shapes, and was for a long while made dumb by the Devils, though at the time of the trials released. There often came to him a man with a book for him to sign, but he always refused. 'Once, with the book, there was a pen offered him, and an inkhorn, with liquor in it that seemed like blood; but he never touched it.' Mr. Ring was thus able to recognize whom he chose, as he chose. He was wasted in Salem; he would have done better in London, a few years earlier, under Titus Oates.

At Andover, a town near at hand, there were the beginnings of a similar outbreak. The wife of a certain Joseph Ballard fell ill and her husband, believing her to be bewitched, sent to Salem for some of the accusers (there were by now others than the afflicted children), some who had the power to see the spectral evidence, to come and say who was oppressing the sick woman. They came and did as they were asked; they were thrown into fits, and cried out that they saw such a one sitting on the invalid's head and such a one on her lower parts. More than Mrs. Ballard fell ill. 'Many parents believed their children to be witches; many husbands their wives.' The accusers, the witch-finders, were taken about; and their capacity also spread. Others, especially the young people of Andover, 'had the same spectral sight'. Presently more than fifty of the inhabitants were accused and under suspicions. A magistrate of the place, who had granted warrants for the arrest of thirty or forty, hesitated, for some reason, to grant more. A cry against him was immediately begun; it was said that the spirits of those he had himself killed, some eight or nine, were floating over him in the air. His wife was also 'cried out on'. He took warning in time; husband and wife fled together.

But another of the accused acted differently. He was then living at Boston, 'a worthy gentleman', and his name had been mentioned by the witch-finders at Andover. He was not in immediate danger; he had time to act; he did act. He procured a writ against the accusers for defamation of character, and set the damages at a thousand pounds. This writ he gave to some of his friends who were going to Andover, and charged them to procure certain proof of the slanders, 'in doing which their business was perceived'. The knowledge wonderfully quenched zeal; the accusers saw *his* spectre at least no more; then other rumours began to dwindle; the accusations at Andover generally ceased. It is unfortunate that no-one had taken the same course with Matthew Hopkins in England.

At Salem there was an incident which showed the determination of the mob to have its panic appeased by death. Rebecca Nurse was a woman of seventy, the mother of a large family, a respected member of the Church, and of some social position. She was a little deaf; she was ill when she was arrested, but she was brought to examination in the usual way, and she maintained her defence with dignity. Asked, 'Do you think that these suffer against their wills?' she answered 'I do not think these suffer against their wills'. A paper testifying to her upright character and signed by thirty-nine acquaintances was handed in. The jury pronounced her guiltless. There was an immediate hubbub in the court. The accusers cried out; the afflicted children screamed. The judges exclaimed against the verdict. One said they would have her indicted over again. Another directed the attention of the jury to a phrase used by the accused: when Deliverance Hobbs, who had been a witch and had confessed, came to give evidence, Rebecca Nurse was heard to say: 'What, do these persons give in evidence against me now? they used to come amongst us.' The jury asked leave to withdraw again. The foreman was still troubled and went back into court to ask the prisoner what she meant by the words. But she was hard of hearing and most unhappy; the court was noisy; she did not hear him. He went out again, and the jury found her guilty. Afterwards she was told what had happened; she said that all she had meant was that Goodwife Hobbs and her daughter had been her fellow prisoners. The governor, perhaps upon hearing of this declaration, issued a reprieve, but there was a fresh outcry and he withdrew it. She was executed on the 19th July.

It was, however, at her trial that the first fault was made by the accusers. They cried out on Mr. Willard. Now Mr. Willard was a minister, of the Old South Church, Boston; he appears to have displayed some hesitation about accepting all the evidence. But he was too great a man for the accusers of Salem to be allowed to reach; whoever spoke was hastily hushed, pushed out of court, and 'it was told about that she was mistaken in the person'.

The modification of the panic seems to have begun in a similar rashness—when the wife of the Reverend John Hale, of Beverly, was accused. This happened in October, and the Reverend John Hale found it impossible to believe. He began to stand out; others joined him. The Governor also took action; he refused to allow any more spectral evidence; he ordered the special court which had been sitting to cease from witchcraft trials. By November the accusers found the tales falling harmless. They fell into fits at the sight of an old woman on a bridge, but she was not arrested; they had visions of three persons sitting on a sick person till she died, but bond was accepted for all three. By the next May all those who were still prisoners were released; it is said there were about a hundred and fifty, though another two hundred had been accused. Twenty during the year of panic had been executed, nineteen hanged and one (the famous Giles Corey) pressed to death for refusing to plead. Two had died in prison. Eight were under condemnation when they were released. This release so moved the chief judge that he protested loudly: 'We were in a way to have cleared the land of them; who it is that obstructs the cause of justice I know not; the Lord be merciful to this country!'

But the affair did not end there. It was followed by the operation of some of the Salem people against their minister Mr. Parris, and of the declaration of others against themselves. Few trials have had such a conclusion. In April 1693, before the final release had taken place, eight men of Salem drew up a paper which they read to Mr. Parris. It accused him of credulity, lack of charity, and the practice of unwarrantable methods; it said they seriously feared to be accused as the Devil's instruments, since they had seen those better than themselves accused; they said that his continual dwelling on the mystery of iniquity working among them all 'was not profitable but offensive'. For this reason they had preferred to withdraw from communion with the church at Salem village. Mr. Parris in his reply acknowledged his faults and changed his opinions. He lamented the beginning of the terror in his own household; he said that 'God hath been righteously spitting in my face: Numbers xii. 14. And I desire to lie low under all this reproach and to lay my hand on my mouth.' He allowed that 'God sometimes suffers the Devil, as of late, to afflict in shape of not only innocent but pious persons; or so to delude the senses of the afflicted, that they strongly conceit their hurt is from such persons, when it is not.'

This, of course, was fatal to any accusation based on spectral evidence. It had been maintained long ago by the authors of the *Malleus* that the apparent good might be evil. But only here and there had any intellect maintained that the apparent evil might be good. Yet one can hardly imagine Satan's kingdom by halves; if he can deceive, he can deceive. Mr. Parris, to do him justice, saw the difficulty at last: God had suffered them to be deluded —'but how far on the one side or the other is much above me to say'.

The opposition, however, were unsatisfied. They did not think it above them to say that Mr. Parris and his side had been deluded throughout. The other churches of the district made some attempt to compose the difference and failed. In 1695 the congregation was demanding the minister's withdrawal, and in another two years the dispute had to be put to arbitration. In the paper put in by attorneys on behalf of the village Mr. Parris was flatly accused of having 'dealt with them that have a familiar spirit', in so far as he had inquired of the afflicted children; it came near the old problem of using sorcery to cure sorcery. This, and his preaching such 'scandalous immoralities', his 'believing the Devil's accusations'— 'by these practices and principles' he had been 'the beginner and procurer of the sorest afflictions not to this village only but to this whole country'. The petition ended:

'We, the subscribers, in behalf of ourselves, and of several others of the same mind with us (touching these things), having some of us had our relations by these practices taken off by an untimely death; others have been imprisoned, and suffered in our persons, reputations, and estates; submit the whole to your honours' decision, to determine whether we are or ought to be any ways obliged to honour, respect and support such an instrument of our miseries; praying God to guide your honours to act herein as may be for his glory, and the future settlement of our village in amity and unity.'

To this attack the minister was compelled to yield; he actually left the village and went elsewhere; it was not perhaps unjustified. But though it exhibited regret and determination in the townsmen, it could not exhibit repentance. One at least of the afflicted children made some motion towards such a greater acknowledgement. Anne Putnam, in 1706, was received into the Church at the age of twenty-six. But the events of 1692 had not been forgotten; either by her own will or under the direction of others, she produced a Confession. It read as follows:

'I desire to be humbled before God for that sad and humbling providence that befell my father's family in the year about '92; that I being then in my childhood, should by such providence be made an instrument for the accusing of several persons of a grievous crime, whereby their lives were taken away from them, whom now I have just grounds and good reason to believe they were innocent persons; and that it was a great delusion of Satan that deceived me in that sad time, whereby I justly fear I have been instrumental, with others, though ignorantly and unwittingly, to bring upon myself and this land the guilt of innocent blood; though what was said or done by me against any person I can truly and up-rightly say, before God and man, I did it not out of any anger, malice or ill-will to any person, for I had no such thing against one of them; but what I did was ignorantly, being deluded by Satan. And particularly, as I was a chief instrument of accusing of Goodwife Nurse and her two sisters, I desire to lie in the dust, and to be humbled for it, in that I was a cause, with others, of so sad a calamity to them and their families; for which cause I desire to lie in the dust, and earnestly beg forgiveness of God, and from all those unto whom I have given just cause of sorrow and offence, whose relations were taken away or accused.'

But the unique thing in all the history was the action

of one of the judges and of the jurors. Judge Sewall, who had taken an active part, could not content himself with blaming Mr. Parris or the Devil or the Providence of God. He stood up one day in Old South Church, in Boston; he handed up a paper, before all the congregation, to be read from the pulpit; he remained standing upright while it was read. It confessed his error and his fault; it implored the forgiveness of God; it entreated the prayers of the Church to avert the anger of God from his country, his family, and himself. He continued to observe privately an annual day of fasting and prayer. The actual document does not remain. But the Confession of the twelve jurors does remain.[1]

'We, whose names are under written, being in the year 1692 called to serve as jurors in court at Salem on trial of many, who were by some suspected guilty of doing acts of witchcraft upon the bodies of sundry persons:

'We confess that we ourselves were not capable to understand, nor able to withstand, the mysterious delusions of the powers of darkness, and prince of the air; but were, for want of knowledge in ourselves, and better information from others, prevailed with to take up with such evidence against the accused, as, on further consideration and better information, we justly fear was insufficient for the touching the lives of any (Deut. xvii. 6) whereby we fear we have been instrumental, with others,

---

[1] Taken from *More Wonders of the Invisible World* (1700); a collection made by Robert Calafe, an opponent of Cotton Mather's. It was ordered to be burnt by Increase Mather.

though ignorantly and unwittingly, to bring upon ourselves and this people of the Lord the guilt of innocent blood; which sin the Lord saith, in scripture, he would not pardon (2 Kings xxiv. 4), that is, we suppose, in regard of his temporal judgements. We do therefore hereby signify to all in general (and to the surviving sufferers in special) our deep sense of, and sorrow for, our errors, in acting on such evidence to the condemning of any person; and do hereby declare, that we justly fear that we were sadly deluded and mistaken; for which we are much disquieted and distressed in our minds; and do therefore humbly beg forgiveness, first of God for Christ's sake, for this our error; and pray that God would not impute the guilt of it to ourselves, nor others; and we also pray that we may be considered candidly, and aright, by the living sufferers, as being then under the power of a strong and general delusion, utterly unacquainted with, and not experienced in, matters of that nature.

'We do heartily ask forgiveness of you all, whom we have justly offended; and do declare, according to our present minds, we would none of us do such things again on such grounds for the whole world; praying you to accept of this in way of satisfaction for our offence, and that you would bless the inheritance of the Lord, that he may be entreated for the land.

Foreman, Thomas Fisk,	Th. Pearly, sen.
William Fisk,	John Peabody,
John Bachelor,	Thomas Perkins,
Thomas Fisk, jun.	Samuel Sayer,
John Dane,	Andrew Eliot,
Joseph Evelith,	Henry Herrick, sen.'

If it had not been for the Salem jury (and for the Supreme Court of the Inquisition in Spain), the Church of God would not, through those centuries, have made a much better showing than the most malicious of those against whom they set themselves. The century that followed, during which on the whole the panics ceased, would have owed that appeasement rather to the growing scepticism than to any more holy impulse. All that certainly was a part of the change. But, coming when and where it did, the repentance of the Salem jurors on the edge of Christendom seems to carry with it an efficacious grace. Salem has been too long remembered for its witches and its trials; it ought to be remembered for its reparation. In that, in those thirteen good and Christian men—twelve jurors and one judge—by whom it was accomplished, it may be thought that our Lord saw Satan, as lightning, fall from heaven.

Chapter Thirteen

CONCLUSION

The third famous trial at the end of the seventeenth century was that of Major Weir and his sister Jane in Edinburgh. Thomas Weir had presided at the execution of Montrose, and in his later years was regarded as a great person in the religious world of Edinburgh. It was said (but that may have been slander) that 'he pretended to pray only in the families of such as were saints of the highest form'. At least, to all appearance, he was, in 1669, an austere liver, old—he was sixty-nine—devout, respected. No-one had any suspicion of his integrity until, at the beginning of the year 1670, he himself began to denounce it. He spoke of dreadful sins; he opened himself in confessions to some of his church; he declared himself stirred by conscience. They thought him wandering in his mind; the Provost of Edinburgh was moved to send physicians. The physicians, however, reported that they could find no insanity; he was clear and, as far as they could judge, absolutely sincere. He himself referred to sin and not to disease. The Provost accordingly sent ministers, who brought the same tale. 'The terrors of

God', they said, 'are on his soul.' He was at last arrested, with his sister Jane; on the arrest Jane cried out to the officers to prevent her brother laying hold of his staff, which had 'a crooked head of thorn wood', and had been given him magically by the Devil. But he did not desire it; he was past (he said) all salvation, earthly or heavenly. On the 9th April 1670 the two were brought to trial.

It was Jane who brought witchcraft into the proceedings. Weir's own confessions were sex-driven, and the Devil's power had been to him, if anything, but a means to that. He had committed incest, adultery, bestiality. Mr. John Sinclair, 'a conventicle minister', testified that Weir had confessed that he had lain with the Devil in the shape of a beautiful woman, and (asked if he had seen the Devil) answered that he had 'felt him in the dark'. He had been invisibly transported to the bedrooms of women; one to whom he had thus gone, and who had rejected his solicitations, had soon after fallen ill and died. The Devil had helped him too in religion. He had not (it was recollected) knelt at prayers, but always leant on the magical staff. He confessed that the Devil had even supplied him with phrases for his public prayers—and at that, if he had taken pleasure in his capacity for such leading of the elect, he need not have been very far wrong.

But Jane was more honest—or, perhaps, madder. She said their mother had been a witch and had known of the 'secret things' done by Jane at a distance. She confessed that she and her brother had made a Pact. They had once been carried to Musselburgh 'in a coach and six horses which seemed all on fire'. Her brother had had converse with the Devil, and had 'Devil's work on his shoulder'; he had been told by the Devil of Preston Battle, so that he had been able to gain a reputation for prophecy. She herself had had little reward; she had always found an extraordinary quantity of yarn ready on the spindle; and once a tall woman had come to the house and offered to speak on Jane's behalf to 'the Queen of Fairie'; which is not so far from the tree of Domrémy and 'those who came in the air' in the days of Joan of Arc's childhood. Fairie may or may not be diabolical, but it was held then, as it is now, that it is no world for men and women. To be related to it was too near the tale of the outrageous union between two different natures which had appalled the authors of Genesis and of the *Malleus*.

They had been, the two old creatures confessed, on the edge of things. They had committed incest with each other; and she had spoken with Fairie and he had taken his satisfaction with 'mares and cows'. They were, of course, condemned; she to be hanged, he to be strangled and burnt. He remained unrepentant; while ministers prayed over and for him, he said that they were troublesome and cruel to him; he lay listening, 'in a most stupid manner, with his mouth wide open'. It is easy to make the usual joke about those long solemn prayers—and yet it is not so easy, for he said that he did not hear their devotion nor care for it, and at the end he added: 'Let me alone; I have lived as a beast and I must die as a beast.'

But Jane Weir repented. She became extreme with the thought of her sin. When she was brought to the gallows, before they could cover her face, she cried that she was determined to die with 'all the shame she could', and there on the death-ladder tried to tear off her clothes and strip herself naked before all the crowd, so that in the confusion and struggle she was at last thrown off 'open-faced', and anyone who cared might try in her convulsions to discern the mark of a horse-shoe which the devil had set on her forehead, 'shaped for nails in her wrinkles'.

The three trials, therefore, in three separate countries, which mark the end of the seventeenth century, mark also three different aspects of the subject. The La Voisin case is as regular, as just (allowing for torture), and as clear as any such case can be; it is overwhelmingly probable that some such facts as were testified to did, in fact, happen. It is one of the classic trials. The Salem trials represent that variation where suspicion, from whatever cause, being once aroused, a legal and popular movement against the suspects begins in which the general imagination has its own bloody and unjustified way. The Weir case began with the interior distress of Thomas Weir—whether he had actually committed the deeds he declared or whether his unbalanced mind did but brood on the dreams till he thought they were facts. There was truth in Paris; there was no truth in Salem; there may or may not have been truth in Edinburgh.

The juxtaposition of these three cases forms a convenient end. What followed was, at first, a repudiation in European thought of the whole witchcraft idea—not entirely as a part of the eighteenth-century repudiation of the whole Christian idea. After that—perhaps even along with that—there was a resurrection of it. Of the present position it is almost impossible to say anything with certainty unless by belonging or having belonged to the secret schools of sorcery; it is a condition that no record of the history of witchcraft is important enough to make desirable. Even if one accepted it, the condition would invalidate its own conclusions. No accuracy could be expected from anyone who had seriously accepted the practice of sorcery—except perhaps in the practice of sorcery. The exactitude of diabolism is confined to itself alone.

In general, at the end of the seventeenth century, virtue went out of the grand pursuit—both honest and dishonest virtue. Disgust rather than sympathy entered the general European mind. This disgust, the mere reaction against horror and monotonous pain, gave an opportunity to a real intellectual force of which the sceptical and humanitarian writers took full advantage. Reaction (so to call it) gave a chance to reform; it is, after all, their proper relation. The assertions made with varying degrees of clarity by such champions of intelligence as King James of England and the Inquisition in Spain began to be widely accepted by both more and less intelligent people. Even in 1584 King James himself had been alarmed by the complete scepticism displayed by Reginald Scot, and by 1668 Joseph Glanvil was declaring in the preface to his *Sadducismus Triumphatus* that derision of witches was spreading, not among the mere vulgar but 'in a little higher rank of understanding'. This certainly cannot be taken too closely, because the faithful—to whatever doctrine—always have complained, always are complaining, and always will complain, of the spread of

infidelity. The Middle Ages themselves were only regarded as ages of Faith when they were ended; to themselves they seemed ages of remarkable disbelief.

Perhaps the chief difference in the intellectual honour
(and therefore slowly in the mere intellectual fashion) of
Europe was a change in the questions asked. The early
Middle Ages had, on the whole, tended to ask the question, *Why does it happen?* and to answer it in theological
terms. But in the later Middle Ages to some extent, and
afterwards to a much greater extent, the question was
altered to *What happens?* Saint Gregory had assumed
that the little boy in his father's arms, dying, had seen
blackamoors coming to carry him off, and had explained
them on moral grounds of blasphemy. The newer spirit,
less in many ways but superior in that, preferred first of
all to ask firmly, if it were certain that there were any
objective blackamoors to see, and if not, then how did it
come about that the boy thought he saw them? They
might, of course, have been spiritual beings. But it was
more and more felt that it was worth while, undogmati-
cally, to examine the actual recorded circumstances of
the apparition of spiritual beings. Upon this growing
tendency there broke the philosophy of Descartes. Descartes very nearly denied that spirit and matter could
have anything to do with each other—except by a kind
of coincidence. The theologians denied the Cartesian
ideas. But they and Descartes, as it were, exchanged
courtesies. He, sincerely, professed Catholicism; they,
sincerely, were affected by Cartesianism. 'The century of
mathematics' became the Age of Reason.

The great philosophical change affected directly only

a few minds; they were, however, 'the minds that move the minds that move the world', and the world allowed itself to be moved. Lord Herbert of Cherbury in 1624 had promulgated in Paris the doctrines of Deism. Under Deism, it has been well said, God was 'the absentee land-lord' of the universe. It was also true, however, that the Devil became a kind of absentee trespasser. Voltaire, the great doctor of the next century, and of that general spiritual absenteeism, had his faults. But the enthusiastic detection of the Devil was not one of them. He did not, in his moral battles, aim his weapons at anything beyond the natural cruelty and tyranny which preoccupied the minds of the supernatural believers. A cold rage of equity shook him. Men were terrified of behaving unfashion-ably, and those who would once have believed in witches now disbelieved for exactly the same reason—because everyone else did.

But this was later. Yet at the beginning of the eighteenth century that admirable example of good taste, Joseph Addison, put the thing neatly enough. 'I believe in general', he wrote, 'that there is such a thing as witch-craft; but at the same time can give no credit to any particular instance of it.' What Addison believed was obviously proper to his day; no-one's thought kept the high-road more elegantly than his. In the year following his penning of that sentence, in 1712, a sentence of death was passed on the English witch Jane Wenham, in spite of the judge's efforts to persuade the jury to hold her innocent. The judge went further, however; he procured her pardon from the queen. It was the last death-sentence for witchcraft passed in England. On the Continent the fires did not cease so soon, but even there they were modified. The modification was chiefly due to three things.

(1) Metaphysical. The Cartesian division of soul from body, it may be thought, assisted even in the schools of the orthodox the tendency to lessen the power of the Devil; just as, from a very different point of view, did the philosophy of Jacob Boehme. A Dutch theologian, Balthasar Bekker, who published a book on the witch-controversy in 1691–3, took the view that, though Satan and the evil spirits existed, they had nothing executively to do with men and women. An Italian writer of the next century went back to the Ignatian view that with the coming of Christ the power of the Devil ceased: 'every sorcery and every spell was dissolved'. Both writers were involved in serious controversies, the one Protestant in Amsterdam, the other Catholic in Germany and Italy. William Law in England shaped, perhaps better than it has been put elsewhere, the idea that the darkness of hell is but the Divine Nature falsely invoked by the self and that the only dissipator of it is the Spirit of Love 'in his own blessed nature'. It is hardly tenable that such a high view, seriously and strongly held as it was, profoundly affected the habits of magistrates and of social circles. But where it came it lifted the argument on to a loftier level; it restored again the light of Redemption, which the bigots of redemption had done so much to obscure. 'It was said of old', said one German writer, 'that whoever denies Christ denies God; now it is said: "whoever denies the horned Devil denies God": was ever such an absurdity heard?'

(2) Legal. The weak point of the witch-prosecutions had always been the untrustworthiness of the evidence, but the agitation of the times had prevented the invalidity of much of it from being manifest. The extreme example is the 'spectral' evidence, the testimony of witnesses that they saw beings invisible to the court, as at Salem. In general, such evidence seems to have come rather late in the history. It was used mostly in the seventeenth century, and its last appearance in England was in the Jane Wenham case of 1712. But before spectral evidence came in, the evidence, almost as suspect, of reputed accomplices was admitted. A convicted witch was urged to name others, though it might have been thought that, of all possible witnesses, declared children of the Father of Lies would be held least trustworthy. The Spanish Inquisition had indeed shown very little trust, but almost everywhere else such testimony had been generally accepted. But in the eighteenth century the law began to find a happier habit. It began to be declared that judges ought to neglect all the evidence of accomplices. For—and this indeed was an advance—it was realized precisely that the Devil could and would deceive, and that creatures of the Devil might be and probably would be deceived. The medium of their sight might be diabolically changed. This struck at the whole force of the prosecution. Addison's comment was, as it were, made almost a principle of law. Witchcraft could and no doubt did exist. But being in its nature illusive, illusion could hardly be believed even in proof of itself.

Thus (to take only two examples) in 1714 a penitentiary of Paris, who wrote a book on cases of conscience, declared: 'There is every reason to believe that the sight of a sorcerer is affected by the illusion of imagination deranged by the demon, so that in sleep the sorcerer sees things otherwise than as they are.' And even earlier, in 1701, a doctor at Magdeburg had said the same thing and had gone so far as to point out that the absence of a husband or wife at night from the common bed might show a breach of the seventh commandment rather than the second.

(3) Medical. There had always been a tendency to suggest from time to time that disease had a great deal to do with the marvels of witchcraft. The suggestion had usually been suppressed. In the eighteenth century it was no longer suppressed. Observation of facts was at last seriously allowed and explanation of facts was no longer confined to theology. The movement towards this had been present since Athens, but for centuries it had not been widely encouraged. Francis Bacon, with others, had been, as he wished to be, 'a bell ringing' to call men to that difficult labour; he had, as it were, planned the road on which Addison conveniently walked. Malebranche had followed. Descartes had followed. The famous 'pineal gland' had been defined to be the point at which soul and body (to put it crudely) came together. It would be altogether too crude to say that the pineal gland was the salvation of many, but it is not quite untrue to say that the kind of research suggested by the words 'pineal gland' did help the study of physical disease. A proper devotion to the Sacred Heart might have had the same effect; in fact, however, it seems not to have had. The medical faculties began to be able to

propose various explanations of extraordinary occur-
rences which were not necessarily supernatural. Depositions became more exact; rumours were a little
checked. Sudden death, impotence, physical seizures,
were attributed to other causes than the Devil. Decep-
tions, conscious or not, were more and more discovered,
and more and more tales which might once have started
panic and pain were turned back on their authors.
Children especially found that to be enchanted was an
occupation that was apt to lead to no pleasure and to
considerable inconvenience.

What all this meant was that original Canon Law had
been, in fact, justified; the Canon of Elvira still expressed
(translated, as it now had to be, into other language) the
general Mind of the Church. An Abbot of the Theatines
in Munich in 1766 declared that it was the Canon Episcopi which had caused him to doubt the truth of witchcraft as popularly held. The diversion from that Canon
had been long and terrible. The best and the worst of the
Church had conflicted with each other; say also that the
best had—in the true sense of tragedy—conflicted with
the best. The tale of witchcraft is a tale of the deception
of virtue by itself.

Yet it had had, as such deception always has, every
kind of good excuse. Before Christendom began, magic,
with its lower accompaniment of witchcraft, preoccupied the whole Roman Empire; we have forgotten
the darkness out of which we came. It was as popular as
it was perilous. It was certainly regarded by the authorities as a public danger, but, on the whole, action against
it was taken only by private persons in lawsuits or by the

government in suspicion of treason. The peddlers of spells and practitioners of magic were in general not much disturbed; love-philtres and venoms were to be obtained for payment by the credulous. There was no clear line between those who controlled and those who compacted with the invisible powers, and it is doubtful whether there was even much distinction—except in the best minds—between those who sought union with the gods and those who desired profit by converse with the daimons. 'Magic' was a general word and roughly covered all. The loathsome sexual exhibitions related in Petronius were dissociated only by fastidious taste from the apparition of Isis granted to Apuleius. A world of powers and spirits rarely seen surrounded the world that was seen; the boundary was vague and uncertain; the incantations and rites united all.

Upon this general world of dangerous attraction impinged the new doctrines. 'Une grande espérance a traversé la monde', but that hope was by no means vague. It asserted itself more and more by definition and dogma. The single authoritative cry at the beginning was that Redemption came by Jesus Christ. Redemption was from all evil and from all deities except Jesus Christ. Man had, in fine, only the choice of that Redemption. The only futurity of importance was that which lived in him. Love of one's neighbour forbade venom; love of one's neighbour's freedom forbade love-philtres. Spirits there no doubt were; they were either angels and saints, whose control was in God, or devils, who were now overthrown. Sorcery and spells were done; the searchers after wisdom fell before the Child, and the searchers after vain profit fled from the Cross. Christ had harrowed hell every way.

So high a passion lasted long, and still lasts. Nevertheless, without aspersing the development of the Church, and without sighing for any fabulous primitivism, it does seem as if it might be said that the Church began not only to pay more and more attention to sin but to become more and more interested in sin. The world of images, in which at its lowest so much of mankind moves, threw up more and more often the image of the Devil. He was to be rejected and he was rejected. But he was more and more imagined to be there in order to be rejected.

Two thousand years of Christianity—even weak Christianity—have done more for us (let it be repeated once more) than we normally believe. The world of Rome was, in many ways, very like our own. But it was also very unlike our own: the presuppositions were different. And the presuppositions involved the 'nightmare' of magic; the habitual images of man's life easily included the images of magic. They are very near us today, but they are a little further off, and that they are at all further off is due to the Church, and to the Church alone. Fully supernatural, it denounced the hideous supernatural. and denounced it as an indulgence of the mind and of the fancy as much as of act itself. In that sense as in all it instructed its members to 'think no evil'; do not *imagine* these things. God and only God; love and only love.

It remained, however, that, in such a world, the Christian champions began to find themselves divided into two schools: the school that rejected evil with a stern awareness of it, and the school that rejected evil with a sweet neglect of it. They were not, of course, exclusive; no such distinction can ever follow a definite line. Saint Francis, in later days, was vividly conscious of evil; and Torquemada was vividly conscious of peace. But Saint Francis and Torquemada used, in fact, different methods. It would not perhaps be unfair to say that in this as in so much else the fashion of Augustine rather than Augustine himself influenced the Church to the sterner side. The great doctor set his foot on superstition, and every one of his ardent followers was anxious to have a part in the same trampling. Without that war superstition might have lasted much longer; as it was, it must be admitted that for very long superstition was admitted as an ally within the Church itself. Like the Emperors and the barbarian chiefs, the hateful energies of hate were enlisted on the side of Christendom. Cruelty, denounced as a sin, was welcomed and embraced as a saviour.

All this took time, and there were many excuses. There were also many delays. The Canon Episcopi was the chief of these. It got into Canon Law, and ever after it had to be explained. Up to the full Middle Ages the struggle between the two ways of regarding magic and witchcraft—as a falsity of imagination, basely and wickedly indulged, or as an act, possible, successful, and propagandist—seems to have been almost level. But when the civil power launched its laws against heresy, when heresy became a crime, then the sterner methods against magic and witchcraft were quickened. Then also other great doctors defined what Augustine had permitted them, had even encouraged them, to define. Saint Thomas, rigidly intellectual, had no choice but to declare the reality of the evil. It may be believed nevertheless that Saint Thomas, in charge of a trial for witchcraft, would have demanded evidence as he demanded logic, and have been on the bench as difficult to the prosecution as in his cell he was a danger to the defence (such defence as was then allowed!). As the reality of the act began to be universally accepted, as the question of heresy and the question of witchcraft began to be intermingled, so the problem turned more and more on the provision of sufficient evidence of the right kind.

The Middle Ages had many great virtues; they retained for long the greatest of virtues—a deliberate belief in God. They were a great deal more 'democratic' in the sense that they took a much more note of popular belief and popular repute. The history of witchcraft, perhaps, does not altogether encourage a belief in democratic opinion. Nor in aristocratic opinion. It is the history of a fashion, and it has yet to be shown that either democracy or aristocracy are proof against fashion. As the Middle Ages hurried to their feverish and calamitous close, fashion rode them like a fury.

It has become fashionable of late to denounce the Renaissance. But at least it may be said that there was every excuse for the Renaissance. The Black Death, the Great Schism, the growth of torture, the spread of witchcraft tales, these things, with others, had spoiled the dream of the Kingdom of God on earth which had occupied the best medieval minds; had indeed turned it into a nightmare. It was out of that nightmare that the Renaissance woke—to dream, in its turn, of Man. We who live in the collapse of the Renaissance forget the collapse of the Middle Ages from which the growth of the sceptical and inquiring human mind gradually saved us. The *Malleus Maleficarum* was published about 1486, but it is not a Renaissance document. At the same time the results of the *Malleus*, and of all the similar books that accompanied it, were neither specially Renaissance nor specially medieval; they were merely human. The Devil ruled with power.

To say so is not to say that the Devil was on one side only. Invalid as most of the evidence is, there remains enough, scattered through the centuries, to make it clear that efforts at the old Goetic life were certainly made. Omit and reduce as much as we choose, it is still difficult to think that Gilles de Rais and the Abbé Guibourg did not work the Rites, that the blood of the innocent was not sacramentally shed nor invocations of unclean spirits seriously uttered. And if it was possible for the rich it was possible for the poor; the Devil is no respecter of persons. Underneath all the tales there does lie something different from the tales. How different? In this—that the thing which is invoked is a thing of a different nature, however it may put on a human appearance or indulge in its servants their human appetites. It is cold, it is hungry, it is violent, it is illusory. The warm blood of children and the intercourse at the Sabbath do not satisfy .t. It wants something more and other; it wants 'obedience', it wants 'souls', and yet it pines for matter. It never was, and yet it always is.

Some such absurd contradiction is perhaps the nearest

one can come to describing the impression left by the whole history. Among the great host of images raised up by man for seen and unseen things, for real existences and unreal, there is this image also, the image of an almost abstract perversion. Opinions have differed and will (humanly speaking) always differ about its reality. Some have supposed that it had no identity in itself, that its image was only a reflection of man's desire and man's capacity; others have thought that the image was of an actual being, allied to men only in the sense that men are spirit and that it is spirit, differing from men in the sense that men are matter and that it is not, and never can be, matter. Therefore it twists, defiles, and destroys matter. Some again have supposed that it has very great power and some that it has hardly any power at all—at least within the Christian Church. Those who have thought it powerful have used all the powers of the State and the Church to fight it. They have been led by it, or by their dreams of it and their fear of it, into madness and massacre beyond description: or rather, not beyond description. 'All sorcery and all spells were dissolved', wrote the holy Ignatius in the first new generation of Christian things. The Church annotated that sentence. If ever the image of the Way of Perversion of Images came into common human sight, outside the Rites of the Way, it was before the crowds of serious Christians who watched a child, at the instance of pious and intelligent men, scourged three times round the stake where its mother was burned.

INDEX

313

INDEX

INDEX

CHARLES WILLIAMS

1886?

*Charles Williams, born in London in 1895, was
an editor, teacher, poet, novelist, playwright, and
theologian. After two years at the University of
London, he was compelled by lack of funds to take
a position with a publishing house while continuing
his studies evenings at Workingmen's College.
Despite his lack of formal academic degrees, he
was appointed lecturer at Oxford and awarded an
honorary M. A. Among his thirty-eight published
books the best known are the supernatural novels*
DESCENT INTO HELL, WAR IN HEAVEN, ALL
HALLOW'S EVE, MANY DIMENSIONS, *and* SHADOWS
OF ECSTASY. *His history of the Holy Spirit in the
Church,* THE DESCENT OF THE DOVE, *is available
in Living Age Books published by Meridian
Books. Charles Williams died in 1945.*